WITHDRAWN

Corner House Publishers

SOCIAL SCIENCE REPRINTS

General Editor MAURICE FILLER

Travel in the South in the Thirties.

Frontispiece.

STAGE-COACH·AND TAVERN·DAYS

By ALICE MORSE EARLE

Author of *Home Life in Colonial Days*, *Child Life in Colonial Days*, and other Social and Domestic Histories of Colonial Times

" Long ago, at the end of the route,
The stage pulled up, and the folks stepped out.
They have all passed under the tavern door —
The youth and his bride and the gray three-score.
Their eyes were weary with dust and gleam,
The day had gone like an empty dream.
Soft may they slumber, and trouble no more
For their eager journey, its jolt and roar,
In the old coach over the mountain."

CORNER HOUSE PUBLISHERS
WILLIAMSTOWN, MASSACHUSETTS 01267
1977

REPRINTED 1977

BY

CORNER HOUSE PUBLISHERS

ISBN 0–87928–083–2

Printed in the United States of America

TO MY HUSBAND

HENRY EARLE

Contents

List of Illustrations

Stage-coach and Tavern Days

Stage-coach and Tavern Days

CHAPTER I

THE PURITAN ORDINARY

IN reverent and affectionate retrospective view
of the influences and conditions which had
power and made mark upon the settlement of
New England, we are apt to affirm with earnest
sentiment that religion was the one force, the one
aim, the one thought, of the lives of our forbears.
It was indeed an ever present thought and influence
in their lives; but they possessed another trait
which is as evident in their records as their piety,
and which adds an element of human interest to
their story which their stern Puritanism never could
have done; with them their neighborliness was as
ever present and as sincere as their godliness.
Hence the establishment of an hostelry, — an ordinary it was usually called, — for the entertainment of
travellers and for the mutual comfort of the settlers, was scarcely second to their providing a gath-
ering-place for the church.

The General Court of Massachusetts at an early
date took decisive measures with regard to houses
of common entertainment. No one was permitted

to keep without license "a common victuallyng
house," under a penalty of twenty shillings a week.
Soon the power of granting licenses was transferred
to the County Courts, as the constant increase in
the number of ordinaries made too constant detailed
work for so important a body as the General Court.

Consideration for the welfare of travellers, and a
desire to regulate the sale of intoxicating liquors,
seemed to the magistrates important enough reasons
not only to counsel but to enforce the opening of
some kind of a public house in each community,
and in 1656 the General Court of Massachusetts
made towns liable to a fine for not sustaining an
ordinary. Towns were fined and admonished for
not conforming to this law; Concord, Massachusetts, was one of the number. The Colonial Records of Connecticut, in 1644, ordered "one sufficient
inhabitant" in each town to keep an ordinary, since
"strangers were straitened" for want of entertainment. A frequent and natural choice of location
for establishing an ordinary was at a ferry. Tris-
tram Coffyn kept both ferry and ordinary at Newbury, Massachusetts; there was an ordinary at
Beverly Ferry, known until 1819 as the "Old
Ferry Tavern."

Great inducements were offered to persons to
keep an ordinary; sometimes land was granted
them, or pasturage for their cattle, or exemption
from church rates and school taxes. In 1682,
Hugh March, of Newbury, Massachusetts, petitioned for a renewal of his license to keep an ordinary, saying thus: "The town of Newbury, some

Ordinary at Duxbury, Massachusetts.

years since, were destitute of an ordinary, and could not persuade any person to keep it. For want of an ordinary they were twice fined by the county, and would have been a third time had I not undertaken it." In 1668 the town had persuaded one Captain White to "undertake an ordinary" on high moral grounds; and it is painful to record that, though he did so unwillingly, he found the occupation so profitable that he finally got into disgrace through it.

The early taverns were not opened wholly for the convenience of travellers; they were for the comfort of the townspeople, for the interchange of news and opinions, the sale of solacing liquors, and the incidental sociability; in fact, the importance of the tavern to its local neighbors was far greater than to travellers. There were many restrictions upon the entertainment of unknown strangers. The landlord had to give the name of all such strangers to the selectmen, who could, if they deemed them detrimental or likely to become a charge upon the community, warn them out of the town. The old town records are full of such warnings, some of them most amusing. Nor could the landlord "knowingly harbor in house, barn, or stable, any rogues, vagabonds, thieves, sturdy beggars, masterless men or women." Our ancestors were kindly neighbors to godly folk, but sternly intolerant of wrong-doers, or even of those suspected of wrong.

We cannot wonder that citizens did not seek to become ordinary-keepers when we learn how they were hampered, or how the magistrates tried to hamper them. They were at one time not to be permitted to sell " sack or strong waters," nor have any dancing or singing within their walls. No games could be played in their precincts. They were even hindered in the selling of cakes and buns. Innholders and victuallers were prohibited the brewing of beer, but that soon had to be revoked. The price and quality of beer was constantly being established by law and as constantly changed. In 1634 the Court set the price of a single meal at six-pence, and not above a penny for an ale-quart of beer out of meal time. Then, a little later, the landlords were forbidden to change more than twelve pence for a meal; and they were ordered to furnish meals to "pore people," as simply as called for.

One Richard Cluffe, in an utterance which sounds like the voice of Shakespeare's clown, exclaimed at a mean meal served to him, " What ! shall

I pay twelve pence for the fragments which the grand jury roages have left?" The majesty of the law could not thus be attacked in Massachusetts in the year 1640. Three pounds six shillings and eight pence did Cluffe pay for his rash and angry words — truly a costly dinner.

The ordinary called The Anchor, at Lynn, was kept by one Joseph Armitage. Being a half-way house between Boston and Salem, the magistrates made it their stopping-place on their various trips from court to court. The accounts of this ordinary are still preserved. Governor Endicott's bills for "vitals, beare, and logen," for "bear and caeks," were paid by the Auditor. Governor Bradstreet had "beare and wyne." The succeeding landlord of this ordinary was described by John Dunton in 1686 as a hearty, talkative, fine old gentleman, one of Oliver Cromwell's soldiers. Dunton had at The Anchor a good fowl and a bottle of sack, instead of the beer and cakes of the abstemious Puritan governor.

The "Sports of the Innyard" were sternly frowned upon by Puritan magistrates. Among the games which were named as forbidden in the ordinaries were "carding," dicing, tally, bowls, billiards, slidegroat, shuffle-board, quoits, loggets, nine-pins. After a time shuffle-board and bowls were tolerated in private houses, though not deemed reputable at the ordinary.

The Puritan ordinary saw some wedding scenes, and apparently some tentatively gay scenes, since in 1631 the magistrates of Massachusetts Bay, in "consequence of some miscarriages at weddings" which had been held in an ordinary, passed a law prohibiting dancing on such occasions in public houses.

Lord Ley lodged at the Boston ordinary in 1637; and when Governor Winthrop urged him to come to his home from the inn, his lordship declined, saying that the house where he was staying was so well ordered that he could be as private there as elsewhere.

In the towns a night-watch was soon instituted, and the instructions given by the Boston magistrates smack strongly of Dogberry's famous charge. Their number each night was eight; they were "to walk two by two together, a youth joined to an older and more sober person." Lights had to be out,— or hidden,— especially in the ordinaries. "If they see lights, to inquire if there be warrantable cause; and if they hear any noise or disorder, wisely to demand the reason; if they are dancing and singing vainly, to admonish them to cease; if they do not discontinue after moderate admonition, then the constable to take their names and acquaint the authorities therewith. If they find young men and maidens, not of known fidelity, walking after ten o'clock, modestly to demand the cause, and if they appear ill-minded, to watch them narrowly, command them to go to their lodgings, and if they refuse then to secure them till morning." In 1663 Josselyn found that young sparks walking with their sweethearts, or "Marmalet-Madams" as he called them, had to go home at nine o'clock.

Constant and strenuous efforts were made from earliest days to prevent drunkenness and all tavern disorders. As early as 1637 complaints had been made that "much drunkenness, waste of the good creatures of God, mispense of time, and other disorders" had taken place at the ordinaries. Frequent laws were made about selling liquor to the "devilish bloudy salvages," and many were the arrests and fines and punishments therefor.

Taproom Furnishings of an Old Ordinary.

Landlords were forbidden by the Court in 1645 "to suffer anyone to be drunk or drink excessively, or continue tippling above the space of half an hour in any of their said houses under penalty of 5s. for every such offence suffered; and every person found drunk in the said houses or elsewhere shall forfeit 10s.; and for every excessive drinking he shall forfeit 3s. 4d.; for sitting idle and continuing drinking above half an hour, 2s. 6d.; and it is declared to be excessive drinking of wine when above

half a pint of wine is allowed at one time to one
person to drink : provided that it shall be lawful
for any strangers, or lodgers, or any person or persons, in an orderly way to continue in such houses
of common entertainment during meal times or upon
lawful business, what time their occasions shall
require."

Drunkards were severely punished by being thrust
into the bilboes, set in the stocks, and whipped. In
1632 one " James Woodward shalbe sett in the bilbowes for being drunke at New-Towne." Robert
Wright was fined twenty shillings and ordered to
sit in the stocks an hour for being " twice dis-
tempered in drink." On September 3, 1633, in
Boston : —

" Robert Coles was fyned ten shillings and enjoynd to
stand with a white sheet of paper on his back, whereon
Drunkard shalbe written in great lres, and to stand therewith soe long as the Court find meet, for abusing himself
shamefully with drinke."

This did not reform Robert Coles, for a year
later his badge of disgrace was made permanent : —

" Robert Coles for drunkenness by him committed at
Rocksbury shalbe disfranchizd, weare about his neck, and
so to hang upon his outwd garment a D. made of redd
cloth & sett upon white : to continyu this for a yeare, &
not to have it off any time hee comes among company,
Vnder the penalty of xl *s.* for the first offence, and 5 £
for the second, and afterward to be punished by the
Court as they think meet : also *hee is to wear the D out-
wards.*"

It might be inferred from the clause I have itali- cized that the Puritan drunkard was not without guile, and that some had worn the scarlet letter and hidden it from public view as skilfully as the moral brand is often hidden from public knowledge to-day. Women, also, were punished severely for "intem- perate drinking from one ordinary to another," but such examples were rare.

Lists of names of common drunkards were given to landlords in some towns (among them New Cas- tle, New Hampshire), and landlords were warned not to sell liquor to them. Licenses were removed and fines imposed on those who did not heed the warning.

The tithing-man, that amusing but most bump- tious public functionary of colonial times, was at first the official appointed to spy specially upon the ordinaries. He inspected these houses, made com- plaint of any disorders he discovered, and gave in to the constable the names of idle drinkers and gamers. He warned the keepers of public houses to sell no more liquor to any whom he fancied had been tippling too freely. John Josselyn, an Eng- lish visitor in Boston in 1663, complained bitterly thus :—

"At houses of entertainment into which a stranger went, he was presently followed by one appointed to that office, who would thrust himself into the company uninvited, and if he called for more drink than the officer thought in his judgement he could soberly bear away, he would presently countermand it, and appoint the proportion, beyond which he could not get one drop."

Old Tavern at Easton, Massachusetts.

Now that certainly was trying. Nor could it have been agreeable to would-be cheerful frequenters of Greyhound Tavern, in Roxbury, to have godly Parson Danforth, when he saw from his study windows any neighbors or strangers lingering within the tavern doors, come sallying forth from his house across the way, and walk sternly into their company, and, as he said, "chide them away." Patient must have been the Greyhound's landlord to have stood such pious meddling and hindrance to trade.

Governor Winthrop gives an account of the exploits of a Boston constable in 1644, which shows the restraint held over a lodger in a Boston ordinary at that date.

"There fell out a troublesome business in Boston. An English sailor happened to be drunk and was carried to his lodging; and the Constable (a Godly man and much zealous against such disorders) hearing of it, found him out, being upon his bed asleep; so he awaked him, and led him to the stocks, no magistrate being at home. He being left in the stocks, some one of La Tours French gentlemen visitors in Boston lifted up the stocks and let him out. The Constable hearing of it, went to the Frenchman (being then gone and quiet) and would needs carry *him* to the stocks. The Frenchman offered to yield himself to go to prison but the Constable, not understanding his language, pressed him to go to the stocks. The Frenchman resisted and drew his sword. With that company came in and disarmed him, and carried him by force to the stocks, but soon after the Constable took him out and carried him to prison."

Winthrop gravely enumerates the faults of the constable, such as his "transgressing the bounds of his office, the fruits of ignorant and misguided zeal, not putting a hook on the stocks," etc., and the matter bade fair to assume some gravity, since it was deemed in France "most ignominious to be laid in the stocks." Yet Winthrop took care not to rebuke the Constable in public lest he "discourage and discountenance an honest officer."

It has been said that the homely injunction "to mind your own business" was the most difficult lesson New Englanders ever had to learn, and that even now it has been acquired and practised in the cities only, not in the country.

Administration of government in those days certainly consisted much of meddlesome interference in the private affairs of daily life. Experience has since taught that the free-will of the citizen is the best regulator in such matters.

It is one of the curiosities of old-time legislation that the use of tobacco was in earliest colonial days plainly regarded by the magistrates and elders as far more sinful, degrading, and harmful than indulgence in intoxicating liquors. Both the use and the planting of it were forbidden, the latter being permitted in small quantities "for meere necessitie, for phisick, for preservaceon of the health, and that the same be taken privately by aunccient men." Landlords were ordered not to "suffer any tobacco to be taken into their houses" on penalty of a fine to the "victualler," and another to "the party that takes it. The "Creature called Tobacko" seemed to have an immortal life. The laws were constantly altered and were enforced, still tobacco was grown and was smoked. Soon it was forbidden to "take tobacco in any wine or common victual house, except in a private room there, so as the master of said house nor any guest there shall take offense thereat; which, if any do, the said person shall forbear upon pain of two shillings sixpence for every such offense." No one could take tobacco "publicquely" nor in his own house or anywhere else before strangers. Two men were forbidden to smoke together. Windsor required a physician's certificate ere it could be used. No one could smoke within two miles of the meeting-house on the Sabbath day. There were wicked backsliders who were caught smoking around the corner of the meeting-house, and others on the street, and they

were fined, and set in the stocks, and in cages.
Until within a few years there were New England
towns where tobacco-smoking was prohibited on
the streets, and innocent cigar-loving travellers
were astounded at being requested to cease smoking. Mr. Drake wrote in 1886 that he knew men,
then living, who had had to plead guilty or not
guilty in a Boston police court for smoking in the
streets of Boston. In Connecticut in early days
a great indulgence was permitted to travellers — a
man could smoke once during a journey of ten miles.

The relationship of tavern and meeting-house in
New England did not end with their simultaneous
establishment; they continued the most friendly
neighbors. And so long as a public house was
commonly known as an ordinary, those who were
high in church counsels looked sharply to the
control of these houses of sojourn. The minister
and tithing-man were aided in their spying and their
chiding by deacons, elders, and church members.

Usually the ordinary and the meeting-house were
close companions. Licenses to keep houses of entertainment were granted with the condition that
the tavern must be near the meeting-house — a keen
contrast to our present laws prohibiting the sale of
liquor within a certain distance of any church. A
Boston ordinary-keeper, in 1651, was granted permission to keep a house of common entertainment
"provided hee keepe it neare the new meeting-
house."

Those who know of the old-time meeting-house
can fully comprehend the desire of the colonists to

have a tavern near at hand, especially during the winter services. Through autumn rains, and winter frosts and snows, and fierce northwesters, the poorly-built meeting-house stood unheated, growing more damp, more icy, more deadly, with each succeeding week. Women cowered, shivering, half-frozen, over the feeble heat of a metal foot-stove as the long sermon dragged on and the few coals became ashes.

Leather Black-jack.

Men stamped their feet and swung their arms in the vain attempt to warm the blood. Gladly and eagerly did all troop from the gloomy meeting-house to the cheerful tavern to thaw out before the afternoon service, and to warm up before the ride or walk home in the late afternoon. It was a scandal in many a town that godly church-members partook too freely of tavern cheer at the nooning; the only wonder is that the entire congregation did not succumb in a body to the potent flip and toddy of the tavern-keeper.

In midsummer the hot sun beat down on the meeting-house roof, and the burning rays poured in the unshaded windows. The taproom of the tavern and the green trees in its dooryard offered a pleasant shade to tired church-goers, and its well-sweep afforded a grateful drink to those who turned not to the taproom.

There are ever backsliders in all church communities; many walked into the ordinary door instead of up the church " alley." The chimney seat of the inn was more comfortable than the narrow seat of the " pue." The General Court of Massachusetts passed a law requiring all innkeepers within a mile of any meeting-house, to clear their houses " during the hours of the exercise." " Thus," Mr. Field says wittily, " the townsmen were frozen out of the tavern to be frozen in the meeting-house."

Our ancestors had no reverence for a church save as a literal meeting-house, and it was not unusual to transform the house of God into a tavern. The Great House at Charlestown, Massachusetts, the official residence of Governor Winthrop, became a meeting-house in 1633, and then a tavern, the Three Cranes, kept by Robert Leary and his descendants for many years. It was destroyed in June, 1775, in the burning of the town. In this Great House, destined to become a tavern, lived Governor Winthrop when he announced his famous discountenance of health-drinking at the tables and in public places. This first of all temperance pledges in New England is recorded in his Diary in his own language, which was as temperate as his intent: —

" The Governor, upon consideration of the inconveniences which had grown in England by drinking one to another, restrained it at his own table, and wished others to do the like; so it grew, little by little, into disuse."

Frequently religious services were held in the spacious rooms of the tavern, until a meeting-house was built; as in the town of Fitchburg, Massachusetts, and in Providence, Rhode Island, where Roger Williams preached. Many of the Puritan ordinaries were thus used.

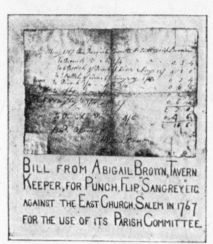

BILL FROM ABIGAIL BROWN, TAVERN KEEPER, FOR PUNCH, FLIP SANGREY ETC. AGAINST THE EAST CHURCH, SALEM IN 1767 FOR THE USE OF ITS PARISH COMMITTEE.

Ecclesiastical affairs were managed at the ordinary, among them that most ticklish and difficult of all adjustments and allotments, namely, seating the meeting. The "Elders, Deacons, and Selectmen" of Cambridge were made a "constant and settled power for regulating the seating of persons in the meeting-house." They were ordered to meet at the ordinary, and such orders and appointments as this were made : —

"Brother Richard Jackson's wife to sit where Sister Kempster was wont to sit. Ester Sparhawke to sit in the place where Mrs. Upham is removed from. Mr. Day to sit the second seat from the table. Ensign Samuel Greene to sit at the Table. Goody Gates to sit at the end of the Deacon's seat. Goody Wines to sit in the Gallery."

It needed much consultation and thought to "seat the meeting." We can imagine the deacons loosening their tongues over the tavern flip and punch, and arguing confidentially over the standing, the wealth, and temper of the various parties to be seated.

There were in Boston at different times several ordinaries and taverns known as the King's Arms. One of the earliest ones stood at the head of Dock Square. In 1651 one Hugh Gunnison, vintner, and his wife, sold this house, known by the sign of the King's Arms, with its furniture and appurtenances, for the sum of £600 sterling, a goodly sum for the day. An inventory of the " p'ticular goods and household stuffe " still exists, and is of much interest not only as indicating the furnishings of a house of that character in that colony at that date, but showing also the naming of the chambers, as in the English inns of Shakespeare's day.

" In the chamber called the Exchange one halfe bedstead with blew pillows, one livery Cupbord coloured blue, one long table, benches, two formes and one carved chaire.

" In the Kitchen three formes dressers shelves.

" In the Larder one square Table banisters dressers & shelves round.

" In the Hall, three Small Roomes with tables and benches in them, one table about six foote long in the .Hall and one bench.

" In the low parlor one bedstead one table and benches two formes, one small frame of a form and shelves, one Closet with shelves.

" In the room Vnder the closet one child's bedsted.

" In the Chamber called London, one bedsted two benches.

" In the Chamber over London one bedsted one crosse table one forme one bench.

" In the Closet next the Exchange, shelves.

" In the barr by the hall, three shelves, the frame of a low
stoole.

" In the vpper p'lor one bedsted two chaires one table one
forme bench and shelves.

" In the Nursery one Crosse Table with shelvs.

" In the Court Chamber one Long table three formes one
livery cupbord, & benches.

" In the closet within the Court chamber one bedsted and
shelvs.

" In the Starr chamber one long table, one bedsted, one livery Cupbord one chaire three formes with benches.

" In the Garret over the Court chamber one bedsted one
table two formes.

" In the garret over the closet in the Court chamber one
bedsted one smale forme.

" In the foure garrett chambers over the Starr chamber three
bedsteds four tables with benches.

" In the brewhouse one Cop', twoe fatts, one vnder back,
one vpper back, one kneading trough one dresser one
brake.

" In the stable one Racke & manger.

" In the yarde one pumpe, pipes to convey the water to the
brew house, fyve hogg styes, one house of office.

" The signes of the Kinges Armes and signe posts."

This was certainly a large house and amply furnished. It contained thirteen bedsteads and a vast
number of tables, forms, benches, shelves, and
cupboards.

The rooms of the Blue Anchor, another Boston
ordinary, also bore names: the Rose and Sun Low
room, the Cross Keys, the Green Dragon, the
Anchor and Castle.

We can form, from the items of this inventory, a
very good and detailed picture of the interior of a Boston ordinary at that date.   But it must not be imagined
that there were at the time of this sale many colonial
ordinaries as amply furnished as the King's Arms.
The accommodations in the public houses of small
towns, indeed perhaps everywhere in New England

Taproom of Wayside Inn.

save in Boston and Salem, were very primitive.   The
ordinary was doubtless as well furnished as the private
homes of its neighbors, and that was very simple of
fashion, while the fare was scant of variety.

We know that even the early ordinaries had sign-
boards.

The ordinary-keeper had his license granted with
the proviso that " there be sett up some inoffensive

sign obvious for direction to strangers" — this in
Salem in 1645. In 1655 the Rhode Island courts
ordered that all persons appointed to keep an ordinary should "cause to be sett out a convenient Signe
at ye most perspicuous place of ye said house, thereby
to give notice to strangers yt it is a house of public
entertainment, and this to be done with all convenient speed."

Women kept ordinaries and taverns from early
days. Widows abounded, for the life of the male
colonists was hard, exposure was great, and many
died in middle age. War also had many victims.
Tavern-keeping was the resort of widows of small
means then, just as the "taking of boarders" is to-day.
Women were skilled in business affairs and compe-
tent; many licenses were granted to them to keep
victualling-houses, to draw wine, and make and sell
beer. In 1684 the wife of one Nicholas Howard
was licensed "to entertain Lodgers in the absence of
her husband"; while other women were permitted to
sell food and drink but could not entertain lodgers
because their husbands were absent from home, thus
drawing nice distinctions. A Salem dame in 1645
could keep an ordinary if she provided a "godly
man" to manage her business. Some women became renowned as good innkeepers, and they were
everywhere encouraged in the calling.

The colonists did not have to complain long, nor
to pine long for lack of ordinaries. In 1675 Cotton
Mather said every other house in Boston was an ale-
house.

One of the first serious protests against the increase

of ordinaries and ale-houses in the colonies, and appreciation of their pernicious effects, came from Nathaniel Saltonstall of Haverhill, Massachusetts. He was a magistrate, and an officer in the militia. He was appointed one of the judges in the Salem witchcraft trials; but in this latter capacity he refused to serve, which may be taken as a proof of his advanced thought. He was said to be "a man-of superior powers of mind and rare talents." In December, 1696, he sent a letter to the Salem Court which ran thus: —

"Much Hon'd Gentlemen:

"I allways thought it great prudence and Christianity in our former leaders and rulers, by their laws to state the number of publique houses in towns and for regulation of such houses, as were of necessity, thereby to prevent all sorts, almost, of wickednesses which daily grow in upon us like a flood. But alas! I see not but that now the case is over, and such (as to some places I may term them) pest-houses and places of enticement (tho not so intended by the Justices) the sin are multiplied. It is multiplied too openly, that the cause of it may be, the price of retailers' fees, etc. I pray what need of six retailers in Salisbury, and of more than one in Haverhill, and some other towns where the people, when taxes and rates for the country and ministers are collecting, with open mouths complain of povertie and being hardly dealt with, and yet I am fully informed, can spend much time, and spend their estates at such blind holes, as are clandestinely and unjustly petitioned for; and more threaten to get licenses, chiefly by repairing to a remote court, where they are not known or suspected, but pass for current, and thereby the towns are abused, and the youth get evil habits; and men sent out on country service

at such places waste much of their time, yet expect pay
for it, in most pernicious loytering and what, and sometimes by foolish if not pot-valiant firing and shooting off
guns, not for the destruction of enemies, but to the wonderful disturbance and affrightment of the inhabitants, which
is not the service a scout is allowed and maintained for.

"Please to see what good is done by giving a license
to Robert Hastings, in such a by-place about three miles
from the publique house in town. The man himself I
am sure has no cause, nor do I believe the town and travellers if they are sober men, will ever give the court thanks
for the first grant to him, or the further renewal thereof.

"But now the bravado is made, what is done is not enough ;
we must have a third tippling house at Peter Patey's about
midway between the other two, which they boast as cock-
sure of, and have it is thought laid in, for this very end,
an unaccountable store of cyder, rum, molasses, and what
not. It is well if this stock be not now spent on, in pro-
curing subscriptions for to obtain the villain's license,
which I fear, knowing the man, we may be bold to say,
wickedness will be practiced and without control. . . . I
have done my part in court, as to what I heard of, to prevent such confiding licenses to persons unknown. . . .

"I am now God's prisoner and cant come abroad, and
have waited long to speak of those, and others, but as
yet cant meet with an opportunity. You have nothing
here of personal animosity of mine against any man, but
zeal and faithfulness to my country and town, and to the
young and rising generation that they be not too much at
liberty to live and do as they list. Accept of the good in-
tentions of, gentlemen, your humble servant,

                              "N. SALTONSTALL."

There is a sturdy ring about this letter, a freedom
from cant and conventional religious expressions,

that serve to paint clearly the character of the writer, and show us by one of those side-glimpses, which, as Ruskin says, often afford more light than a full stare, the sort of man that built up New England in the beginning, on its solid and noble foundations.

In spite of the forebodings of Saltonstall and other Christian gentlemen, the flood of wickedness and disorder which he predicted was slow in its approach. The orderly ways and close restrictions

Buckman Tavern, Lexington, Massachusetts, 1690.

and surveillance of the Puritan ordinary lasted until long after public houses were called taverns.

In the latter quarter of the seventeenth century and the first of the eighteenth a nearly continual diary was kept by a resident of Boston, Judge Samuel Sewall,

who might be called Boston's first citizen.   He was
rich, he was good, he was intelligent, and some portions of his diary are of great value for the light they
throw on contemporary customs and events.   He has
been called a Puritan Pepys; but in one respect he is
markedly unlike Pepys, who gave us ample record
of London taverns, and of tavern life in his day.   It
is doubtful that Sewall knew much about tavern life
in Boston; for his private life was a great contrast to
that of our gay Pepys.   Judge Sewall was a home-
body, tenderly careful of his children — he had fourteen; a "loving servant" to his wives — he had
three; especially devoted to his mother-in-law — he
had but one, the richest woman in Boston; kind to
his neighbors, poor as well as rich; attentive to his
friends in sickness, and thoughtful of them in death;
zealous in religious duties both in the church and
the family; public-spirited and upright in his service
to his town and state, from his high office as judge,
down to fulfilling petty duties such as serving on the
watch.   He had little time for tavern life, and little
inclination to it; and he condemned men who "kept
ordinaries and sold rum."   He was a shining example of the "New-English men," whose fast-thinning
ranks he so sadly deplored, and whose virtues he
extolled.   He occasionally refers in his diary to ordinaries.   Sometimes he soberly drank healths and
grace-cups within Boston and Cambridge tavern
walls with the honored Deputies, at the installation
of a new Governor, on the King's Coronation Day,
or a Royal Birthday.   Sometimes we read of his
pleasuring trips with his wife to the Greyhound Tav-

ern in Roxbury, his gala dinner of boiled pork and roast fowls, and his riding home at curfew in "brave moonshine." That clear June moonlight shining down through the centuries does not display to us any very gay figures, any very jolly riders. We can see the Judge in rich but sad-colored attire, with his wife on a pillion behind him, soberly jogging home, doubtless singing psalms as they went through the short stretches of Roxbury woods; for he sang psalms everywhere apparently, when he was permitted to do so. This is as might be expected of a man who on another pleasure jaunt with his wife left her eating cherries in the orchard, while he, like any other Puritan, "sweetened his mouth with a bit of Calvin," that is, he sat indoors and read *Calvin on Psalms*.

At this time — in the year 1714 — Boston had a population approaching ten thousand. It had thirty-four ordinary- or inn-holders, of whom twelve were women; four common victuallers, of whom one was a woman; forty-one retailers of liquor, of whom seventeen were women, and a few cider sellers. There were, therefore, ample places in which liquor could be bought; but Sewall's entire diary gives proof of the orderliness of life in Boston. There are not half a dozen entries which give any records or show any evidence of tavern disorders. In 1708 an inquiry was made by the magistrates "as to debaucheries at the Exchange," and as a result one young man was fined five shillings for cursing, ten shillings for throwing a beer-pot and scale-box at the maid, and twenty shillings for lying — that was

all.   The longest entry is on the Queen's birthday
in 1714 : —

"My neighbor Colson knocks at my door about nine
P.M., or past, to tell of disorders at the ordinary at the
South End, kept by Mr. Wallace.   He desired me that I

Hound-handle Tavern Pitcher.

would accompany Mr. Bromfield and Constable Howell
hither.   It was 35 minutes past nine before Mr. Bromfield
came, then we went, took Æneas Salter with us.   Found
much company.   They refused to go away.   Said was there
to drink the Queen's health and had many other healths to
drink.   Called for more drink and drank to me : I took
notice of the affront, to them.   Said they must and would
stay upon that solemn occasion.   Mr. Netmaker drank

the Queen's health to me. I told him I drank none; on that he ceased. Mr. Brinley put on his hat to affront me. I made him take it off. I threatened to send some of them to prison. They said they could but pay their fine and doing that might stay. I told them if they had not a care they would be guilty of a riot. Mr. Bromfield spake of raising a number of men to quell them, and was in some heat ready to run into the street. But I did not like that. Not having pen and ink I went to take their names with my pencil and not knowing how to spell their names they themselves of their own accord writ them. At last I addressed myself to Mr. Banister. I told him he had been longest an inhabitant and freeholder and I expected he would set a good example by departing thence. Upon this he invited them to his own house, and away they went. And we after them went away. I went directly home and found it 25 minutes past ten at night when I entered my own house."

No greater tribute to orderly Boston could be given than this record of rare disturbance. Even in that day, half after nine was not a late hour, and it took the Judge but an hour to walk from his house and back and disperse these soberly rioting young men, whom we can picture, solemnly writing down their own names with the Judge's pencil for him to bring them up in the morning. The next day they were each fined five shillings. Some paid, some appealed and gave bonds. Mr. Netmaker was Secretary to the Commander of her Majesty's forces, and he had to pay five shillings for cursing. They also attempted to make him give bonds to keep the peace, but at this he and his friends lost patience and refused. Judges Sewall and Bromfield promptly sent him to jail.

It is not surprising to know that the Governor released him, though under strenuous protest from the two magistrates, who had, they contended, simply executed the laws.

Sign-board of Hayden Tavern, Essex, Connecticut.

Judge Sewall records one scene, a typically Puritanical one, and worthy of a Puritan tithing - man. It took place at the Castle Inn where he went with some other good Bostonians to shut off a " vain show."

"Treat with Brother Wing (the landlord) about his Setting a Room in his House for a Man to shew Tricks in. He saith, seeing 'tis offensive he will remedy it.   It seems the Room is fitted with Seats.   I read what Dr. Ames saith of Callings, and spake as I could from this Principle, that the Man's Practice was unlawfull, and therefore Capt. Wing could not lawfully give him an accommodation for it.   Sung the 90 Ps from the 12 v to the end.   Broke up."

There is a suggestion of sober farce in this picture of those pious gentlemen reading and expounding a sermon, whipping out their psalm books, and singing a psalm to poor hospitable Landlord Wing in the parlor or taproom of his own house.

Naturally the Puritan planters, and all " true New-English men " like Sewall, did not care to have the ordinaries of their quiet towns made into places of gay resort, of what they called " the shewing of vain shews." They deemed those hostelries places of hospitable convenience, not of lively entertainment. A contemporary poet, Quarles, thus compares human life to a stay at an inn : —

> " Our life is nothing but a winter's day,
> Some only break their fast and so away ;
> Others stay dinner and depart full fed ;
> The deepest age but sups and goes to bed.
> He's most in debt who lingers out the day,
> Who dies betimes, has less and less to pay."

This somewhat melancholy view, both of life and of a public house, lingered long in the colonies, for nearly a century ; we might say, with the life of the ordinary. When taverns came, their guests thought very little of dying, and paid very much attention to living.

CHAPTER II

OLD-TIME TAVERNS

BY the close of the seventeenth century the word ordinary was passing into disuse in America ; public houses had multiplied vastly and had become taverns, though a few old-fashioned folk — in letters, and doubtless in conversation — still called them ordinaries — Judge Sewall was one. The word inn, universal in English speech, was little heard here, and tavern was universally adopted. Though to-day somewhat shadowed by a formless reputation of being frequently applied to hostelries of vulgar resort and coarse fare and ways, the word tavern is nevertheless a good one, resonant of sound and accurate of application, since to this present time in the commonwealth of Massachusetts and in other states such large and sumptuous caravansaries as the Touraine and the Somerset Hotel of Boston are in the eye and tongue of the law simply taverns, and their proprietors innholders or tavern-keepers.

In the Middle colonies ordinaries and inns were just as quickly opened, just as important, just as frequent, as in New England ; but in the Southern colonies, the modes of settlement were so different, there were so few towns and villages, that hospitality to the traveller was shown at each plantation, every man's home was an inn; every planter was a landlord.

In general no charge was made for the entertainment of the chance visitor whose stay was deemed a pleasure in the secluded life of the Virginia tobacco planter. Indeed, unless a distinct contract had been made in advance and terms stated, the host could not demand pay from a guest, no matter how long the visitor remained. Rates of prices were set for the first Virginian ordinaries; previous to 1639 six pounds of tobacco were paid for a dinner, or about eighteen pence in coin; but as food soon grew more abundant, the price was reduced to twelve pence, and it was enjoined that the food must be wholesome and plentiful. Then the charges grew exorbitant, — twenty pounds of tobacco for a meal for a master, fifteen for a servant. Throughout the country the prices wavered up and down, but were never low. There were apparently two causes for this: the fact that ordinary-keepers captured so few guests, and also that the tobacco leaf varied and depreciated in value.

By 1668 so many small tippling-houses and petty ordinaries existed in the colony of Virginia that laws were passed restricting the number in each county to one at the court-house, and possibly one at a wharf or ferry. Then the magistrates tried to limit the drinks sold in these houses to beer and cider; and private individuals were warned not to sell "any sort of drink or liquor whatsoever, by

retail under any color, pretence, delusion, or subtle
evasion whatsoever." Those conditions did not
last long. Soon the Virginia ordinaries had plentiful domestic and imported liquors, and at very low
prices. Mr. Bruce says that "Madeira, Canary,
Malaga, and Fayal wines were probably much more
abundant in the Colony than in England at this
time, and were drunk by classes which in the mother
country were content with strong and small-beer."

But the ordinaries did scant business as lodging-
places. Governor Harvey complained that he could
with as much justice be called the host as the Governor of Virginia, from the great number of persons
entertained by him. This condition of affairs continued outside the cities till well into this century. In
the large towns, however, comfortable taverns were
everywhere established; and they were, as in the
Northern colonies, the gathering places of many
serious and many frivolous assemblages. The best
of our American taverns were found in Southern
cities; Baltimore had the Fountain Inn built around
a courtyard like an old English inn, and furnished
very handsomely.

Few of these ancient taverns still remain. The
old Indian Queen Tavern is still standing at Bladensburg, Maryland. Its picture is given opposite
page 33. This view is from a painting by Mr.
Edward Lamson Henry. It shows also an old stage-
wagon such as was used in the eighteenth century,
starting out from the tavern door. Mr. Henry
has made a most exhaustive study of old-time
modes of travel, as well as a fine collection of old

Indian Queen Tavern, Bladensburg, Maryland.

vehicles, harnesses, costumes, etc. The copies of his paintings, which I am honored by using in this book, are in every detail authoritative and invaluable records of the olden time.

With the establishment of turnpikes, road houses multiplied, and for a time prospered. But their day was short; a typical Maryland road house is shown on page 34, far gone in a decrepit and ugly old age.

The history of Pennsylvania shows that its taverns were great in number and good in quality, especially soon after the Revolution. This would be the natural accompaniment of the excellent roads throughout the state. Philadelphia had an extraordinary number of public houses, and many were needed; for the city had a vast number of visitors, and a great current of immigration poured into that port. In the chapter on Signs and Symbols, many names and descriptions are given of old Philadelphia taverns.

The first Dutch directors-general of New Netherland entertained infrequent travellers and traders at their own homes, and were probably very glad to have these visitors. But trade was rapidly increasing, and Director-General Kieft, "in order to accommodate the English, from whom he suffered great annoyance, built a fine inn of stone." The chronicler De Vries had often dined in Kieft's house, and he says dryly of the building of this inn, " It happened well for the travellers."

The Stadt Harberg, or City Tavern, was built in where now stand the warehouses, 71 and 73 Pearl Street. It was ordained that a well and brew-house might be erected at the rear of the inn; right was given to retail the East India Company's wine and brandy; and some dull records exist of the use of the building as an inn.   It had a career afterward

Old Maryland Road House.

of years of use and honor as the Stadt Huys, or City Hall; I have told its story at length in a paper in the *Half-Moon Series* on Historic New York.

The building was certainly not needed as a tavern, for in 1648 one-fourth of the buildings in New Amsterdam had been turned into tap-houses for the sale of beer, brandy, and tobacco.   Governor Stuyvesant placed some restraint on these tapsters; they had to receive unanimous consent of the Council to set up the business; they could not sell to Indians.

"Unreasonable night-tippling," that is, drinking after the curfew bell at nine o'clock, and "intemperate drinking on the Sabbath," that is, drinking by any one not a boarder before three o'clock on the Sabbath (when church services were ended), were heavily fined. Untimely "sitting of clubs" was also prohibited. These laws were evaded with as much ease as the Raines Law provisions of later years in the same neighborhood.

In 1664 the red cross of St. George floated over the city; the English were in power; the city of New Amsterdam was now New York. The same tavern laws as under the Dutch obtained, however, till 1748, and under the English, taverns multiplied as fast as under Dutch rule. They had good old English names on their sign-boards: the Thistle and Crown, the Rose and Thistle, the Duke of Cumberland, the Bunch of Grapes, St. George and the Dragon, Dog's Head in the Porridge Pot, the Fighting Cocks, the White Lion, the King's Head.

On the Boreel Building on Broadway is a bronze commemorative tablet, placed there in 1890 by the Holland Society.

The site of this building has indeed a history of note. In 1754 Edward Willet opened there a tavern under the sign of the Province Arms; and many a distinguished traveller was destined to be entertained for many a year at this Province Arms and its successors. It had been the home residence of the De Lanceys, built about 1700 by the father of Lieutenant-Governor James De Lancey, and was deemed

a noble mansion.   The Province Arms began its
career with two very brilliant public dinners : one
to the new English Governor, Sir Charles Hardy ;
the other upon the laying of the corner-stone of
King's College.   A grand function this was, and
the Province Arms had full share of honor.   All
the guests, from Governor to students, assembled
at the tavern, and proceeded to the college grounds ;
they laid the stone and returned to Landlord Willet's, where, says the chronicle, " the usual loyal
healths were drunk, and Prosperity to the College ;
and the whole was conducted with the utmost
Decency and Propriety."

In 1763 the Province Arms had a new landlord, George Burns, late of the King's Head in the
Whitehall, and ere that of the Cart and Horse.
His advertisements show his pretensions to good
housekeeping, and his house was chosen for a
lottery-drawing of much importance — one for the
building of the lighthouse at Sandy Hook.   This
lottery was for six thousand pounds, and lighthouse
and lottery were special pets of Cadwallader Colden,
then President of his Majesty's Council.   Lotteries
were usually drawn at City Hall, but just at that
time repairs were being made upon that building, so
Mr. Burns's long room saw this important event.
The lighthouse was built.   The *New York Maga-
zine* for 1790 has a picture and description of it.
It is there gravely stated that the light could be
seen at a distance of ten leagues, that is, thirty miles.
As the present light at Sandy Hook is officially
registered to be seen at fifteen miles' distance, the

marvel of our ancestors must have shone with "a light that never was on land or sea."

Troublous times were now approaching. George Burns's long room held many famous gatherings anent the Stamp Act — at the first the famous Non-Importation Agreement was signed by two hundred stout-hearted New York merchants. Sons of Liberty drank and toasted and schemed within the walls of the Province Arms. Concerts and duels alternated with suppers and society meetings; dancing committees and governors of the college poured in and out of the Province Arms. In 1792 Peter De Lancey sold it to the Tontine Association; the fine old mansion was torn down, and the City Hotel sprang up in its place.

The City Hotel filled the entire front of the block on Broadway between Thomas and Cedar streets. Travellers said it had no equal in the United States, but it was unpretentious in exterior, as may be seen through the picture on the old blue and white plate (shown on page 38) which gives the front view of the hotel with a man sawing wood on Broadway, this in about 1824. It was simply yet durably furnished, and substantial comfort was found within. Though the dining room was simply a spacious, scrupulously neat apartment, the waiters were numerous and well-trained. There was a "lady's dining room" in which dances, lectures, and concerts were given. The proprietors were two old bachelors, Jennings and Willard. It was reported and believed that Willard never went to bed. He was never known to be away from his post, and with ease and good

nature performed his parts of host, clerk, book-
keeper, and cashier.   When Billy Niblo opened an
uptown coffee-house and garden, it was deemed a
matter of courtesy that Willard should attend the
housewarming.   When the hour of starting arrived,

City Hotel.

it was found that Willard had not for years owned a
hat.   Two streets away from the City Hall would
have been to him a strange city, in which he could
be lost.   Jennings was purveyor and attended to
all matters of the dining room, as well as relations
with the external world.   Both hosts had the per-

fect memory of faces, names, and details, which often
is an accompaniment of the successful landlord.
These two men were types of the old-fashioned
Boniface.

In the early half of the eighteenth century the
genteel New York tavern was that of Robert Todd,
vintner.   It was in Smith (now William) Street
between Pine and Cedar, near the Old Dutch
Church.   The house was known by the sign of
the Black Horse.   Concerts, dinners, receptions,
and balls took place within its elegant walls.   On
the evening of January 19, 1736, a ball was therein
given in honor of the Prince of Wales's birthday.
The healths of the Royal Family, the Governor,
and Council had been pledged loyally and often at
the fort through the day, and " the very great appearance of ladies and gentlemen and an elegant entertainment" at the ball fitly ended the celebration.
The ladies were said to be " magnificent." The ball
opened with French dances and then proceeded to
country dances, "upon which Mrs. Morris led up
to two new country dances made upon the occasion,
the first of which was called the Prince of Wales,
the second the Princess of Saxe-Gotha."

The Black Horse was noted for its Todd drinks,
mainly composed of choice West India rum ; and
by tradition it is gravely asserted that from these
delectable beverages was derived the old drinking
term " toddy."   (Truth compels the accompanying note that the word " toddy," like many of
our drinking names and the drinks themselves, came
from India, and the word is found in a geographical

description of India written in 1671, before Robert Todd was born, or the Black Horse Tavern
thought of.)

When Robert of toddy fame died, after nine
years of successful hospitality, his widow Margaret
reigned in his stead. She had a turn for trade,
and advertised for sale, at wholesale, fine wines and
playing cards, at reasonable rates. In 1750 the
Boston Post made this tavern its headquarters,
but its glory of popularity was waning and soon
was wholly gone.

At the junction of 51st and 52d streets with the
post-road stood Cato's Road House, built in 1712.
Cato was a negro slave who had so mastered various
specialties in cooking that he was able to earn enough
money to buy his freedom from his South Carolina
master. He kept this inn for forty-eight years.
Those who tasted his okra soup, his terrapin, fried
chicken, curried oysters, roast duck, or drank his
New York brandy-punch, his Virginia egg-nogg, or
South Carolina milk-punch, wondered how any one
who owned him ever could sell him even to himself. Alongside his road house he built a ballroom
which would let thirty couple swing widely in ener-
getic reels and quadrilles. When Christmas sleighing set in, the Knickerbocker braves and belles
drove out there to dance; and there was *always*
sleighing at Christmas in old New York — all octo-
genarians will tell you so. Cato's egg-nogg was
mixed in single relays by the barrelful. He knew
precisely the mystic time when the separated white
and yolk was beaten enough, he knew the exact

modicum of sugar, he could count with precision
the grains of nutmeg that should fleck the compound, he could top to exactness the white egg
foam. A picture of this old road house, taken
from a print, is here given. It seems but a shabby
building to have held so many gay scenes.

Cato's House.

The better class of old-time taverns always had a
parlor. This was used as a sitting room for women
travellers, or might be hired for the exclusive use of
some wealthy person or family. It was not so jovial
a room as the taproom, though in winter a glowing
fire in the open fireplace gave to the formal furnishings that look of good cheer and warmth and
welcome which is ever present, even in the meanest
apartment, when from the great logs the flames shot
up and " the old rude-furnished room burst flower-
like into rosy bloom." We are more comfortable

now, with our modern ways of house-heating, but our rooms do not look as warm as when we had open fires.   In the summer time the fireplace still was an object of interest.   A poet writes : —

> " 'Tis summer now ; instead of blinking flames
> Sweet-smelling ferns are hanging o'er the grate.
>   With curious eyes I pore
> Upon the mantel-piece with precious wares,
> Glazed Scripture prints in black lugubrious frames,
>   Filled with old Bible lore ;
> The whale is casting Jonah on the shore :
> Pharaoh is drowning in the curling wave.
> And to Elijah sitting at his cave
> The hospitable ravens fly in pairs
> Celestial food within their horny beaks."

The walls of one tavern parlor which I have seen were painted with scenes from a tropical forest.   On either side of the fireplace sprang a tall palm tree. Coiled serpents, crouching tigers, monkeys, a white elephant, and every form of vivid-colored bird and insect crowded each other on the walls of this Vermont tavern.   On the parlor of the Washington Tavern at Westfield, Massachusetts, is a fine wall-paper with scenes of a fox-chase.   This tavern is shown on the opposite page; also on page 45 one of the fine hand-wrought iron door-latches used on its doors.   These were made in England a century and a half ago.

The taproom was usually the largest room of the tavern.   It had universally a great fireplace, a bare, sanded floor, and ample seats and chairs. Usually there was a tall, rather rude writing-desk,

Washington Tavern, Westfield, Massachusetts.

at which a traveller might write a letter, or sign a contract, and where the landlord made out his bills and kept his books. The bar was the most interesting furnishing of this room. It was commonly made with a sort of portcullis grate, which could be closed if necessary. But few of these bars remain; nearly all have been removed, even if the tavern still stands. The taproom of the Wayside Inn at Sudbury, Massachusetts, is shown on page 19. It is a typical example of a room such as existed in hundreds of taverns a century ago. Another taproom may still be seen in the Wadsworth Inn. This well-built, fine old house, shown on page 47, is a good specimen of the better class of old taverns. It is three miles from Hartford, Connecticut, on the old Albany turnpike. It was one of twenty-one taverns within a distance of twenty miles on that pike. It was not a staging inn for every passing coach, but enjoyed an aristocratic patronage. The property has been in the same family for five generations, but the present building was erected by Elisha Wadsworth in 1828. It is not as old as the member of the Wadsworth family who now lives in it, Miss Lucy Wadsworth, born in 1801. Its old taproom is shown on page 51. This tavern was a public house till the year 1862.

Some of the furnishings of the taproom of the old Mowry Inn still are owned by Landlord Mowry's descendants, and a group of them is shown on page 70. Two heavy glass beakers brought from Holland, decorated with vitrifiable colors like the Bristol glass, are unusual pieces. The wooden tankard, certainly two centuries old, has the curious ancient lid hinge. The Bellarmine jug was brought to America filled with fine old gin from Holland by Mayor Willet, the first Mayor of New York City. The bowl is one of the old Indian knot bowls. It has been broken and neatly repaired by sewing the cracks together with waxed thread. The sign-board of this old inn is shown on page 57. The house stood on the post-road between Woonsocket and Providence, in a little village known as Lime Rock. As it was a relay house for coaches, it had an importance beyond the size of the settlement around it.

Sometimes the taproom was decorated with broad hints to dilatory customers. Such verses as this were hung over the bar : —

"I've trusted many to my sorrow.
Pay to-day. I'll trust to-morrow."

Another ran : —

"My liquor's good, my measure just ;
But, honest Sirs, I will not trust."

Another showed a dead cat with this motto : —

"Care killed this Cat.
Trust kills the Landlord."

Still another : —

"If Trust,
I must,
My ale,
Will pale."

The old Phillips farm-house at Wickford, Rhode Island, was at one time used as a tavern. It has a splendid chimney over twenty feet square. So much room does this occupy that there is no central staircase, and little winding stairs ascend at three corners of the house. On each chimney-piece are hooks to hang firearms, and at one side curious little drawers are set for pipes and tobacco. I

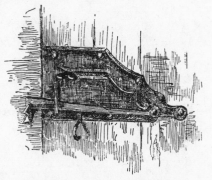

Door-latch of Washington Tavern.

have seen these tobacco drawers in several old taverns. In some Dutch houses in New York these tobacco shelves are found in an unusual and seem-

ingly ill-chosen place, namely, in the entry over the
front door ; and a narrow flight of three or four steps
leads up to them.   Hanging on a nail alongside the
tobacco drawer or shelf would usually be seen a pipe-
tongs — or smoking tongs.   They were slender little
tongs, usually of iron or steel; with them the smoker
lifted a coal from the fireplace to light his pipe.
Sometimes the handle of the tongs had one end
elongated, knobbed, and ingeniously bent S-shaped
into convenient form to press down the tobacco
into the bowl of the pipe.   Other old-time pipe-
tongs were in the form of a lazy-tongs.   A companion of the pipe-tongs on the mantel was what
was known as a comfortier ; a little brazier of metal
in which small coals could be handed about for
pipe lighting.   An unusual luxury was a comfortier
of silver, which were found among the wealthy
Dutch settlers.

Two old taverns of East Poultney, Vermont,
are shown on page 59.   Both sheltered Horace
Greeley in his sojourn there.   The upper house,
the Pine Tree, is a "sun-line" house, facing
due north, with its ends pointing east and west.
Throughout a century the other house, the Eagle
Tavern, has never lost its calling ; now it is the
only place in the village where the tourist may find
shelter for the night unless he takes advantage of
the kindness of some good-hearted housekeeper.

The main portion of the Eagle Tavern of Newton,
New Hampshire, is still standing and is shown with
its sign-board on page 126.   It was the "halfway
house" on the much-travelled stage-road between

Haverhill, Massachusetts, and Exeter, New Hampshire. The house was kept by Eliphalet Bartlett in Revolutionary times as account-books show, though the sign-board bears the date 1798. The tavern originally had two long wings, in one of which was kept a country store. Five generations of Bartletts were born in it before it was sold to the present

Wadsworth Inn, Hartford, Connecticut.

owners. The sign-board displays on one side the eagle which confers the name; on the other, what was termed in old descriptions a punch-bowl, but which is evidently a disjointed teapot.

About the time when settlements in the New World had begun to assume the appearance of towns, and some attempt at closely following English modes of life became apparent, there were springing up in London at every street corner coffee-houses, which flourished through the times of Dryden, Johnson, and Goldsmith, till the close of the eighteenth century.   Tea and coffee came into public use in close companionship.   The virtues of the Turkish beverage were first introduced to Londoners by a retired Turkey merchant named Daniel Edwards, and his Greek servant, Pasque Rosser.   The latter opened the first coffee-house in London in 1652.   The first advertisement of this first coffee venture is preserved in the British Museum.

The English of a certain class were always ready to turn an evil eye on all new drinks, and coffee had to take its share of abuse.   It was called " syrup of soot," and " essence of old shoes," etc.; and the keeper of the Rainbow Coffee-house was punished as a nuisance " for making and selling of a drink called coffee whereby in making the same he annoyeth his neighbours by evil smells."   Soon, however, the smell of coffee was not deemed evil, but became beloved; and every profession, trade, class, and party had its coffee-house.   The parsons met at one, "cits" at another; soldiers did not drink coffee with lawyers, nor gamesters with politicians.   A penny was paid at the bar at entering, which covered newspaper and lights; twopence paid for a dish of coffee.   Coffee-houses sprang up everywhere in America as in London.   In 1752 in New York the New or Royal Exchange was held to be so laudable an undertaking that £100 was voted toward its construction by the Common Council.   It was built like the English exchanges, raised on brick arches, and was opened as a coffee-room in 1754.   The name of the Merchant's Coffee-house — on the southeast corner of Wall and Water streets — appears in every old newspaper. It was a centre of trade. Ships, cargoes, lands, houses, negroes, and varied merchandise were " vendued " at this coffee-house. It also served as an insurance office. Alexander Macraby wrote in 1768 in New York : —

" They have a vile practice here, which is peculiar to this city ; I mean that of playing back-gammon (a noise I detest) which is going forward in the public coffee-houses from morning till night, frequently ten or a dozen tables at a time."

From this it will be seen that the English sin of gaming with cards did not exist in New York coffee-houses.

The London Coffee-house was famous in the history of Philadelphia. On April 15, 1754, the printer, Bradford, put a notice in his journal for sub-scribers to the coffee-house to meet at the court-house on the 19th to choose trustees. Bradford applied for a license to the Governor and Council thus : —

" Having been advised to keep a Coffee-House for the benefit of merchants and traders, and as some people may be desirous at times to be furnished with other liquors besides coffee, your petitioner apprehends that it is neces-sary to have the government license."

The coffee-house was duly opened ; Bradford's account for opening day was £9 6s. The trustees also lent him £259 of the £350 of subscriptions, and this coffee-house became a factor in American history. The building, erected about 1702, stood on the corner of Front and Market streets, on land which had been given by Penn to his daughter Letitia. Bradford was a grandson of the first printer Bradford, and father of the Attorney-General of the United States under Washington. His standing at once gave the house prestige and much custom. Westcott says "it was the headquarters of life and action, the pulsating heart of excitement, enterprise, and patriotism." Soldiers and merchants here met; slaves here were sold; strangers resorted for news; captains sold cargoes; sheriffs held "vandues."

The Exchange Coffee-house of Boston was one of the most remarkable of all these houses. It was a mammoth affair for its day, being seven stories in height. It was completed in 1808, having been nearly three years in building, and having cost half a million dollars. The principal floor was an exchange. It ruined many of the workmen who helped to build it. During the glorious days of stage-coach travel, its successor, built after it was burnt in 1818, had a brilliant career as a staging tavern, for it had over two hundred bedrooms, and was in the centre of the city. At this Coffee-house Exchange was kept a register of marine news, arrivals, departures, etc., and many distinguished naval officers were registered there. At a sumptuous dinner given to President Monroe, who had rooms there, in July, 1817, there were present Commodores Bainbridge, Hull, and Perry; ex-Presi-

Taproom of Wadsworth Inn.

dent John Adams; Generals Swift, Dearborn, Cobb, and Humphreys; Judges Story, Parker, Davis, Adams, and Jackson; Governor Brooks, Governor Phillips, and many other distinguished men.

It would be a curious and entertaining study to trace the evolution of our great hotels, from the cheerful taverns and country inns, beloved of all

travellers, to more pretentious road houses, to coffee-houses, then to great crowded hotels. We
could see the growth of these vast hotels, especially
those of summer resorts, and also their decay. In
many fashionable watering-places great hotels have
been torn down within a few years to furnish space
for lawns and grounds around a splendid private
residence. Many others are deserted and closed,
some flourish in exceptional localities which are in
isolated or remote parts of the country, such as
southern Florida, the Virginia mountains, etc.;
many have been forced to build so-called cottages
where families can have a little retirement and
privacy between meals, which are still eaten in a
vast common dining room. But the average American of means in the Northern states, whose parents
never left the city till after the 4th of July, and
then spent a few weeks in the middle of the summer in a big hotel at Saratoga, or Niagara Falls,
or Far Rockaway, or in the White Mountains, now
spends as many months in his own country home.
A few extraordinary exceptions in hotel life in
America remain prosperous, however, the chief
examples on our Eastern coast being at Atlantic
City and Old Point Comfort.

The study of tavern history often brings to light
much evidence of sad domestic changes. Many a
cherished and beautiful home, rich in annals of
family prosperity and private hospitality, ended its
days as a tavern. Many a stately building of historic note was turned into an inn in its later career.
The Indian Queen in Philadelphia had been at

various times the home of Sir Richard Penn, the
headquarters of General Howe and of General Bene-
dict, the home of Robert Morris and Presidents
Washington and Adams. Benjamin Franklin's home
became a tavern ; so also did the splendid Bingham
mansion, which was built in 1790 by the richest
man of his day. Governor Lloyd's house became
the Cross Trees Inn. Boston mansions had the
same fate. That historic building — the Province
House — served its term as a tavern.

Sometimes an old-time tavern had a special petty
charm of its own, some peculiarity of furnishing or
fare. One of these was the Fountain Inn of Medford, Massachusetts. It was built in 1725 and soon
became vastly frequented. No town could afford a
better site for inns than Medford. All the land
travel to Boston from Maine, eastern New Hampshire, and northeastern Massachusetts poured along
the main road through Medford, which was just distant enough from Boston centre to insure the halting
and patronage of every passer-by. The Fountain
Inn bustled with constant customers, and I can well
believe that all wanderers gladly stopped to board
and bait at this hospitable tavern. For I know
nothing more attractive, "under the notion of an
inn," than this old tavern must have been, especially through the long summer months. It was a
road house and stood close to the country road, so
was never quiet; yet it afforded nevertheless a charming and restful retreat for weary and heated wanderers. For on either side of the front dooryard
grew vast low-spreading trees, and in their heavy

branches platforms were built and little bridges connected tree to tree, and both to the house. Perhaps the happy memories of hours and days of my
childhood spent in a like tree nest built in an old
apple tree, endow these tree rooms of the Fountain

Fountain Inn.

Inn with charms which cannot be equally endorsed
and appreciated by all who read of them ; but to me
they form an ideal traveller's joy. To sit there
through the long afternoon or in the early twilight,
cool and half remote among the tree branches, drinking a dish of tea ; watching horsemen and cartmen
and sturdy pedestrians come and go, and the dash-

ing mail-coach rattle up, a flash of color and noise and life, and pour out its motley passengers, and speedily roll away with renewed patrons and splendor — why, it was like a scene in a light opera.

The tree abodes and the bridges fell slowly in pieces, and one great tree died; but its companion lived till 1879, when it, too, was cut down and the bald old commonplace building crowded on the dusty street stood bare and ugly, without a vestige or suggestion of past glory around it. Now that, too, is gone, and only the picture on the opposite page, of the tavern in its dying poverty, remains to show what was once the scene of so much bustle and good cheer.

The State House Inn of Philadelphia was built in 1693, and was long known as Clark's Inn. It was a poor little building which stood in a yard, not green with grass, but white with oysters and clam shells. Its proximity to the State House gave it the custom of the members and hangers-on of the colonial assemblies. William Penn often smoked his pipe on its porch. Clark had a signboard, the Coach and Horses, and he had something else which was as common perhaps in Philadelphia as tavern sign-boards, namely, turnspit dogs — little patient creatures, long-bodied and crook-legged, whose lives were spent in the exquisite tantalization of helping to cook the meat, whose appetizing odors of roasting they sniffed for hours without any realization of tasting at the end of their labors.

Dr. Caius, founder of the college at Cambridge, England, that bears his name, is the earliest English

writer upon the dog, and he tells thus of turnspits:
" Certain dogs in kitchen service excellent.   When
meat is to be roasted they go into a wheel, where,
turning about with the weight of their bodies they
so diligently look to their business that no drudge
or scullion can do the feat more cunningly."   The
Philadelphia landlord says in his advertisement of
dogs for sale, " No clock or jack so cunningly."
The summary and inhuman mode of teaching these
turnspits their humble duties is described in a book
of anecdotes published at Newcastle-on-Tyne in
1809.   The dog was put in the wheel.   A burning
coal was placed with him.   If he stopped, his legs
were burned.   That was all.   He soon learned his
lesson.   It was hard work, for often the great piece
of beef was twice the weight of the dog, and took at
least three long hours' roasting.   I am glad to know
that these hard-working turn-broches usually grew
shrewd with age ; learned to vanish at the approach
of the cook or the appearance of the wheel.   At one
old-time tavern in New York little brown Jesse
listened daily at the kitchen doorstep while the
orders were detailed to the kitchen maids, and he
could never be found till nightfall on roast-meat
days ; nay, more, he, as was the custom of dogs in
that day, went with his mistress to meeting and lay
at her feet in the pew.   And when the parson one
Sunday chose to read and expound from the first
chapter of Ezekiel, Jesse fled with silent step and
slunken tail and drooping ears at the unpleasant
verse, " And when the living creatures went, the
wheels went by them ; and when the living creatures

were lifted up from the earth, the wheels were lifted up." Naturally Jesse never suspected that these Biblical wheels were only parts of innocent allegorical chariots, but deemed them instead a very untimely and unkind reminder on a day of rest of his own hated turnspit wheel.

One of the sweetest of all tales of an inn is that begun by Professor Reichel and ended by Mr. John W. Jordan of the Historical Society of Pennsylvania; it is called "A Red Rose from the

Sign-board of N. Mowry's Inn.

Olden Time." It is a story of *Der neue Gasthof* or "The Tavern behind Nazareth," as it was modestly called, the tavern of the Moravian settlement at Bethlehem, Pennsylvania. It was a substantial building, "quartered, brick-nogged, and snugly weatherboarded, with a yard looking North and a Garden looking South." In 1754, under the regency of its first ruler, one Schaub, the cooper, and Divert Mary, his faithful wife, it bore a sign-board charged with a full-blown rose, and was ever after known as the Rose. This was not because the walls were coated with Spanish red; this rose bloomed with a life derived from sentiment and history, for it was built on land released by William Penn on an annual payment as rental of ONE RED ROSE.

There is something most restful and beautiful in the story of this old inn. Perhaps part of the hidden charm comes from the Biblical names of the towns. For, without our direct consciousness, there is ever something impressive in Biblical association; there is a magical power in Biblical comparison, a tenderness in the use of Biblical words and terms which we feel without actively noting. So this Red Rose of Nazareth seems built on the road to Paradise. An inventory was made of the homely contents of the Rose in 1765, when a new landlord entered therein; and they smack of the world, the flesh, and the devil. Ample store was there of rum, both of New England and the West Indies, of Lisbon wine, of cider and madigolum, which may have been metheglin. Punch-bowls, tumblers, decanters, funnels, black bottles, and nutmeg-graters and nutmegs also. Feather-beds and pillows were there in abundance, and blankets and coverlets, much pewter and little china, ample kitchen supplies of all sorts. In war and peace its record was of interest, and its solid walls stood still colored a deep red till our own day.

The night-watch went his rounds in many of our colonial towns, and called the hour and the weather. Stumbling along with his long staff and his dim horn-

lantern, he formed no very formidable figure either
to affright marauders or warn honest citizens that
they tarried too long in the taproom.   But his
voice gave a certain sense of protection to all who
chanced
to wake in
the night,
a knowl-
edge that
a   friend
was near.
All   who
dwelt in
t h e o l d

Pine-tree Tavern and Eagle Tavern.

towns of
B e t h l e -
hem   and
Nazareth
in Penn-
s y l v a n i a
could lis-
ten and be
truly cheered by the sound of the beautiful verses
written for the night watchman by Count Zinzen-
dorf.   In winter the watchman began his rounds at
eight o'clock, in summer at nine.   No scenes of
brawling or tippling could have prevailed at the

Rose Inn when these words of peace and piety rang
out : —

> Eight o'clock :
>   The clock is eight !   To Bethlehem all is told,
>   How Noah and his seven were saved of old.
>
> Nine o'clock :
>   Hear, Brethren, hear !   The hour of nine is come ;
>   Keep pure each heart and chasten every home.
>
> Ten o'clock :
>   Hear, Brethren, hear !   Now ten the hour-hand shows ;
>   They only rest who long for night's repose.
>
> Eleven o'clock :
>   The clock's eleven !   And ye have heard it all,
>   How in that hour the mighty God did call.
>
> Twelve o'clock :
>   It's midnight now !   And at that hour ye know
>   With lamps to meet the bridegroom we must go.
>
> One o'clock :
>   The hour is one !   Through darkness steals the day.
>   Shines in your hearts the morning star's first ray ?
>
> Two o'clock :
>   The clock is two !   Who comes to meet the day,
>   And to the Lord of Days his homage pay ?
>
> Three o'clock :
>   The clock is three :   The three in one above
>   Let body, soul, and spirit truly love.
>
> Four o'clock :
>   The clock is four !   Where'er on earth are three,
>   The Lord has promised He the fourth will be.

Five o'clock :
   The clock is five !   While five away were sent,
   Five other virgins to the marriage went.

Six o'clock :
   The clock is six !   And from the watch I'm free,
   And every one may his own watchman be.

CHAPTER III

THE TAVERN LANDLORD

THE landlord of colonial days may not have been the greatest man in town, but he was certainly the best-known, often the most popular, and ever the most picturesque and cheerful figure. Travellers did not fail to note him and his virtues in their accounts of their sojourns. In 1686 a gossiping London bookseller and author, named John Dunton, made a cheerful visit to Boston. He did not omit to pay tribute in his story of colonial life to colonial landlords. He thus pictures George Monk, the landlord of the Blue Anchor of Boston : —

"A person so remarkable that, had I not been acquainted with him, it would be a hard matter to make any New England man believe I had been in Boston ; for there was no one house in all the town more noted, or where a man might meet with better accommodation. Besides, he was a brisk and jolly man, whose conversation was coveted by all his guests as the life and spirit of the company."

This picture of an old-time publican seems more suited to English atmosphere than to the stern air of New England Puritanism.

Grave and respectable citizens were chosen to keep the early ordinaries and sell liquor. The first "house of intertainment" at Cambridge, Massachusetts, was kept by a deacon of the church, afterward Steward of Harvard College. The first license in that town to sell wine and strong water was to Nicholas Danforth, a selectman, and Representative to the General Court. In the Plymouth Colony Mr. William Collier and Mr. Constant South-

Sign-board of Washington Hotel.

worth, one of the honored Deputies, sold wine to their neighbors. These sober and discreet citizens

were men of ample means, who took the duty of
wine-selling to aid the colony rather than their own
incomes.

The first ordinary in the town of Duxbury was
kept by one Francis Sprague, said by a local chronicler to be of "ardent temperament." His license
was granted October 1, 1638, "to keep a victualling
on Duxburrow side." His ardent temperament
shaped him into a somewhat gay reveller, and his
license was withdrawn. It was regranted and again
recalled in 1666. His son succeeded him, another
jovial fellow. Duxbury folk were circumspect and
sober, and desired innkeepers of cooler blood.
Mr. Seabury, one of the tavern inspectors, was
granted in 1678 "to sell liquors unto such sober-
minded neighbours as hee shall thinke meet; soe
as hee sell not lesse than the quantie of a gallon
att a tyme to one pson, and not in smaller quantities
by retaile to the occationing of drunkeness."

The license to sell liquor and keep a tavern
explained clearly the limitations placed on a tavern-
keeper. The one given the Andover landlord in
1692 ran thus : —

"The Condition of this Obligation is sent. That
Whereas the above said William Chandler is admitted and
allowed by their Majesties' Justices at a General Sessions
of the Peace to keep a common Home of Entertainment
and to use common selling of Ale, Beer, Syder, etc., till
the General Session of Peace next, in the now-Dwelling
house of said Chandler in Andover, commonly known by
the sign of the Horse Shoe and no other, if therefore the
said William Chandler, during the time of keeping a Pub-

lick House shall not permit, suffer, or have any playing at Dice, Cards, Tables, Quoits, Loggets, Bowls, Ninepins, Billiards, or any other unlawful Game or Games in his House, yard, Garden, or Backside, nor shall suffer to be or remain in his House any person or persons not being of his own family upon Saturday nights after it is Dark, nor any time on the Sabbath Day or Evening after the Sabbath, nor shall suffer any person to lodge or stay in his House above one Day or Night, but such whose Name and Surname he shall deliver to some one of the Selectmen or Constables or some one of the Officers of the Town, unless they be such as he very well knoweth, and will answer for his or their forthcoming: nor shall sell any Wine or Liquors to any Indians or Negroes nor suffer any apprentices or servants or any other persons to remain in his house tippling or drinking after nine of the Clock in the night time; nor buy or take to Pawn any stolen goods, nor willingly Harbor in

Sign-board of Hays' Tavern.

his said House, Barn, Stable, or Otherwhere any Rogues, Vagabonds, Thieves, nor other notorious offenders whatsoever, nor shall suffer any person or persons to sell or utter any ale, beer, syder, etc., by Deputation or by colour of this License, and also keep the true assize and measure in his Pots, Bread and otherwise in uttering of ale, beer, syder, rum, wine, &c., and the same sell by sealed

measure.   And in his said house shall and do use and maintain good order and Rule : Then this present Obligation to
be either void, or else to stand in full Force, Power, and
Virtue."

Dr. Dwight in his Travels said that Englishmen often laughed at the fact that inns in New
England were kept by men of consequence.   He
says : —

"Our ancestors considered the inn a place where cor-
ruption might naturally arise and easily spread ; also as a
place where travellers must trust themselves, their horses,
baggage, and money, and where women must not be subjected to disagreeable experiences.   To provide for safety
and comfort and against danger and mischief they took
particular pains in their laws to prevent inns from being
kept by unprincipled or worthless men.   Every innkeeper
in Connecticut must be recommended by the selectmen and
civil authorities, constables and grand jurors of the town
in which he resides, and then licensed at the discretion of
the Court of Common Pleas.   It was substantially the
same in Massachusetts and New Hampshire."

Lieutenant Francis Hall, travelling through America in 1817, wrote : —

"The innkeepers of America are in most villages what
we call vulgarly, topping men — field officers of militia,
with good farms attached to their taverns, so that they are
apt to think what, perhaps, in a newly settled country is not
very wide of the truth, that travellers rather receive than
confer a favour by being accommodated at their houses.   The
daughters of the host officiate at tea and breakfast and generally wait at dinner."

An English traveller who visited this country shortly after the Revolution speaks in no uncertain terms of "the uncomplying temper of the landlords of the country inns in America." Another adds this testimony : —

"They will not bear the treatment we too often give ours at home. They feel themselves in some degree independent of travellers, as all of them have other occupations to follow; nor will they put themselves into a bustle on your account; but with good language, they are very civil, and will accommodate you as well as they can."

Brissot comprehended the reason for this appearance of independence ; he wrote in 1788 : —

"You will not go into one without meeting neatness, decency, and dignity. The table is served by a maiden well-dressed and pretty; by a pleasant mother whose age has not effaced the agreeableness of her features; and by men *who have that air of respectability which is inspired by the idea of equality*, and are not ignoble and base like the greater part of our own tavern-keepers."

Captain Basil Hall, a much-quoted English traveller who came to America in 1827, designated a Salem landlord as the person who most pleased him in his extended visit. Sad to say he gives neither the name of the tavern nor the host who was " so devoid of prejudice, so willing to take all matters on their favourable side, so well informed about everything in his own and other countries, so ready to impart his knowledge to others ; had such mirthfulness of fancy, such genuine heartiness of good-humour," etc.

Cooper Tavern.

In 1828 a series of very instructive and entertaining letters on the United States was published
under the title, *Notions of the Americans.* They
are accredited to James Fenimore Cooper, and were
addressed to various foreigners of distinction. The
travels took place in 1824, at the same time as the
visit of Lafayette, and frequently in his company.
Naturally inns, hotels, and modes of travel receive
much attention.   He speaks thus lucidly and pleasantly of the landlords : —

" The innkeeper of Old England and the innkeeper
of New England form the very extremes of their class.
The former is obsequious to the rich ; the other unmoved
and often apparently cold. The first seems to calculate at
a glance the amount of profit you are likely to leave behind

you, while his opposite appears to calculate only in what manner he can most contribute to your comfort without materially impairing his own. . . . He is often a magistrate, the chief of a battalion of militia or even a member of a state legislature. He is almost always a man of character, for it is difficult for any other to obtain a license to exercise the calling."

John Adams thus described the host and hostess of the Ipswich Inn : —

" Landlord and landlady are some of the grandest people alive, landlady is the great-granddaughter of Governor Endicott and has all the notions of high family that you find in the Winslows, Hutchinsons, Quincys, Saltonstalls, Chandlers, Otises, Learneds, and as you might find with more propriety in the Winthrops. As to landlord, he is as happy and as big, as proud, as conceited, as any nobleman in England, always calm and good-natured and lazy, but the contemplation of his farm and his sons, his house and pasture and cows, his sound judgment as he thinks, and his great holiness as well as that of his wife, keep him as erect in his thoughts as a noble or a prince."

The curiosity and inquisitiveness of many landlords was a standing jest.

" I have heard Dr. Franklin relate with great pleasantry," said one of his friends, " that in travelling when he was young, the first step he took for his tranquillity and to obtain immediate attention at the inns, was to anticipate inquiry by saying, ' My name is Benjamin Franklin. I was born in Boston. I am a printer by profession, am travelling to Philadelphia, shall have to return at such a time, and have no news. Now, what can you give me for dinner?'"

The landlord was usually a politician, sometimes a rank demagogue. He often held public office, was selectman, road commissioner, tax assessor, tax collector, constable, or town moderator; occasionally he performed all these duties. John Adams wrote bitterly that at public houses men sat drinking heavily while "plotting with the landlord to get him at the next town-meeting an election either for selectman or representative."

They were most frequently soldiers, either officers in the militia or brave fighters who had served in the army. It was a favorite calling for Revolutionary soldiers who lived till times of peace. They were usually cheerful men; a gloomy landlord made customers disappear like flowers before a frost. And these cheery hosts were fond of practical jokes.

One of the old hotels with the long piazza across the entire front was owned by a jesting landlord who never failed to spring an April-fool joke on his forgetful customers each year. The tavern had two doors, and every winter these were protected by portable storm porches the width of the door and about four feet deep. On the first day of April the landlord moved the porches a few feet down the piazza, so they opened upon the blank wall of the house. The house and piazza sat at such an angle with the walk from the street that the uncovered front doors were not visible to the visitor, so the delusion was complete. Grocerymen, butchers, bakers, travellers, even the tavern servants, invariably fell into the trap, thrust open the door, which swung with a slam and left them facing the blank wall. Any tavern frequenter, caught early in the day, was always ready to tole in a group of victims. As they walked up the steps he would say, "Come, boys, let's all pile into the office in a bunch and holler, 'Hullo, old Jed,' all together." All agreed and charged with a rush into the 4 x 6 storm box, while the plotter of the trick went in the real door and sat coolly sipping a rum punch as the confused and angry contingent came in with battered hats and bruised elbows, after its scuffle in the trap.

Shelby's Traveller's Rest.

One landlord had the name of frequently trick-ing travellers who stopped for a single meal by hav-ing the driver call out " Stage is ready " before they could eat the dinner they had ordered and paid for. A Yankee passenger disregarded this hasty sum-

mons and leisurely ate his dinner while the stage
drove off without him.   He finished the roast and
called at last for a bowl of bread and milk to top
off with as dessert.   Not a spoon could be found
for this dish, though plenty of silver spoons had
been on the table when the stage stopped.   To the
distracted landlord the Yankee drawled out, " Do
you think them passengers was going away without
something for their money ?   I could p'int out the
man that took them spoons."   A stable boy on a
fleet horse was promptly despatched after the stage,
and overtook it two miles down the road.   A low-
spoken explanation and request to the driver caused
him to turn quickly around and drive back to the
tavern door with all the angry protesting passengers.
The excited landlord called out to the Yankee as
the coach stopped, " You just p'int out the man that
took them spoons." — " Sartainly, Squire," said he,
as he climbed into the coach, " I'll p'int him out.
I took 'em myself.   You'll find 'em all in the big
coffee pot on the table.   Hurry up, driver, I've
had my dinner.   All aboard."

Grant Thorburn quaintly tells of this custom at
another tavern : —

" At Providence coaches were ready : on flew through
the dust and sweat of the day like Jehus.   At the tavern
dinner was ready, but there was no contract for time to
eat ; after grace from Dr. Cox (too long for the occasion)
we begun to eat.   Scarcely had I swallowed half my first
course when in came driver hallowing " All ready."   I
thought there was a stable-yard understanding between
him and the landlord, for while we were brushing the dust

from our clothes, mustering and saying grace, he was eating and drinking as fast as he could, and I did not observe that he paid anything. We arrived at the Eagle Tavern (Boston) about sundown; the ladies' hats and frocks which had shewed colours enough to have decked fifteen rainbows were now one, viz.: ashes on ashes and dust on dust."

The graceless modern reader might suspect that the "stable-yard understanding" included the parson.

Miller's Tavern.

A very amusing and original landlord was "Devil" Dave Miller, of the old General Washington Tavern which stood on East King Street, Lancaster, Pennsylvania. He was very stout and was generally seen in public bestriding an unusu-

ally small horse, which he would ride into his barroom to get a drink for both.   When he wished to
dismount, he rode to the doorway and hung on the
frame of the door with his hands.   The horse
would walk from under him and go unguided to the
stable.   An old print of this tavern marked D.
Miller's Hotel, is shown on page 73.   The various
vehicles standing in front of the hotel are interesting in shape, — old chaises, chairs, and a coach.

An old landlord named·Ramsay had a spacious
and popular inn on a much-travelled turnpike road,
and was the proprietor of a prosperous line of stage-
coaches.   He waxed rich, but though looked up to
by all in the community, plainly showed by the
precarious condition of his health in his advancing
years that he partook too freely of his own " pure
old rye."   His family and friends, though thoroughly
alarmed, did not dare to caution the high-spirited
old gentleman against this over-indulgence ; and
the family doctor was deputed to deal with the
squire in the most delicate and tactful manner possible.   The doctor determined to employ a parable,
as did Nathan to David, and felt confident of success ; and to deliver his metaphorical dose he
entered the taproom and cheerfully engaged the
squire in conversation upon an ever favorite topic,
the stage-coach.   He finally ran on to know how
long a well-built coach would last on the road, and
then said : " Now, Squire, if you had a fine well-
built old coach that had done good service, but
showed age by being a little shackling, being sprung
a little, having the seams open, would you hitch it

up with young horses and put it on a rough road, or would you favor it with steady old stagers and the smoothest road you could find?" — "Well, Doctor," answered the squire, "if I had such a coach as that *I would soak it*." And that seemed to bring the doctor's parable to a somewhat sudden and unprofitable ending.

CHAPTER IV

TAVERN FARE, AND TAVERN WAYS

IN the year 1704 a Boston widow named Sarah Knights journeyed " by post," that is, went on horseback, in the company of the government postman, from Boston to New York, and returned a few months later. She kept a journal of her trip, and as she was a shrewd woman with a sharp eye and sharper tongue, her record is of interest. She stopped at the various hostelries on the route, some of which were well-established taverns, others miserable makeshifts; and she gives us some glimpses of rather rude fare. On the first night of her journey she rode late to " overtake the post," and this is the account of her reception at her first lodging-place : —

" My guide dismounted and very complasently shewed the door signing to me to Go in, which I Gladly did. But had not gone many steps into the room ere I was interrogated by a young Lady with these or words to this purpose, viz., Law for mee — what in the world brings you here this time-a-night? I never see a Woman on the Rode so Late in all my Varsall Life! Who are you? Where are you goeing? Im scar'd out of my witts. . . . She then turned agen to mee and fell anew into her silly questions

without asking mee to sit down.   I told her she treated me
very Rudely and I did not think it my duty to answer her
unmannerly questions.   But to get ridd of them I told her
I come there to have the Posts company with me to morrow
on my journey."

She thus describes one stopping-place : —

"I pray'd her to show me where I must lodge. Shee conducted mee to a parlour in a little back Lento, which was
almost filled with the bedstead, which was so high that I was
forced to climb on a chair to gitt up to ye wretched bed
that lay on it, on which having Strecht my tired Limbs and
lay'd my Head on a Sad-coloured pillow, I began to think
on the transactions of ye past day."

At another place she complained that the dinner
had been boiled in the dye-kettle, that the black
slaves ate at the table with their master, "and into
the dish goes the black hoof as freely as the white
hand. . . ." Again she says : —

"We would have eat a morsell, but the Pumpkin and
Indian-mixt Bread had such an aspect, and the Bare-legg'd
Punch so awkerd or rather awfull a sound that we left
both."

At Rye, New York, she lodged at an ordinary
kept by a Frenchman.   She thus writes : —

"Being very hungry I desired a Fricassee which the
landlord undertaking managed so contrary to my notion of
Cookery that I hastened to Bed superless.   Being shew'd
the way up a pair of Stairs which had such a narrow passage that I had almost stopt by the Bulk of my Body; But
arriving at my Apartment found it to be a little Lento

Chamber furnisht among other Rubbish with a High Bedd
and a Low one, a Long Table, a Bench and a Bottomless
Chair.   Little Miss went to scratch up my Kennell whch
Russelled as if shee'd bin in the Barn among the Husks
and supose such was the contents of the Tickin — nevertheless being exceedingly weary down I laid my poor
Carkes never more tired and found my Covering as scanty
as my bed was hard.   Anon I heard another Russelling
noise in the room — called to know the matter — Little
Miss said she was making a bed for the men; who when
they were in Bed complain'd their Leggs lay out of it by
reason of its shortness — my poor bones complained bitterly
not being used to such Lodgings, and so did the man who
was with us; and poor I made but one Grone which was
from the time I went to bed to the time I riss which was
about three in the morning Setting up by the fire till light."

Manners were rude enough at many country taverns until well into the century.   There could be no
putting on of airs, no exclusiveness.   All travellers sat
at the same table.   Many of the rooms were double-
bedded, and four who were strangers to each other
often slept in each other's company.

An English officer wrote of this custom in
America : —

"The general custom of having two or three beds in
a room to be sure is very disagreeable ; it arises from the
great increase of travelling within the last few years, and
the smallness of their houses, which were not built for
houses of entertainment."

Mr. Twining said that after you were asleep the
landlord entered, candle in hand, and escorted a
stranger to your side, and he calmly shared the bed

till morning. Thurlow Weed said that any one who objected to a stranger as a bedfellow was regarded as obnoxious and as unreasonably fastidious. Still Captain Basil Hall declared that even at remote taverns his family had exclusive apartments; while in crowded inns it was never even

Ellery Tavern.

suggested to him that other travellers should share his quarters.

Many old tavern account-books and bills exist to show us the price of tavern fare at various dates.

Mr. Field gives a bill of board at the Bowen Inn at Barrington, Rhode Island. John Tripp and his wife put up at the inn on the 11th of May, 1776.

	s.	d.
" To 1 Dinner		9
To Bread and Cheese		7
To breakfast & dinner	1	3
To 1 Bowl Toddy		9
To Lodging you and wife		6
To 1 ½ Bowl Toddy	1	1 ½
To ½ Mug Cyder		1 ½
To lodge self and wife		6
To 1 Gill Brandy		5 ½
To breakfast		9 ½
Mug Cyder		1 ½
To ½ bowl Toddy		4 ½
Dinner		8
To 15 Lb Tobacco at 6d.	7	6
To ¼ Bowl Toddy		4 ½
To ½ Mug Cyder		1 ½
To Supper		6 "

I suppose the quarter bowls of toddy were for
Madam Tripp.

The house known for many years as the Ellery
Tavern is still standing in Gloucester, Massachusetts, and is a very good example of the overhang-
ing second story, as is shown in the front view of
it given on page 79 ; and also of the lean-to, or
sloping-roofed ell, which is shown by the picture on
page 83 of the rear of the house. This house
was built by Parson White in 1707, and afterward
kept as a tavern by James Stevens till 1740 ; then
it came into the hands of Landlord Ellery. As in
scores of other taverns in other towns, the selectmen
of the town held their meetings within its doors.
There were five selectmen in 1744, and their annual

salary for transacting the town's business was five dollars apiece. The tavern charges, however, for their entertainment amounted to £30, old tenor. It is not surprising, therefore, to read in the town records of the following year that the citizens voted the selectmen a salary of £5, old tenor, apiece, and "to find themselves." Nevertheless, in 1749, there was another bill from the Ellery Tavern of £78, old tenor, for the selectmen who had been sworn in the year previously and thus welcomed, " Expense for selectmen and Licker, £3. 18s." The Ellery Tavern has seen many another meeting of good cheer since those days.

The selectmen of the town of Cambridge, Massachusetts, met at the Blue Anchor Tavern, which was established as an ordinary as early as 1652. Their bill for 1769 runs thus : —

"The Selectmen of the Town of Cambridge to Ebenezer Bradish, Dr. 1769 :

March, To dinners and drink . . £0.	17.	8
April, To flip and punch	2.	
May, To wine and eating	6.	8
May, To dinners, drink and suppers . .	18.	
May, To flip and cheese	1.	8
May, To wine and flip	4.	
June, To punch	2.	8
July, To punch and eating	4.	
August, To punch and cheese . . .	3.	7
October, To punch and flip	4.	8
October, To dinners and drink . . .	13.	8
Sundries	12.	

£4. 10. 7 "

"Ordination Day" was almost as great a day for the tavern as for the meeting-house. The visiting ministers who came to assist at the religious service of ordination of a new minister were usually entertained at the tavern. Often a specially good beer was brewed called "ordination beer," and in Connecticut an "ordination ball" was given at the tavern — this with the sanction of the parsons. The bills for entertaining the visitors, for the dinner and lodging at the local taverns, are in many cases preserved. One of the most characteristic was at a Hartford ordination. It runs: —

	£	s.	d.
"To keeping Ministers		2.	4
2 Mugs tody		5.	10
5 Segars		3	
1 Pint Wine			9
3 Lodgings		9	
3 Bitters			9
3 Breakfasts		3.	6
15 boles Punch	1.	10	
24 dinners	1.	16	
11 bottles wine		3.	6
5 Mugs flip		5.	10
5 Boles Punch		6	
3 Boles Tody		3.	6"

The bill is endorsed with unconscious humor, "This all paid for except the Ministers Rum."

The book already referred to, called *Notions of the Americans*, tells of taverns during the triumphal tour of Lafayette in 1824. The author writes thus of the stage-house, or tavern, on

Lean-to of Ellery Tavern.

the regular stage line.   He said he stopped at fifty
such, some not quite so good and some better than
the one he chooses to describe, namely, Bispham's
at Trenton, New Jersey.

" We were received by the landlord with perfect civility,
but without the slightest shade of obsequiousness.   The
deportment of the innkeeper was manly, courteous, and
even kind; but there was that in his air which sufficiently
proved that both parties were expected to manifest the same
qualities.   We were asked if we all formed one party, or
whether the gentlemen who alighted from stage number
one wished to be by themselves.   We were shown into a
neat well-furnished little parlour, where our supper made
its appearance in the course of twenty minutes.   The
table contained many little delicacies, such as game, oysters,

and choice fish, and several things were named to us as at hand if needed. The tea was excellent, the coffee as usual indifferent enough. The papers of New York and Philadelphia were brought at our request, and we sat with our two candles before a cheerful fire reading them as long as we pleased. Our bed-chambers were spacious, well-furnished, and as neat as possible; the beds as good as one usually finds them out of France. Now for these accommodations, which were just as good with one solitary exception (sanitary) as you would meet in the better order of English provincial inns, and much better in the quality and abundance of the food, we paid the sum of 4s. 6d. each."

A copy is given opposite page 86 of a bill of the "O. Cromwell's Head Tavern" of Boston, which was made from a plate engraved by Paul Revere. This tavern was kept for over half a century by members of the Brackett family. It was distinctly the tavern of the gentry, and many a distinguished guest had " board, lodging, and eating " within its walls, as well as the wine, punch, porter, and liquor named on the bill. It will be noted that the ancient measure — a pottle — is here used. Twenty years before the Revolutionary War, and just after the crushing defeat of the British general, Braddock, in what was then the West, an intelligent young Virginian named George Washington, said to be a good engineer and soldier, lodged at the Cromwell's Head Tavern, while he conferred with Governor Shirley, the great war Governor of the day, on military affairs and projects. When this same Virginian soldier entered Boston at the head of a victorious army, he quartered his troops in Governor Shirley's mansion and grounds.

The sign-board of this tavern bore a portrait of the Lord Protector, and it is said it was hung so low that all who passed under it had to make a necessary reverence.

While British martial law prevailed in Boston, the grim head of Cromwell became distasteful to Tories, who turned one side rather than walk under the shadow of the sign-board, and at last Landlord Brackett had to take down and hide the obnoxious symbol.

The English traveller Melish was loud in his praise of the taverns throughout New York State as early as 1806. He noted at Little Falls, then in the backwoods, and two hundred miles from New York, that on the breakfast table were " table-cloth, tea tray, tea-pots, milk-pot, bowls, cups, sugar-tongs, teaspoons, casters, plates, knives, forks, tea, sugar, cream, bread, butter, steak, eggs, cheese, potatoes, beets, salt, vinegar, pepper," and all for twenty-five cents. He said Johnstown had but sixty houses, of which nine were taverns.

Another English traveller told of the fare in American hotels in 1807. While in Albany at " Gregory's," which he said was equal to many of the London hotels, he wrote : —

" It is the custom in all American taverns, from the highest to the lowest, to have a sort of public table at which the inmates of the house and travellers dine together at a certain hour. It is also frequented by many single gentlemen belonging to the town. At Gregory's upwards

of thirty sat down to dinner, though there were not more
than a dozen who resided in the house.   A stranger is thus
soon introduced to an acquaintance with the people, and if
he is travelling alone he will find at these tables some relief
from the ennui of his situation.   At the better sort of
American taverns very excellent dinners are provided, con-
sisting of almost everything in season.   The hour is from
two to three o'clock, and there are three meals in the day.
They breakfast at eight o'clock upon rump steaks, fish,
eggs, and a variety of cakes with tea or coffee.   The last
meal is at seven in the evening, and consists of as substantial fare as the breakfast, with the addition of cold fowl, ham,
&c.   The price of boarding at these houses is from a dollar and a half to two dollars per day.   Brandy, hollands,
and other spirits are allowed at dinner, but every other
liquor is paid for extra.   English breakfasts and teas, generally speaking, are meagre repasts compared with those
of America, and as far as I observed the people live with
respect to eating in a much more luxurious manner than
we do.   Many private families live in the same style as
at these houses ; and have as great variety.   Formerly pies,
puddings, and cyder used to grace the breakfast table, but
now they are discarded from the genteeler houses, and are
found only in the small taverns and farm-houses in the
country."

In spite of the vast number of inns in Philadelphia, another English gentleman bore testimony in
1823 that he deemed the city ill-provided with hostelries.   This gentleman " put up " at the Mansion
House, which was the splendid Bingham Mansion
on Third Street.   He wrote : —

" The tavern-keepers will not receive you on any other
terms except boarded at so much a day or week ; you can-

Bill of Cromwell's Head Tavern.

not have your meals by yourself, or at your own hours. This custom of boarding I disliked very much. The terms are, however, very moderate, only ten dollars per week. The table is always spread with the greatest profusion and variety, even at breakfast, supper, and tea; all of which meals indeed were it not for the absence of wine and soup, might be called so many dinners."

There lies before me a collection of twoscore old hotel bills of fare about a half century old. They are of dates when stage-coaching had reached its highest point of perfection, and the coaching tavern its glory. There were railroads, — comparatively few lines, however, — but they had not destroyed the constant use of coaches.

These hotels were the best of their kind in the country, such as the United States Hotel of Philadelphia, Foley's National Hotel of Norfolk, Virginia, Union Place Hotel and New York Hotel of New York, Union Hotel of Richmond, Virginia, American House of Springfield, Massachusetts, Dorsey's Exchange Hotel and Barnum's City Hotel of Baltimore, Maryland, the Troy House, the Tremont House of Boston, Massachusetts, etc. At this time all have become hotels and houses, not a tavern nor an inn is among them.

The menus are printed on long narrow slips of poor paper, not on cardboard; often the names of many of the dishes are written in. They show much excellence and variety in quality, and abundant quantity; they are, I think, as good as hotels of similar size would offer to-day. There are more boiled meats proportionately than would be served

now, and fewer desserts.   Here is what the American House of Springfield had for its guests on
October 2, 1851 :   Mock-turtle soup ; boiled blue-
fish with oyster sauce ; boiled chickens with oyster
sauce ; boiled mutton with caper sauce ; boiled
tongue, ham, corned beef and cabbage ; boiled
chickens with pork ; roast beef, lamb, chickens, veal,
pork, and turkey ; roast partridge ; fricasseed chicken,
oyster patties, chicken pie, boiled rice, macaroni ;
apple, squash, mince, custard, and peach pies ; boiled
custard ; blanc mange, tapioca pudding, peaches,
nuts, and raisins.   Vegetables were not named ;
doubtless every autumnal vegetable was served.

At the Union Place Hotel in 1850 the vegetables
were mashed potatoes, Irish potatoes, sweet potatoes, boiled rice, onions, tomatoes, squash, cauli-
flower, turnips, and spinach.   At the United States
Hotel in Philadelphia the variety was still greater,
and there were twelve entrées.   The Southern hotels
offered nine entrées, and egg-plant appears among
the vegetables.   The wine lists are ample ; those of
1840 might be of to-day, that is, in regard to familiar names ; but the prices were different.   Mumm's
champagne was two dollars and a half a quart ;
Ruinard and Cliquot two dollars ; the best Sauterne
a dollar a quart ; Rudesheimer 1811, and Hock-
heimer, two dollars ; clarets were higher priced, and
Burgundies.   Madeiras were many in number, and
high priced ; Constantia (twenty years in glass)
and Diploma (forty years in wood) were six dollars
a bottle.   At Barnum's Hotel there were Madeiras
at ten dollars a bottle, sherries at five, hock at six ;

this hotel offered thirty choice Madeiras — and these dinners were served at two o'clock. Corkage was a dollar.

Certain taverns were noted for certain fare, for choice modes of cooking special delicacies. One was resorted to for boiled trout, another for planked shad. Travellers rode miles out of their way to have at a certain hostelry calves-head soup, a most elaborate and tedious dish if properly prepared, and a costly one, with its profuse wine, but as appetizing and rich as it is difficult of making. More humble taverns with simpler materials but good cooks had wonderful johnny-cakes, delightful waffles, or even specially good mush and milk. Certain localities afforded certain delicacies; sal-

Bill of Fare of City Hotel.

mon in one river town, and choice oysters. One
landlord raised and killed his own mutton ; another
prided himself on ducks. Another cured his own
hams. An old Dutch tavern was noted for rolliches
and head-cheese.

During the eighteenth century turtle-feasts were
eagerly attended — or turtle-frolics as they were
called. A travelling clergyman named Burnaby
wrote in 1759 : —

" There are several taverns pleasantly situated upon East
River, near New York, where it is common to have these
turtle-feasts. These happen once or twice a week. Thirty
or forty gentlemen and ladies meet and dine together, drink
tea in the afternoon, fish, and amuse themselves till evening, and then return home in Italian chaises, a gentleman
and lady in each chaise. On the way there is a bridge,
about three miles distant from New York, which you
always pass over as you return, called the Kissing Bridge,
where it is part of the etiquette to salute the lady who has
put herself under your protection."

Every sea-captain who sailed to the West Indies
was expected to bring home a turtle on the return
voyage for a feast to his expectant friends. A turtle
was deemed an elegant gift ; usually a keg of limes
accompanied the turtle, for lime-juice was deemed
the best of all " sourings " for punch. In Newport
a Guinea Coast negro named Cuffy Cockroach, the
slave of Mr. Jahleel Brenton, was deemed the prince
of turtle cooks. He was lent far and wide for these
turtle-feasts, and was hired out at taverns.

Near Philadelphia catfish suppers were popular.
Mendenhall Ferry Tavern was on the Schuylkill

River about two miles below the Falls. It was opposite a ford which landed on the east side, and from
which a lane ran up to the Ridge Turnpike. This
lane still remains between the North and South
Laurel Hill cemeteries, just above the city of Philadelphia. Previous to the Revolution the ferry was
known as Garrigue's Ferry. A cable was stretched
across the stream ; by it a flatboat with burdens
was drawn from side to side. The tavern was the
most popular catfish-supper tavern on the river
drive. Waffles were served with the catfish. A
large Staffordshireware platter, printed in clear, dark,
beautiful blue, made by the English potter, Stubbs,
shows this ferry and tavern, with its broad piazza,
and the river with its row of poplar trees. It is
shown on page 93. Burnaby enjoyed the catfish-
suppers as much as the turtle-feasts, but I doubt if
there was a Kissing Bridge in Philadelphia.

Many were the good reasons that could be given
to explain and justify attendance at an old-time
tavern ; one was the fact that often the only newspaper that came to town was kept therein. This
dingy tavern sheet often saw hard usage, for when
it went its rounds some could scarce read it, some
but pretend to read it. One old fellow in Newburyport opened it wide, gazed at it with interest,
and cried out to his neighbor in much excitement :
" Bad news. Terrible gales, terrible gales, ships all
bottom side up," as indeed they were, in his way of
holding the news sheet.

The extent and purposes to which the tavern
sheet might be applied can be guessed from the

notice written over the mantel-shelf of one taproom, "Gentlemen learning to spell are requested to use last week's newsletter."

The old taverns saw many rough jokes. Often there was a tavern butt on whom all played practical jokes. These often ended in a rough fight. The old Collin's Tavern shown on page 97 was in coaching days a famous tavern in Naugatuck on the road between New Haven and Litchfield. One of the hostlers at this tavern, a burly negro, was the butt of all the tavern hangers-on, and a great source of amusement to travellers. His chief accomplishment was "bunting." He bragged that he could with a single bunt break down a door, overturn a carriage, or fell a horse. One night a group of jokers promised to give him all the cheeses he could bunt through. He bunted holes through three cheeses on the tavern porch, and then was offered a grindstone, which he did not perceive either by his sense of sight or feeling to be a stone until his alarmed tormentors forced him to desist for fear he might kill himself.

A picturesque and grotesque element of tavern life was found in those last leaves on the tree, the few of Indian blood who lingered after the tribes were scattered and nearly all were dead. These tawnies could not be made as useful in the tavern yard as the shiftless and shifting negro element that also drifted to the tavern, for the Eastern Indian never loved a horse as did the negro, and seldom became handy in the care of horses. These waifs of either race, and half-breeds of both races, circled around the tavern chiefly because a few stray pennies might be earned there, and also because within the tavern were plentiful supplies of cider and rum.

Almost every community had two or three of these semi-civilized Indian residents, who performed

Mendenhall Ferry Platter.

some duties sometimes, but who often in the summer, seized with the spirit of their fathers or the influence of their early lives, wandered off for weeks and months, sometimes selling brooms and baskets, sometimes reseating chairs, oftener working not, simply tramping trustfully, sure of food whenever they asked for it. It is curious to note how industrious, orderly Quaker and Puritan house-

wives tolerated the laziness, offensiveness, and ex-
cesses of these half-barbarians. Their uncouth-
ness was endured when they were in health, and
when they fell sick they were cared for with somewhat the same charity and forbearance that would
be shown a naughty, unruly child.

Often the landlady of the tavern or the mistress
of the farm-house, bustling into her kitchen in the
gray dawn, would find a sodden Indian sleeping on
the floor by the fireplace, sometimes a squaw and
pappoose by his side. If the kitchen door had no
latch-string out, the Indian would crawl into the
hay in the barn; but wherever he slept, he always
found his way to the kitchen in good time for an
ample breakfast.

Indian women often proved better helpers than
the men. One Deb Browner lived a severely
respectable life all winter, ever ready to help in the
kitchen of the tavern if teamsters demanded meals;
always on hand to help dip candles in early winter,
and ~make soap in early spring; and her strong
arms never tired. But when early autumn tinted
the trees, and on came the hunting season, she tore
off her respectable calico gown and apron, kicked
off her shoes and stockings, and with black hair
hanging wild, donned moccasins and blanket, and
literally fled to the woods for a breath of life, for
freedom. She took her flitting unseen in the night,
but twice was she noted many miles away by folk
who knew her, tramping steadily northward, bearing by a metomp of bark around her forehead a
heavy burden in a blanket.

One Sabbath morning in May a travelling teamster saw her in her ultra-civilized state on her way
home from meeting, crowned, not only with a discreet bonnet, but with a long green veil hanging
down her back. She was entering the tavern door
to know whether they wished her to attack the big
spring washing and bleaching the following day.
" Hello, Teppamoy ! " he said, staring at her, " how
came you here and in them clothes ? " Scowling
fiercely, she walked on in haughty silence, while the
baffled teamster told a group of tavern loafers that
he had been a lumberman, and some years there
came to the camp in Maine a wild old squaw named
Teppamoy who raised the devil generally, but the
constable had never caught her, and that she " looked
enough like that Mis' Browner to be her sister."

Another half-breed Indian, old Tuggie Bannocks,
lived in old Narragansett. She was as much negro
as Indian and was reputed to be a witch ; she certainly had some unusual peculiarities, the most
marked being a full set of double teeth all the way
round, and an absolute refusal ever to sit on a
chair, sofa, stool, or anything that was intended to
be sat upon. She would sit on a table, or a churn,
or a cradle-head, or squat on the floor; or she
would pull a drawer out of a high chest and recline
on the edge of that. It was firmly believed that in
her own home she hung by her heels on the oaken
chair rail which ran around the room. She lived
in the only roofed portion of an old tumble-down
house that had been at one time a tavern, and she
bragged that she could " raise " every one who had

ever stopped at that house as a guest, and often did so for company. Oh! what a throng of shadows, some fair of face, some dark of life, would have filled the dingy tavern at her command! I have told some incidents of her life in my *Old Narragansett*, so will no longer keep her dusky presence here.

Other Indian "walk-abouts," as tramps were called, lived in the vicinity of Malden, Massachusetts; old "Moll Grush," who fiercely resented her nickname; Deb Saco the fortune-teller, whose "counterfeit presentment" can be seen in the East Indian Museum at Salem; Squaw Shiner, who died from being blown off a bridge in a gale, and who was said to be "a faithful friend, a sharp enemy, a judge of herbs, a weaver of baskets, and a lover of rum."

Another familiar and marked character was Sarah Boston. I have taken the incidents of her life from *The Hundredth Town*, where it is told so graphically. She lived on Keith Hill in Grafton, Massachusetts, an early "praying town" of the Indians. A worn hearthstone and doorstone, surrounded now by green grass and shadowed by dying lilacs, still show the exact spot where once stood her humble walls, where once "her garden smiled."

The last of the Hassanamiscoes (a noble tribe of the Nipmuck race, first led to Christ in 1654 by that gentle man John Eliot, the Apostle to the Indians), she showed in her giant stature, her powerful frame, her vast muscular power, no evidence of a debilitated race or of enfeebled vitality. It is said she weighed over three hundred pounds. Her father was Boston

Phillips, also told of in story and tradition for his curious ways and doings. Sarah dressed in short skirts, a man's boots and hat, a heavy spencer (which was a man's wear in those days); and, like a true Indian, always wore a blanket over her shoulders in winter. She was mahogany-red of color, with coarse black hair, high cheek-bones, and all the char-

Collin's Tavern.

acteristic features of her race. Her great strength and endurance made her the most desired farm-hand in the township to be employed in haying time, in wall-building, or in any heavy farm work. Her fill of cider was often her only pay for some powerful feat of strength, such as stone-lifting or stump-pull-ing. At her leisure times in winter she made and peddled baskets in true Indian fashion, and told improbable and baseless fortunes, and she begged cider at the tavern, and drank cider everywhere. "The more I drink the drier I am," was a favorite expression of hers. Her insolence and power of abuse made her dreaded for domestic service, though she freely entered every home, and sat smoking and glowering for hours in the chimney corner of the tavern ; but in those days of few house-servants and scant " help," she often had to be endured that she might assist the tired farm wife or landlady.

A touch of grim humor is found in this tale of her — the more humorous because, in spite of Apostle Eliot and her Christian forbears, she was really a most godless old heathen. She tended with care her little garden, whose chief ornament was a fine cherry tree bearing luscious blackhearts, while her fellow-townsmen had only sour Morellos growing in their yards. Each year the sons of her white neighbors, unrestrained by her threats and entreaties, stripped her tree of its toothsome and beautiful crop before Sarah Boston could gather it. One year the tree hung heavy with a specially full crop ; the boys watched eagerly and expectantly the glow deepening on each branch, through tinted red to dark wine color, when one morning the sound of a resounding axe was heard in Sarah's garden, and a passer-by found her with powerful blows cutting down the heavily laden tree. "Why, Sarah," he asked in surprise, "why are you cutting down your splendid great cherry tree?" — "It shades the house," she growled; "I can't see to read my Bible."

A party of rollicking Yankee blades, bold with tavern liquor, pounded one night on the wooden gate of the old Grafton burying-ground, and called out in profane and drunken jest, "Arise, ye dead, the judgment day is come." Suddenly from one of the old graves loomed up in the dark the gigantic form of Sarah Boston, answering in loud voice, "Yes, Lord, I am coming." Nearly paralyzed with fright, the drunken fellows fled, stumbling with dismay before this terrifying and unrecognized apparition.

Mrs. Forbes ends the story of Sarah Boston with a beautiful thought. The old squaw now lies at rest in the same old shadowy burial place — no longer the jest and gibe of jeering boys, the despised and drunken outcast. Majestic with the calm dignity of death, she peacefully sleeps by the side of her white neighbors. At the dawn of the last day may she once more arise, and again answer with clear voice, "Yes, Lord, I am coming."

CHAPTER V

"KILL-DEVIL" AND ITS AFFINES

ANY account of old-time travel by stage-coach and lodging in old-time taverns would be incomplete without frequent reference to that universal accompaniment of travel and tavern sojourn, that most American of comforting stimulants — rum.

The name is doubtless American. A manuscript description of Barbadoes, written twenty-five years after the English settlement of the island in 1651, is thus quoted in *The Academy*: "The chief fudling they make in the island is Rumbullion, alias Kill-Divil, and this is made of sugar canes distilled, a hot, hellish, and terrible liquor." This is the earliest-known allusion to the liquor rum; the word is held by some antiquaries in what seems rather a strained explanation to be the gypsy rum, meaning potent, or mighty. The word rum was at a very early date adopted and used as English university slang. The oldest American reference to the word rum (meaning the liquor) which I have found is in the act of the General Court of Massachusetts in May, 1657, prohibiting the sale of strong liquors "whether knowne by the name of rumme,

strong water, wine, brandy, etc., etc." The traveller
Josselyn wrote of it, terming it that "cursed liquor
rhum, rumbullion or kill-devil." English sailors
still call their grog rumbowling. But the word
rum in this word and in rumbooze and in rumfustian did not mean rum; it meant the gypsy adjective
powerful. Rumbooze or rambooze, distinctly a
gypsy word, and an English university drink also, is
made of eggs, ale, wine, and sugar. Rumfustian
was made of a quart of strong beer, a bottle of white
wine or sherry, half a pint of gin, the yolks of
twelve eggs, orange peel, nutmeg, spices, and sugar.
Rum-barge is another mixed drink of gypsy name.
It will be noted that none of these contains any
rum.

In some localities in America rum was called in
early days Barbadoes-liquor, a very natural name,
occasionally also Barbadoes-brandy. The Indians
called it ocuby, or as it was spelled in the Norridge-
wock tongue, ah-coobee. Many of the early white
settlers called it by the same name. Kill-devil was
its most universal name, not only a slang name,
but a trading-term used in bills of sale. A description of Surinam written in 1651 says: "Rhum
made from sugar-canes is called kill-devil in New
England." At thus early a date had the manufacture of rum become associated with New England.

The Dutch in New York called the liquor
brandy-wine, and soon in that colony wherever
strong waters were named in tavern lists, the
liquor was neither aqua vitæ nor gin nor brandy,
but New England rum.

It soon was cheap enough.   Rev. Increase
Mather, the Puritan parson, wrote, in 1686: "It
is an unhappy thing that in later years a Kind of
Drink called Rum has been common among us.
They that are poor and wicked, too, can for a penny
make themselves drunk." From old account-books,
bills of lading, grocers' bills, family expenses, etc.,

Old Rum Bottles.

we have the price of rum at various dates, and find
that his assertion was true.

In 1673 Barbadoes rum was worth 6s. a gallon.
In 1687 its price had vastly fallen, and New England rum sold for 1s. 6d. a gallon.   In 1692 2s. a
gallon was the regular price.   In 1711 the price was
3s. 3d.   In 1757, as currency grew valueless, it
was 21s. a gallon.   In 1783 only a little over a
shilling; then it was but 8d. a quart.   During this

time the average cost of molasses in the West Indies was 12*d*. a gallon; so, though the distillery
plant for its production was costly, it can be seen
that the profits were great.

Burke said about 1750: "The quantity of spirits
which they distill in Boston from the molasses which
they import is as surprising as the cheapness at
which they sell it, which is under two shillings a
gallon; but they are more famous for the quantity
and cheapness than for the excellency of their rum."
An English traveller named Bennet wrote at the
same date of Boston society: "Madeira wine and
rum punch are the liquors they drink in common."
Baron Riedésel, who commanded the foreign troops
in America during the Revolution, wrote of the
New England inhabitants: "Most of the males
have a strong passion for strong drink, especially
rum." While President John Adams said causti-
cally: "If the ancients drank wine as our people
drink rum and cider, it is no wonder we hear of so
many possessed with devils;" yet he himself, to the
end of his life, always began the day with a tankard
of hard cider before breakfast.

The Dutch were too constant beer drinkers to
become with speed great rum consumers, and they
were too great lovers of gin and schnapps. But
they deprecated the sharp and intolerant prohibition
of the sale of rum to the Indians, saying: "To
prohibit all strong liquor to them seems very hard
and very Turkish. Rum doth as little hurt as the
Frenchman's Brandie, and in the whole is much
more wholesome." The English were fiercely

abhorrent of intemperance among the Indians, and court records abound in laws restraining the sale of rum to the "bloudy salvages," of prosecutions and fines of white traders who violated these laws, and of constant and fierce punishment of the thirsty red men, who simply tried to gratify an appetite instilled in them by the English.

William Penn wrote to the Earl of Sutherland in 1683 : " Ye Dutch, Sweed, and English have by Brandy and Specially Rum, almost Debaucht ye Indians all. When Drunk ye most Wretched of Spectacles. They had been very Tractable but Rum is so dear to them."

Rum formed the strong intoxicant of all popular tavern drinks; many are still mixed to-day. Toddy, sling, grog, are old-time concoctions.

A writer for the first *Galaxy* thus parodied the poem, *I knew by the smoke that so gracefully curled :* —

> "I knew by the pole that's so gracefully crown'd
> Beyond the old church, that a tavern was near,
> And I said if there's black-strap on earth to be found,
> A man who had credit might hope for it here."

Josiah Quincy said that black-strap was a composition of which the secret, he fervently hoped, reposed with the lost arts. Its principal ingredients were rum and molasses, though there were other simples combined with it. He adds, "Of all the detestable American drinks on which our inventive genius has exercised itself, this black-strap was truly the most outrageous."

Casks of it stood in every country store and

tavern, a salted cod-fish hung alongside, slyly to tempt by thirst additional purchasers of black-strap. "Calibogus," or "bogus," was unsweetened rum and beer.

Mimbo, sometimes abbreviated to mim, was a drink made of rum and loaf-sugar — and possibly water. The "Rates in Taverns" fixed in York County in Pennsylvania, in 1752, for "the protecting of travellers against the extortions of tavern-keepers," gives its price: —

> "1 Quart Mimbo made best W. I. Rum
> and Loaf: .   .   10d.
> 1 Quart Mimbo, made of New England
> Rum and Loaf: .   9d."

Many years ago, one bitter winter day, there stepped down from a rocking mail-coach into the Washington Tavern in a Pennsylvania town, a dashing young man who swaggered up to the bar and bawled out for a drink of "Scotchem." The landlord was running here and there, talking to a score of people and doing a score of things at once, and he called to his son, a lubberly, countrified young fellow, to give the gentleman his Scotchem. The boy was but a learner in the taproom, but he was a lad of few words, so he hesitatingly mixed a glass of hot water and Scotch whiskey, which the traveller scarcely tasted ere he roared out: "Don't you know what Scotchem is? Apple-jack, and boiling water, and a good dash of ground mustard. Here's a shilling to pay for it." The boy stared at the uninviting recipe, but faithfully compounded it,

when toot-toot sounded the horn—the coach waited
for no man, certainly not for a man to sip a scalding drink—and such a drink, and off in a trice
went full coach and empty traveller. The young
tapster looked dubiously at the great mug of steaming drink ; then he called to an old trapper, a town

Burgoyne Tavern.

pauper, who, crippled with rheumatism, sat ever in
the warm chimney corner of the taproom, telling
stories of coons and catamounts and wolverines, and
taking such stray drops of liquid comfort as old
companions or new sympathizers might pityingly
give him. " Here, Ezra," the boy said, " you take
the gentleman's drink. It's paid for." Ezra was
ever thirsty and never fastidious. He gulped down

the Scotchem. "It's good," he swaggered bravely, with eyes streaming from the scalding mustard, "an' it's tasty, too, ef it does favor tomato ketchup."

Forty years later an aged man was swung precariously out with a violent jerk from a rampant trolley car in front of the Washington Hotel. He wearily entered the gaudy office, and turned thence to the bar. The barkeeper, a keen-eyed, lean old fellow of inscrutable countenance, glanced sharply at him, pondered a moment, then opened a remote closet, drew forth from its recess an ancient and dusty demijohn of apple-jack, and with boiling water and a dash of mustard compounded a drink which he placed unasked before the traveller. "Here's your Scotchem," he said laconically. The surprised old man looked sharply around him. Outside the window, in the stable yard, a single blasted and scaling buttonwood tree alone remained of the stately green row whose mottled trunks and glossy leaves once bordered the avenue. The varying grades of city streets had entirely cut off the long porch beloved of old-time tavern loafers. The creaking sign-board had vanished. Within was no cheerful chimney corner and no welcoming blazing fire, but the old taproom still displayed its raftered ceiling. The ancient traveller solemnly drank his long-paid-for mug of Scotchem. "It's good," he said, "and tasty, if it does favor tomato ketchup."

A ray of memory darted across the brain of the old barkeeper, and albeit he was not a member of the Society of Psychical Research and could not formulate his brain impressions, yet he pondered on the curious problem of thought transference, of forced sequence of ideas, of coincidences of mental action resulting from similar physical conditions and influences.

Flip was a dearly loved drink of colonial times, far more popular in America than in England, much different in concoction in America than in England, and much superior in America—a truly American drink. As its chief ingredient is beer, it might be placed in the chapter on small drink, but the large amount consumed entitles it to a place with more rankly intoxicating liquors.

The earliest date that I find flip named in New England is 1690. From that year till the middle of this century there never was a day, never a minute of the day, and scarce of the night, that some old Yankee flip drinker was not plunging in a loggerhead, or smacking his lips over a mug of creaming flip.

In the *New England Almanac* for 1704 we read under December : —

> "The days are short, the weather's cold,
>   By tavern fires tales are told.
>   Some ask for dram when first come in,
>   Others with flip and bounce begin."

American flip was made in a great pewter mug or earthen pitcher filled two-thirds full of strong beer; sweetened with sugar, molasses, or dried pumpkin, according to individual taste or capabilities; and flavored with "a dash"—about a gill—of New England rum. Into this mixture was thrust and stirred a red-hot loggerhead, made of iron and shaped like a poker, and the seething iron made the liquor foam and bubble and mantle high, and gave it the burnt, bitter taste so dearly loved. A famous tavern host of Canton, Massachusetts, had a special fancy in flip. He mixed together a pint of cream, four eggs, and four pounds of sugar, and kept this on hand. When a mug of flip was called for, he filled a quart mug two-thirds full of bitter beer, added four great spoonfuls of his creamy com-

pound, a gill of rum, and thrust in the loggerhead. If a fresh egg were beaten into the mixture, the froth poured over the top of the mug, and the drink was called "bellows-top."

Happy Farmer Pitcher.

Let me not fail to speak of the splendid glasses in which flip was often served — I mean the great glass tumblers without handles which, under the name of flip glasses, still are found in New England homes. They are vast drinking-vessels, sometimes holding three or four quarts apiece, and speak to us dis-tinctly of the unlimited bibulous capacities of our ancestors. They are eagerly sought for by glass and china collectors, and are among the prettiest and most interesting of old-time relics.

Sign-board of Hancock Tavern.

English flip is not so simple nor so original nor so good a drink as American flip. It might be anything but flip, since it is compounded in a saucepan, and knows naught of the distinctive branding of flip, the seething loggerhead.   If it contained no spirits, it was called "egg-hot."

A rule for flip which seems to combine the good points of the American and English methods, uses ale instead of home-brewed.   It may be given "in the words of the Publican who made it" : —

"Keep grated Ginger and Nutmeg with a fine dried Lemon Peel rubbed together in a Mortar.   To make a quart of Flip: Put the Ale on the Fire to warm, and beat up three or four Eggs with four ounces of moist Sugar, a tea-spoonful of grated Nutmeg or Ginger, and a Quartern of good old Rum or Brandy.   When the Ale is near to boil, put it into one pitcher, and the Rum and Eggs, etc., into another: turn it from one Pitcher to another till it is as smooth as cream.   To heat plunge in the red hot Logger-head or Poker.   This quantity is styled One Yard of Flannel."

A quartern is a quarter of a gill, which is about the "dash" of rum.

No flip was more widely known and more respected than the famous brew of Abbott's Tavern at Holden, Massachusetts.   This house, built in 1763, and kept by three generations of Abbotts, never wavered in the quality of its flip.   It is said to have been famous from the Atlantic to the Pacific — and few stage-coaches or travellers ever passed that door without adding to its praises and thereafter spreading its reputation.   It is sad to add that I don't know exactly how it was made.   A bill still existing tells its price in Revolutionary days; other items show its relative valuation : —

" Mug New England Flip	.	.	.	.	9d.
" West India "	.	.	.	.	11d.
Lodging per night	.	.	.	.	3d.
Pot luck per meal	.	.	.	.	8d.
Boarding commons Men	.	.	.	4s.	8d.
" " Weomen	.	.	.	2s. "	

This is the only tavern bill I have ever seen in which nice distinctions were made in boarding men and women. I am glad to know that the "weomen" traveller in those days had 2s. 8d. of daily advantage over the men.

Other names for the hospital loggerhead were flip-dog and hottle. The loggerhead was as much a part of the chimney furniture of an old-time New England tavern and farm-house as the bellows or andirons. In all taverns and many hospitable homes it was constantly kept warm in the ashes, ready for speedy heating in a bed of hot coals, to burn a mug of fresh flip for every visitor or passer by. Cider could be used instead of beer, if beer could not be had. Some wise old flip tasters preferred cider to beer. Every tavern bill of the eighteenth century was punctuated with entries of flip. John Adams said if you spent the evening in a tavern, you found it full of people drinking drams of flip, carousing, and swearing. The old taprooms were certainly cheerful and inviting gathering-places; where mine host sat behind his cagelike counter surrounded by cans and bottles and glasses, jars of whole spices and whole loaves of sugar; where an inspiring row of barrels of New England rum, hard cider, and beer ranged in rivalry at an end of the room, and

Flip Glasses, Loggerhead, and Toddy Stick.

"Where dozed a fire of beechen logs that bred
   Strange fancies in its embers golden-red,
   And nursed the loggerhead, whose hissing dip,
   Timed by wise instinct, creamed the bowl of flip."

These fine lines of Lowell's seem to idealize the
homely flip and the loggerhead as we love to idealize the customs of our forbears. Many a reader of
them, inspired by the picture, has heated an iron
poker or flip-dog and brewed and drunk a mug of
flip. I did so not long ago, mixing carefully by a
rule for flip recommended and recorded and used
by General Putnam — Old Put — in the Revolution. I had the Revolutionary receipt and I had
the Revolutionary loggerhead, and I had the old-
time ingredients, but alas, I had neither the tastes
nor the digestion of my Revolutionary sires, and
the indescribable scorched and puckering bitterness

of taste and pungency of smell of that rank compound which was flip, will serve for some time in my memory as an antidote for any overweening longing for the good old times.

The toddy stick, beloved for the welcome ringing music it made on the sides of glass tumblers, was used to stir up toddy and other sweetened drinks. It was a stick six or eight inches long, with a knob at one end, or flattened out at the end so it would readily crush the loaf sugar used in the drink. The egg-nog stick was split at one end, and a cross-piece of wood was set firmly.in. It was a crude egg-beater. Whirled rapidly around, while the upright stick was held firmly between the palms of the hands, it was a grateful, graceful, and inviting machine in the hands of skilful landlords of old.

Another universal and potent colonial drink was punch. It came to the English colonies in America from the English colonies in India. To the Orientals we owe punch — as many other good things. The word is from the Hindustani *panch*, five, referring to the five ingredients then used in the drink, namely : tea, arrack, sugar, lemons, water. In 1675 one Tryer drank punch in India and, like the poor thing that he was, basely libelled it as an enervating liquor. The English took very quickly to the new drink, as they did to everything else in India, and soon the word appeared in English ballads, showing that punch was well known.

Englishmen did not use without change the punch-bowls of India, but invented an exceptionally elegant form known by the name of Monteith. It was called

after a man of fashion who was marked and remarkable for wearing a scalloped coat.   In the *Art of
Cookery* we find reference to him and the Monteith punch bowl : —

"New things produce new words, and so Monteith
    Has by one vessel saved himself from death."

Monteiths seem to have come into fashion about
1697. The rim was scalloped like its namesake's
coat, or cut in battlements, thus forming indenta-
tions, in which a
punch ladle and
lemon strainer
and tall wine-
glasses were
hung on their
sides, the foot
out.   The rim
was usually sepa-
rate from the
bowl, and was
lifted off with the
glasses and ladle

Porcelain Monteith.

and strainer, for the punch to be brewed in the bowl.
When the punch was duly finished, the ornamental rim
was replaced.   A porcelain imitation of a Monteith
is here shown, which was made in China for an
American ship-owner, doubtless from a silver model.
    Punch became popular in New England just as it
did in old England, in fact, wherever English-speak-
ing sea rovers could tell of the new drink.   In 1682
John Winthrop wrote of the sale of a punch bowl

in Boston, and in 1686 John Dunton told of more
than one noble bowl of punch in New England.

Every buffet of people of good station in prosperous times soon had a punch bowl. Every dinner
was prefaced by a bowl of punch passed from hand
to hand, while the liquor was drunk from the bowl.
Double and "thribble" bowls of punch were served
in taverns ; these held two and three quarts each.

To show the amount of punch drunk at a minister's
ordination in New England in 1785, I will state
that the eighty people attending in the morning had
thirty bowls of punch before going to meeting ; and
the sixty-eight who had dinner disposed of forty-four
bowls of punch, eighteen bottles of wine, eight bowls
of brandy, and a quantity of cherry rum.

Punch was popular in Virginia, it was popular in
New York, it was popular in Pennsylvania. William
Black recorded in his diary in 1744 that in Philadelphia he was given cider and punch for lunch ;
rum and brandy before dinner ; punch, Madeira,
port, and sherry at dinner ; punch and liqueurs with
the ladies ; and wine, spirit, and punch till bedtime ;
all in punch bowls big enough for a goose to swim in.

In 1757 S. M. of Boston, who was doubtless
Samuel Mather, the son of Cotton Mather, sent to
Sir Harry Frankland, the hero of the New England romance of Agnes Surriage, a box of lemons
with these lines : —

> " You know from Eastern India came
>   The skill of making punch as did the name.
>   And as the name consists of letters five,
>   By five ingredients is it kept alive.

Cincinnati Punch Bowl.

To purest water sugar must be joined,
With these the grateful acid is combined.
Some any sours they get contented use,
But men of taste do that from Tagus choose.
When now these three are mixed with care
Then added be of spirit a small share.
And that you may the drink quite perfect see,
Atop the musky nut must grated be.''

From the accounts that have come down to us, the " spirits a small share " of the Puritan Mather's punch receipt was seldom adhered to in New England punches.

The importation to England and America of lemons, oranges, and limes for use as punch " sowrings," as they were called, was an important part of the West Indian and Portuguese trade. The juices of lemons, oranges, limes, and pineapples were all used in punches, and were imported in demijohns and bottles. The appetizing advertisements of J. Crosby, a Boston fruit importer, are frequent for many years in New England newspapers. Here is one from the *Salem Gazette* in 1741 : —

"Extraordinary good and very fresh Orange juice which some of the very best Punch Tasters prefer to Lemmon, at one dollar a gallon. Also very good Lime Juice and Shrub to put into Punch at the Basket of Lemmons, J. Crosby, Lemmon Trader."

I don't know whether the punch tasters referred to were professional punch mixers or whether it was simply a term applied to persons of well-known experience and judgment in punch-drinking.

In Salem, New Jersey, in 1729, tavern prices were regulated by the Court. They were thus: —

"A rub of punch made with double-refined sugar and one and a half gills of rum . . . . 9d.

A rub of punch made with single refined sugar and one and a half gills of rum . . . . 8d.

A rub made of Muscovado sugar and one and a half gills of rum . . . . . . 7d.

A quart of flipp made with a pint of rum . . 9d.

A pint of wine . . . . . 1s.

A gill of rum . . . . . 3d.

A quart of strong beer . . . . 4d.

A gill of brandy or cordial . . . . 6d.

A quart of metheglin . . . . 9d.

A quart of cider royal . . . . 8d.

A quart of cider . . . . . 4d."

Punches were many of name, scores of different ones were given by drink compounders, both amateur and professional. Punches were named for persons, for places; for taverns and hosts; for bartenders and stage-coach drivers; for unusual ingredients or romantic incidents. Sometimes honor

was conferred by naming the punch for the person;
sometimes the punch was the only honor the original ever had.   In these punches all kinds of flavoring and spices were used, and all the strong liquors
of the world, all the spirits, wines, liqueurs, drops,
distilled waters and essences — but seldom and scant
malt liquors, if it were truly punch.

With regard to the proper amounts of all these
various fluids to be used in composition opinions
always differed.   Many advised a light hand with
cordials, some disliked spices; others wished a
plentiful amount of lemon juice, others wished tea.
In respect of the proportions of two important and
much-discussed ingredients, old-time landlords apparently heeded directions similar to those I once
heard given impressively by an old Irish ecclesias-
tic of high office: "Shtop! shtop! ye are not com-
mincin' right and in due ordher!   Ye musthn't iver
put your whiskey or rum foorst in your punch-
bowl and thin add wather; for if ye do, ivery dhrop
of wather ye put in is just cruel spoilin' of the
punch; but — foorst — put some wather in the
bowl — some, I say, since in conscience ye must —
thin pour in the rum; and sure ye can aisily par-
caive that ivery dhrop ye put in is afther makin' the
punch bowl bether and bether."

Charles Lamb tells in his *Popular Fallacies* of
"Bully Dawson kicked by half the town and half
the town kicked by Bully Dawson."   This Bully
Dawson was a famous punch brewer; his rule was
precisely like that of a famous New England landlord, and is worth choosing among a score of rules:—

" The man who sees, does, or thinks of anything else
while he is making Punch may as well look for the North-
west Passage on Mutton Hill. A man can never make
good punch unless he is satisfied, nay positive, that no
man breathing can make better. I can and do make good
Punch, because I do nothing else, and this is my way of
doing it. I retire to a solitary corner with my ingredients ready sorted ; they are as follows, and I mix them in
the order they are here written. Sugar, twelve tolerable
lumps ; hot water, one pint ; lemons, two, the juice and
peel ; old Jamaica rum, two gills ; brandy, one gill ; porter
or stout, half a gill ; arrack, a slight dash. I allow myself
five minutes to make a bowl in the foregoing proportions,
carefully stirring the mixture as I furnish the ingredients
until it actually foams ; and then Kangaroos ! how beautiful it is ! "

With this nectar and a toast we may fitly close
this chapter. May the grass grow lightly o'er the
grave of Bully Dawson, and weigh like lead on the
half the town that kicked him !

CHAPTER VI

SMALL DRINK

" UNDER this tearme of small-drink," wrote
an old chronicler, "do I endow such
drinks as are of comfort, to quench an
honest thirst, not to heat the brain, as one man
hath ale, another cider, another metheglin, and one
sack." Under this title I also place such tavern
and home drinks of colonial times as were not
deemed vastly intoxicating; though New England
cider might well be ranged very close to New England rum in intoxicating powers.

The American colonists were not enthusiastic
water drinkers, and they soon imported malt and
established breweries to make the familiar ale and
beer of old England. The Dutch patroons found
brewing a profitable business in New York, and
private families in all the colonies built home brew-
houses and planted barley and hops.

In Virginia a makeshift ale was made from maize
as early as 1620. George Thorpe wrote that it was
a good drink, much preferable to English beer.
Governor Berkeley wrote of Virginians a century
later:—

" Their small-drink is either wine or water, beer, milk
and water, or water alone. Their richer sort generally
brew their small-beer with malt, which they have from
England, though barley grows there very well; but for the
want of convenience of malt-houses, the inhabitants take
no care to sow it. The poorer sort brew their beer with
molasses and bran; with Indian corn malted with drying
in a stove: with persimmons dried in a cake and baked;
with potatoes with the green stalks of Indian corn cut
small and bruised, with pompions, with the Jerusalem
artichoke which some people plant purposely for that use,
but this is the least esteemed."

Similar beers were made in New England. The
court records are full of enactments to encourage
beer-brewing. They had not learned that liberty to
brew, when and as each citizen pleased, would prove
the best stimulus. Much personal encouragement
was also given. The President of Harvard College
did not disdain to write to the court on behalf of
" Sister Bradish," that she might be " encouraged
and countenanced" in her baking of bread and
brewing and selling of penny beer. And he adds in
testimony that " such is her art, way, and skill that
shee doth vend such comfortable penniworths for
the relief of all that send unto her as elsewhere they
can seldom meet with." College students were permitted to buy of her to a certain amount; and with
the light of some contemporary evidence as to the
quality of the college commons we can believe they
needed very "comfortable penniworths."

Some New England taverns were famous for
their spruce, birch, and sassafras beer, boiled with

scores of roots and herbs, with birch, spruce, or sassafras bark, with pumpkin and apple parings, with sweetening of molasses or maple syrup, or beet tops and other makeshifts. A colonial song writer boasted —

> " Oh, we can make liquor to sweeten our lips
> Of pumpkins, of parsnips, of walnut-tree chips."

Sign-board of Amherst Hotel.

According to Diodorus Siculus, the ancient Britons drank on festive occasions liquors made from honey, apples, and barley, viz., mead, cider, and ale. The Celts drank mead and cider — natural drinks within the capabilities of manufacture by slightly civilized nations; for wild honey and wild apples could be found everywhere. Ale indicated agriculture and a more advanced civilization.

Mead, or metheglin, of fermented honey, herbs, and water, has been made by every race and tribe on this globe, living where there was enough vegetation to cherish bees. It had been a universal drink in England, but was somewhat in disuse when this country was settled.

Harrison wrote : —

"The Welsh make no less account of metheglin than the Greeks did of their ambrosia or nectar, which for the pleasantness thereof was supposed to be such as the gods themselves did delight in. There is a kind of swishswash made also in Essex, and divers other places, with honeycomb and water, which the homely country-wives putting some pepper and a little other spice among, called mead : very good in mine opinion for such as love to be loose-bodied at large, or a little eased of the cough. Otherwise it differeth so much from true metheglin as chalk from cheese; and one of the best things that I know belonging thereto is, that they spend but little labour and less cost in making of the same, and therefore no great loss if it were never occupied."

Metheglin was one of the drinks of the American colonists. It was a favorite drink in Kentucky till well into this century. As early as 1633, the Piscataqua planters of New Hampshire, in their list of values which they set in furs, — the currency of the colony, — made "6 Gallon Mathaglin equal 2 Lb Beaver." In Virginia, whole plantations of honey locust were set out to supply metheglin. The long beans of the locust were ground and mixed with honey herbs and water, and fermented.

In a letter written from Virginia in 1649, it is told of "an ancient planter of twenty-five years standing," that he had good store of bees and "made excellent good Matheglin, a pleasant and strong drink."

Oldmixon, in *History of Carolina* (1708), says, "the bees swarm there six or seven times a year, and the metheglin made there is as good as Malaga sack," which may be taken *cum grano salis*.

In New England drinking habits soon underwent a marked and speedy change. English grains did not thrive well those first years of settlement, and were costly to import, so New Englanders soon drifted from beer-drinking to cider-drinking. The many apple orchards planted first by Endicott and Blackstone in Massachusetts, and Wolcott in Connecticut, and seen in a few decades on every prosperous and thrifty farm, soon gave forth their bountiful yield of juicy fruit. Perhaps this change in drinking habits was indirectly the result of the influence of the New England climate. Cider seemed more fitted for sharp New England air than ale. Cider was soon so cheap and plentiful throughout the colony that all could have their fill. Josselyn said in 1670: "I have had at the tap-houses of Boston an ale-quart of cider spiced and sweetened with sugar for a groat."

All the colonists drank cider, old and young, and in all places, — funerals, weddings, ordainings, vestry-meetings, church-raisings, etc. Infants in arms drank mulled hard cider at night, a beverage which would kill a modern babe. It was supplied to stu-

Eagle Tavern and Sign-board, Newton, New Hampshire.

dents at Harvard and Yale colleges at dinner and
bever, being passed in two quart tankards from
hand to hand down the commons table.   Old

men began the day with a quart or more of hard
cider before breakfast.   Delicate women drank hard
cider.   All laborers in the field drank it in great
draughts that were often liberally fortified with
drams of New England rum.   The apple crop was
so wholly devoted to the manufacture of cider that
in the days of temperance reform at the beginning
of this century, Washingtonian zealots cut down
great orchards of full-bearing trees, not conceiving
any adequate use of the fruit for any purpose save
cider-making.

A friend — envious and emulous of the detective
work so minutely described by Conan Doyle — was
driving last summer on an old New England road
entirely unfamiliar to him.   He suddenly turned to
the stage-driver by his side and, pointing to a house
alongside the road, said, "The man who lives there
is a drunkard." — "Why, yes," answered the driver
in surprise, "do you know him?" — "No," said
the traveller, "I never saw him and don't know
his name, but he's a drunkard and his father was
before him, and his grandfather." — "It's true," answered the driver, with much astonishment; "how
could you tell?" — "Well, there is a large orchard
of very old apple trees round that house, while all
his neighbors, even when the houses are old, have
younger orchards.   When the 'Washingtonian or
Temperance Movement' reached this town, the
owner of this place was too confirmed a drunkard to
reform and cut down his apple trees as his neighbors
did, and he kept on at his hard cider and cider brandy,
and his son and grandson grew up to be drunkards

after him." Later inquiry in the town proved the truth of the amateur detective's guesswork.

Cider was tediously made at first by pounding the apples in wooden mortars; the pomace was afterward pressed in baskets. Then rude mills with a spring board and heavy maul crushed the apples in a hollowed log. Then presses for cider-making began to be set up about the year 1650.

Apples were at that time six to eight shillings a bushel; cider 1s. 8d. a gallon — as high-priced as New England rum a century later.

Connecticut cider soon became specially famous. Roger Williams in 1660 says John Winthrop's loving letter to him was as grateful as "a cup of your Connecticut cider." By 1679 it was cheap enough, ten shillings a barrel; and in the year 1700, about seven shillings only. It had then replaced beer in nearly all localities in daily diet; yet at the Commencement dinner at Harvard in 1703, four barrels of beer were served and but one of cider, with eighteen gallons of wine.

In 1721 one Massachusetts village of forty families made three thousand barrels of cider, and Judge Joseph Wilder of Lancaster, Massachusetts, made six hundred and sixteen barrels in the year 1728.

Bennett, an English traveller, writing of Boston in the year 1740, says that "the generality of the people with their victuals" drank cider, which was plentiful and good at three shillings a barrel. It took a large amount of cider to supply a family when all drank, and drank freely. Ministers often stored forty barrels of cider for winter use.

By the closing years of the seventeenth century nearly all Virginia plantations had an apple orchard. Colonel Fitzhugh had twenty-five hundred apple trees. So quickly did they mature, that six years after the scions were planted, they bore fruit. Many varieties were common, such as russets, costards, pippins, mains, marigolds, kings, and batchelors. So great was the demand for cider in the

South that apple orchards were deemed the most desirable leasing property. Cider never reached a higher price, however, than two shillings and a half in Virginia during the seventeenth century. Thus it could be found in the house of every Maryland and Virginia planter. It was supplied to the local courts during their times of sitting. Many households used it in large quantity instead of beer or metheglin, storing many barrels for everyday use.

At a very early date apple trees were set out in New York, and cultivated with much care and much success. Nowhere else in America, says Dankers, the Labadist traveller, had he seen such fine apples. The names of the Newton pippin, the Kingston spitzenburgh, the Poughkeepsie swaar apple, the red streak, guelderleng, and others of well-known quality, show New York's attention to apple-raising. Kalm, the Swedist naturalist, spoke of the splendid apple orchards which he saw throughout New York in 1749, and told of the use of the horse press in the Hudson Valley for making cider. Cider soon rivalled in domestic use in this province the beer of the Fatherland. It was constantly used during the winter season, and, diluted with water, sweetened and flavored with nutmeg, made a grateful summer drink. Combined with rum, it formed many of the most popular and intoxicating colonial drinks, of which "stone-wall" was the most potent. Cider-royal was made by boiling four barrels of cider into one barrel. P. T. Barnum said cider-spirits was called "gumption."

A New Hampshire settler carried on his back for twenty miles to his home a load of young apple trees. They thrived and grew apace, and his first crop was eight bushels. From these, he proudly recounted, he made one barrel of cider, one barrel of water-cider, and "one barrel of charming good drink." Water-cider, or ciderkin, was a very weak, slightly cidery beverage, which was made by pouring water over the solid dregs left after the cider had been pressed from the pomace, and pressing it over again. It was deemed especially suitable for children to drink; sometimes a little molasses and ginger was added to it.

A very mild tavern drink was beverige; its concoction varied in different localities. Sometimes beverige was water-cider or ciderkin; at other times

Parson's Tavern.

cider, spices, and water. Water flavored with molasses and ginger was called beverige, and is a summer drink for New England country-folk to-day.

John Hammond wrote of Virginia in 1656 in his *Leah and Rachel*: —

" Beare is indeed in some places constantly drunken, in other some nothing but Water or Milk, and Water or Beverige; and that is where the good-wives (if I may so

call them) are negligent and idle; for it is not want of Corn
to make Malt with, for the Country affords enough, but
because they are slothful and careless; and I hope this
Item will shame them out of these humours; that they
will be adjudged by their drinke, what kind of Housewives
they are."

Vinegar and water — a drink of the ancient
Roman soldiery — was also called beverige.   Dr.
Rush wrote a pamphlet recommending its use by
harvest laborers.

Switchel was a similar drink, strengthened with
a dash of rum.   Ebulum was the juice of elder
and juniper berries, spiced and sweetened.   Perry
was made from pears, and peachy from peaches.

A terrible drink is said to have been popular in
Salem.   It is difficult to decide which was worse,
the drink or its name.   It was sour household beer
simmered in a kettle, sweetened with molasses, filled
with crumbs of "ryneinjun" bread, and drunk
piping hot; its name was whistle-belly-vengeance,
or whip-belly-vengeance.   This name was not a
Yankee vulgarism, but a well-known old English
term.   Bickerdyke says small beer was rightly stig-
matized by this name.   Dean Swift in his *Polite
Conversations* gives this smart dialogue : —

" *Hostess* (offering ale to Sir John Linger).   I never
taste malt-liquor, but they say ours is well-hopp'd.

Sir John.   Hopp'd! why if it had hopp'd a little further, it would have hopp'd into the river.

Hostess.   I was told ours was very strong.

Sir John.   Yes! strong of the water.   I believe the

brewer forgot the malt, or the river was too near him.
Faith! it is more whip-belly-vengeance; he that drinks
most has the worst share."

This would hardly seem a word for " polite conversation," though it was certainly a term in common use. Its vulgarity is in keen contrast to the
name of another " small drink," a name which brings
to the mental vision thoughts of the good cheer, the
genial hospitality, the joy of living, of Elizabethan
days. A black letter copy of the *Loyal Garland*,
a collection of songs of the seventeenth century,
thus names the drink in this gay song : —

> " To the Tavern lets away !
> There have I a Mistress got,
> Cloystered in a Pottle Pot ;
> Plump and bounding, soft and fair,
> Bucksome, sweet and debonair,
> And they call her *Sack*, my Dear ! "

It is vain to enter here into a discussion of exactly
what sack was, since so much has been written
about it. The name was certainly applied to sweet
wines from many places. A contemporary authority,
Gervayse Markham, says in *The English Housewife*,
" Your best Sackes are of Seres in Spain, your
smaller of Galicia or Portugall : your strong Sackes
are of the islands of the Canaries."

Sack was, therefore, a special make of the strong,
dry, sweet, light-colored wines of the sherry family,
such as come from the South, from Portugal, Spain,
and the Canary Islands. By the seventeenth century the name was applied to all sweet wines of this

class, as distinguished from Rhenish wines on one hand and red wines on the other. Many do not wish to acknowledge that sack was sherry, but there was little distinction between them. Sherris-sack, named by Shakespeare, was practically also sherry.

Sack was so cheap that it could be used by all classes. From an original license granted by Sir Walter Raleigh, in 1584, to one Bradshaw to keep

Toby Fillpots.

a tavern we learn that sack was then worth two shillings a gallon.

Perhaps the most famous use of sack was in the making of sack-posset, that drink of brides, of grooms, of wedding and christening parties. A rhymed rule for sack-posset found its way into many collections, and into English and American newspapers. It is said to have been written by Sir Fleetwood Fletcher. It was thus printed in the *New York Gazette* of February 13, 1744 : —

" A Receipt for all young Ladies that are going to be Married.
To make a

SACK–POSSET

From famed Barbadoes on the Western Main
Fetch sugar half a pound ; fetch sack from Spain
A pint ; and from the Eastern Indian Coast
Nutmeg, the glory of our Northern toast.
O'er flaming coals together let them heat
Till the all-conquering sack dissolves the sweet.
O'er such another fire set eggs, twice ten,
New born from crowing cock and speckled hen ;
Stir them with steady hand, and conscience pricking
To see the untimely fate of twenty chicken.
From shining shelf take down your brazen skillet,
A quart of milk from gentle cow will fill it.
When boiled and cooked, put milk and sack to egg,
Unite them firmly like the triple League.
Then covered close, together let them dwell
Till Miss twice sings : *You must not kiss and tell.*
Each lad and lass snatch up their murdering spoon,
And fall on fiercely like a starved dragoon.''

Sack was drunk in America during the first half-
century of colonial life. It was frequently imported
to Virginia ; and all the early instructions for the
voyage cross-seas, such as Governor Winthrop's to
his wife and those of the Plymouth Plantations, urge
the shipping of sack for the sailors. Even in Judge
Sewall's day, a century after the planting of Boston,
sack-posset was drunk at Puritan weddings, but a
psalm and a prayer made it properly solemn.
Judge Sewall wrote of a Boston wedding : —

" There was a pretty deal of company present. Many
young gentlemen and young gentlewomen. Mr. Noyes

made a speech, said love was the sugar to sweeten every condition in the marriage state. After the Sack-Posset sang 45th Psalm from 8th verse to end."

Canary soon displaced sack in popular affection, and many varieties of closely allied wines were imported. Sir Edmund Andros named in his excise list "Fayal wines, or any other wines of the Western Islands, Madeira, Malaga, Canary, Tent, and Alcant." Claret was not popular. The con-

Flip Glasses and Nutmeg Holders.

sumption of sweet wines was astonishing, and the quality was exceeding good. Spiced wines were much sold at taverns, sangaree and mulled wines. Brigham's Tavern at Westborough had a simple recipe for mulled wine: simply a quart of boiling hot Madeira, half a pint of boiling water, six eggs beaten to a froth, all sweetened and spiced. Nutmeg was the favorite flavoring, and nutmegs gilded and beribboned were an esteemed gift. The importation of them was in early days wholly controlled by the Dutch. High livers — *bon vivants* — carried nutmegs in their pockets, fashionable dames also. One of the prettiest trinkets of colonial times is the dainty nutmeg holder, of wrought silver or Battersea enamel, just large enough to hold a single nutmeg. The inside of the cover is pierced or corrugated to form a grater. The ones now before me, both a century and a half old, when opened exhale a strong aroma of nutmeg, though it is many a year since they have been used. With a nutmeg in a pocket holder, the exquisite traveller, whether man or woman, could be sure of a dainty spiced wine flavored to taste; "atop the musky nut could grated be," even in the most remote tavern, for wine was everywhere to be found, but nutmegs were a luxury. Negus, a washy warm wine-punch invented in Queen Anne's day by Colonel Negus, was also improved by a flavoring of nutmeg.

CHAPTER VII

SIGNS AND SYMBOLS

BEFORE named streets with numbered houses came into existence, and when few persons could read, painted and carved sign-boards and figures were more useful than they are to-day; and not only innkeepers, but men of all trades and callings sought for signs that either for quaintness, appropriateness, or costliness would attract the eyes of customers and visitors, and fix in their memory the exact locality of the advertiser. Signs were painted and carved in wood; they were carved in stone; modelled in terra-cotta and plaster; painted on tiles; wrought of various metals; and even were made of animals' heads stuffed.

As education progressed, signs were less needed, and when thoroughfares were named and sign-posts set up and houses numbered, the use of business signs vanished. They lingered sometimes on account of their humor, sometimes because they were a guarantee of an established business, but chiefly because people were used to them.

The shops in Boston were known by sign-boards. In 1761 Daniel Parker, goldsmith, was at the

Golden Ball, William Whitmore, grocer, at the Seven Stars, Susannah Foster was "next the Great Cross," and John Loring, chemist, at the Great Trees. One hatter had a "Hatt & Beaver," another a "Hatt & Helmit"; butter was sold at the "Blue Glove" and "Brazen Head"; dry-goods at the "Sign of the Stays" and at the "Wheat Sheaf"; rum at the "Golden Keys"; pewter ware at the "Crown and Beehive"; knives at the "Sign of the Crown and Razor." John Crosby, for many years a noted lemon trader, had as a sign a basket of lemons. In front of a nautical instrument store on the corner of State and Broad streets, Boston, still stands a quaint wooden figure of an ancient naval officer resplendent in his blue coat, cocked hat, short breeches, stockings, and buckles, holding in his hand a quadrant. The old fellow has stood in this place, continually taking observations of the sun, for upwards of one hundred years. It will be seen that these signs were often incongruous and non-significant, both as to their relation to the business they indicated, and in the association of objects which they depicted.

A rhyme printed in the *British Apollo* in 1710 notes the curious combination of names on London sign-boards : —

> " I'm amazed at the signs
> As I pass through the town ;
> To see the odd mixture
> A Magpie and Crown,
> The Whale and the Crow,
> The Razor and Hen,
> The Leg and Seven Stars,

> The Axe and the Bottle,
> The Sun and the Lute,
> The Eagle and Child,
> The Shovel and Boot.''

Addison wrote nearly two centuries ago on the absurdity and incongruity of these sign-boards, in *The Spectator* of April 2, 1710. He says, advocating a censorship of sign-boards : —

Sign-board of Stratton Tavern.

" Our streets are filled with blue boars, black swans, and red lions ; not to mention flying pigs, and hogs in armour, with many other creatures more extraordinary than any in the deserts of Africa. My first task therefore should be like that of Hercules, to clear the city from monsters. In the second place I would forbid that creatures of jarring and incongruous natures should be joined together in the same sign ; such as the bell and the neat's tongue ; the dog and the gridiron. The fox and goose may be supposed to have met, but what have the fox and the seven stars to do together ? And when did the lamb and dolphin ever meet, except upon a sign-post ?

As for the cat and fiddle there is a conceit in it, and therefore I do not intend that anything I have said should affect it. I must, however, observe to you upon this subject, that it is usual for a young tradesman, at his first setting up, to add to his sign that of the master whom he has served; as the husband, after marriage, gives a place to his mistress's arms in his own coat. This I take to have given rise to many of those absurdities which are committed over our heads; and as, I am informed, first occasioned the three nuns and a hare, which we see so frequently joined together."

Many of the apparently meaningless names on tavern signs come through the familiar corruptions of generations of use, through alterations both by the dialect of speakers and by the successive mistakes of ignorant sign-painters. Thus "The Bag o' Nails," a favorite sign, was originally "The Bacchanalians." The familiar "Cat and Wheel" was the "Catherine Wheel," and still earlier "St. Catherine's Wheel," in allusion to the saint and her martyrdom. The "Goat and Compass" was the motto "God encompasseth us." "The Pig and Carrot" was the "Pique et Carreau" (the spade and diamond in playing cards). Addison thus explains the "Bell Savage," a common sign in England, usually portrayed by an Indian standing beside a bell. "I was formerly very much puzzled upon the conceit of it, till I accidentally fell into the reading of an old romance translated out of the French, which gives an account of a very beautiful woman who was found in a wilderness, and is called in French, La Belle Sauvage, and is everywhere translated by our countrymen the Bell Savage."

"The Bull and Mouth" celebrates in corrupt

wording the victory of Henry VIII. in "Boulougne Mouth" or Harbor.   In London the Bull and Mouth Inn was a famous coach office, and the sign-board bore these lines : —

> "Milo the Cretonian
> An ox slew with his fist,
> And ate it up at one meal,
> Ye Gods ! what a glorious twist."

Twist was the old cant term for appetite.

The universal use of sign-boards furnished employment to many painters of inferior rank, and occasionally even to great artists, who, either as a freak of genius, to win a wager, to crown a carouse, or perhaps to earn with ease a needed sum, painted a sign-board.   At the head of this list is Hogarth. Richard Wilson painted "The Three Loggerheads" for an ale-house in North Wales.   George Morland has several assigned to him : "The Goat in Boots," "The White Lion," "The Cricketers."   Ibbetson paid his bill to Landlord Burkett after a sketching and fishing excursion by a sign with one pale and wan face and one equally rubicund.   The accompanying lines read : —

> "Thou mortal man that livest by bread,
> What makes thy face to look so red ?
> Thou silly fop that looks so pale,
> 'Tis red with Tommy Burkett's ale."

Gérôme, Cox, Harlow, and Millais swell the list of English sign-painters, while Holbein, Correggio, Watteau, Gerriault, and Horace Vernet make a noble company.   The splendid "Young Bull" of

Paul Potter, in the museum of The Hague, is said to have been painted for a butcher's sign.

Benjamin West painted many tavern signs in the vicinity of Philadelphia, among them in 1771 that of the Three Crowns, a noted hostelry that stood on the King's Highway in Salisbury Township, Lancaster County. This neighborhood was partly settled by English emigrants, and the old tavern was kept by a Tory of the deepest dye. The sign-board still bears the marks of the hostile bullets of the Continental Army, and the proprietor came near sharing the bullets with the sign. This Three Crowns was removed in 1816 to the Waterloo Tavern, kept by a

Sign-board of Three Crowns Tavern.

relative of the old landlord. The Waterloo Tavern was originally the Bull's Head, and was kept by a Revolutionary officer. Both sides of the Three Crowns sign-board are shown on page 143. By tradition West also painted the sign-board of the old Hat Tavern shown on page 147. This was kept by Widow Caldwell in Leacock Township, Lancaster County, on the old Philadelphia road.

The Bull's Head Inn of Philadelphia had a sign suited to its title; it was sold in the middle of this century to an Englishman as the work of Benjamin West. The inn stood in Strawberry Alley, and West once lived in the alley; and so also did Bernard Wilton, a painter and glazier, in the days when the inn was young and had no sign-board. And as the glazier sat one day in the taproom, a bull ran foaming into the yard and thrust his head with a roar in the tavern window. The glazier had a ready wit, and quoth he: "This means something. This bull thrust his head in as a sign, so it shall be the sign of the inn, and bring luck and custom forever." I think those were his words; at any rate, those were the deeds.

West also painted the "Ale Bearers." One side had a man holding a glass of ale and looking through it. The other side showed two brewers' porters carrying an ale cask slung with case hooks on a pole — as was the way of ale porters at that day. It is said that West was offered five hundred dollars for a red lion sign-board he had painted in his youth. In the vicinity of Philadelphia several taverns claimed to have sign-boards painted by the

Peales and by Gilbert Stuart, and an artist named Hicks is said to have contributed some wonderful specimens to this field of art.

General Wolfe was a favorite name and figure for pre-Revolutionary taverns and sign-boards. There was a Wolfe Tavern near Faneuil Hall in Boston; and the faded sign-board of the Wolfe Tavern of Brooklyn, Connecticut, is shown on page 211 as it swung when General Israel Put-

Browne's Hall, Danvers, Massachusetts, 1743.

nam was the tavern landlord. These figures of the English officer were usually removed as obnoxious after the Declaration of Independence. But the Wolfe Tavern at Newburyport continued to swing the old sign "in the very centre of the place to be an insult to this truly republican town." This sign is shown in its spruce freshness on page 180. It is a great contrast to "Old Put's" Wolfe sign-board.

A Philadelphia tavern with a clumsy name, though a significant one, was the Federal Conven-

tion of 1787 Inn.   I cannot imagine any band of
tavern tipplers or jovial roisterers ever meeting
there, but it was doubtless used for political gatherings.   It had a most pretentious sign painted by
Matthew Pratt, a pupil of Benjamin West.   It was
said that his signs were painted in a style that should
have given them place in a picture gallery, had it
not been that the galleries of those days were few,
and artists found their most lucrative employment
in painting signs for taverns and stores.   This inn
kept first by a man named Hanna, then by George
Poppal, was at 178 South Street, near Fifth Street.
The sign was a painting of the National Convention
which met May 14, 1787, in the State House or
Independence Hall to frame the Constitution of the
United States.   George Washington was president,
Mayor William Jackson was secretary.   The convention met in the East Room, which was distinctly
and correctly represented on the sign-board; its
wainscoting, the Ionic pilasters supporting a full
entablature beneath a coved ceiling, all were taken
down by a "Commissioner of Repairs," and all now
are happily reproduced and restored.   On one side
of the sign-board Washington was seen seated
under the panel bearing the arms of Pennsylvania.
The dignified Judge Wilson occupied the chair, and
Franklin sat near.   All the heads were portraits.
On both sides of the sign-board were the lines: —

"These thirty-eight men together have agreed
 That better times to us shall very soon succeed."

Watson, writing in 1857, tells of the end of this
historic sign-board: —

" This invaluable sign, which should have been copied by some eminent artist and engraved for posterity, was bandied about like the Casa Santa of Lorretto from post to pillar till it located at South Street near the Old Theatre. The figures are now completely obliterated by a heavy coat of brown paint on which is lettered Fed. Con. 1787."

Sign of the Hat Tavern.

Hat Tavern and Sign-board.

This offence against historic decency can be added to the many other crimes against good taste which lie heavily on the account of the middle of the nineteenth century. The *fin du siècle* has many evils which are daily rehearsed to us; but the middle of the century was an era of bad taste, dulness, affected and melancholic sentimentality and commonplaceness in dress, architecture, household furnishings, literature, society, and art — let us turn from it with haste. It is equalled only in some aspects by some of the decades of dulness in England in the reign of George III.

Another sign-board painted by Woodside is described in Philadelphia newspapers of August, 1820 : —

"UNION HOTEL

"Samuel E. Warwick respectfully informs his friends and the public generally that he has opened a house of Entertainment at the northeast corner of Seventh and Cedar Streets, and has copied for his sign Mr. Binn's beautiful copperplate engraving of the Declaration of Independence, by that justly celebrated artist, Mr. Woodside : —

> "Whate'er may tend to soothe the soul below,
>   To dry the tear and blunt the shaft of woe,
>   To drown the ills that discompose the mind,
>   All those who drink at Warwick's Inn shall find."

The Revolutionary War developed originality in American tavern signs. The "King's Arms," "King's Head," "St. George and the Dragon," and other British symbols gave place to rampant American eagles and portraits of George Washington. Every town had a Washington Tavern, with varied Washington sign-boards. That of the Washington Hotel at Salem, Massachusetts, is on page 63.

The landlord of the Washington Inn at Holmesburg, Pennsylvania, one James Carson, issued this address in 1816 : —

"Ye good and virtuous Americans — come! whether business or pleasure be your object — call and be refreshed at the sign of Washington. Here money and merit will secure you respect and honor, and a hearty welcome to choice liquors and to sumptuous fare. Is it cold? You shall find a comfortable fire. Is it warm? Sweet repose under a cool and grassy shade. In short, every exertion shall be made to grace the sign of the hero and statesman who was first in war, first in peace, and first in the hearts of his countrymen."

On Beach Street a tavern, with the name Washington Crossing the Delaware, had as a sign-board a copy of Sully's famous picture. This must have been a costly luxury. A similar one used as a bridge sign-board is on page 239.

About 1840 one Washington Tavern in Philadelphia, on Second and Lombard streets, displayed a sign which was a novelty at that time. It was what was known as a "slat-sign"; perpendicular strips or slats were so set on the sign that one view or picture was shown upon taking a full front view, a second by looking at it from one side, a third from the other. The portrait of Washington and other appropriate pictures were thus shown.

Other patriotic designs became common, — the Patriotic Brothers having a sign representing the Temple of Liberty with weapons of war. On the steps of the temple a soldier and sailor grasp hands, with the motto, "Where Liberty dwells, there is my country."

A very interesting sign is in the possession of the Connecticut Historical Society. It is shown on page 28. This sign is unusual in that it is carved in good outline on one side with the British coat of arms, and on the other a full-rigged ship under full sail, flying the Union Jack. At the top on each side are the letters U. A. H., and 1766. It is enclosed in a heavy frame, with heavy hangers of iron keyed to suspend from a beam.

The initials U. A. H. stand for Uriah and Ann Hayden, who kept the tavern for which this board was the sign. It stood near the river in Essex, then Pettspung Parish, in the town of Saybrook, Connecticut. The sign was relegated to a garret when the British lion and unicorn were in such disrepute in the new land of freedom, and, being forgotten, was thus preserved to our own day.

An old sign shown on pages 151 and 153 swung for nearly a century by the roadside before a house called Bissell's Tavern, at Bissell's Ferry, East Windsor, Connecticut. Originally it bore an elaborate design of thirteen interlacing rings, each having in its centre the representation of some tree or plant peculiar to the state it designated. These interlacing links surrounded the profile portrait of George Washington. Above this was the legend, "The 13 United States." Beneath this, "Entertainment by David Bissell, A.D. 1777." Ten years later the words David Bissell were painted out and E. Wolcott substituted. The date 1787 was also placed in both upper corners of the board. In 1801 the sign and house came to Joseph Phelps. A new design was given: a copy of the first gold eagle of 1795, and on the other the reverse side of same coin and the name J. Phelps. In 1816 J. Pelton bought the Ferry Tavern, and he painted out all of J. Phelps's name save the initials, which were his own. He hung the sign on the limb of a big elm tree over the Ferry road.

Arad Stratton, who kept the old tavern at Northfield Farms, had a splendid eagle on his sign-board, which is shown on page 140. This tavern built in 1724 was pulled down in 1820.

William Pitt's face and figure frequently appeared on sign-boards. One is shown on page 156 which hung at the door of the Pitt Tavern in Lancaster, Pennsylvania. This tavern was kept from 1808 to 1838

Sign-board of Bissell's Tavern.

by Landlord Henry Diffenbaugh. The sign-board was painted by an artist named Eicholtz, a pupil of Sully and of Gilbert Stuart, whose work he imitated and copied.

A small, single-storied ancient tavern used to stand near the old Swedes' church. Over the door was a sign with an old hen with a brood of chickens; an eagle hovered over them with a crown in its beak; the inscription was: "May the Wings of

Liberty cover the Chickens of Freedom, and pluck the Crown from the Enemy's Head." This was a high flight of fancy, and the Hen and Chickens was doubtless vastly admired in those days of high sentiment and patriotism after the Revolution.

Lafayette and Franklin showed their fame in many a sign-board. When the sign of the Franklin Inn was set up in Philadelphia in 1774, it bore this couplet : —

> " Come view your patriot father ! and your friend,
> And toast to Freedom and to slavery's end."

John Hancock was another popular patriot seen on tavern signs. The sign-board which hung for many years before John Duggan's hostelry, the Hancock Tavern in Corn Court, is shown on page 110. This portrait crudely resembles one of Hancock, by Copley, and is said to have been painted by order of Hancock's admirer, Landlord Duggan. At Hancock's death it was draped with mourning emblems. It swung for many years over the narrow alley shown on page 182, till it blew down in a heavy wind and killed a citizen. Then it was nailed to the wall, and thereby injured. It was preserved in Lexington Memorial Hall, but has recently been returned to Boston.

It was natural that horses, coaches, and sporting subjects should be favorites for tavern signs. A very spirited one is that of the Perkins Inn, at Hopkinton, New Hampshire, dated 1786, and showing horse, rider, and hounds. The Williams Tavern of Centrebrook, Connecticut, stood on the

old Hartford and Saybrook turnpike. One side
of its swinging sign displayed a coach and horses.
It is shown on page 400. The other, on page 396,
portrays a well-fed gentleman seated at a well-spread
table sedately drinking a glass of wine. Sign-boards
with figures of horses were common, such as that of
the Hays Tavern, page
65; of the Conkey
Tavern, page 190; of
Mowry's Inn, page 57;
and of the Pembroke
Tavern, page 217.

Of course beasts and
birds furnished many
symbolsforsignpainters.
On the site where the
Northfield Seminary
buildings now stand,
stood until 1880 the old
Doolittle Tavern. It
was on the main-trav-
elled road from Con-
necticut through Mas-
sachusetts to southern
New Hampshire and
Vermont. Its sign-

Sign-board of Bissell's Tavern.

board, dated 1781, is on page 158. It bore a large
rabbit and two miniature pine trees.

Joseph Cutter, a Revolutionary soldier, kept an
inn in Jaffray, New Hampshire, on the "Brattleboro' Pike" from Boston. His sign-board bore
the figure of a demure fox. It is shown on page 412.

Indian chiefs were a favorite subject for sign-boards; three are here shown, one on page 203, from the Stickney Tavern of Concord, New Hampshire; another on page 382, from the Wells Tavern at Greenfield Meadows, Massachusetts; a third on page 310, from the Tarleton Inn of Haverhill, New Hampshire.

Two Beehive Taverns, one in Philadelphia, one in Frankford, each bore the sign-board a beehive with busy bees. The motto on the former, "By Industry We Thrive," was scarcely so appropriate as —

> "Here in this hive we're all alive,
> Good liquor makes us funny.
> If you are dry, step in and try
> The flavor of our honey."

The sign-board of Walker's Tavern, a famous house of entertainment in Charlestown, New Hampshire, is shown on page 162. It bears a bee-hive and bees. This sign is now owned by the Worcester Society of Antiquity.

The Washington Hotel, at the corner of Sixth and Carpenter streets, had several landlords, and in 1822 became the New Theatre Hotel. Woodside painted a handsome sign, bearing a portrait of the famous old actor and theatrical manager, William Warren, as Falstaff, with the inscription, "Shall I not take mine ease at my inn?" A writer in the *Despatch* says the tavern did not prosper, though its rooms were let for meetings of clubs, societies, audits, and legal proceedings. It was leased by Warren himself in 1830, and still the tavern decayed. He left it and died, and the fine sign-board faded, and was succeeded by the plain lettering, Fallstaff Inn, and the appropriate motto, chosen by Warren, gave place to "Bring me a cup of sack, Hal." The place was a "horrible old rattletrap," and was soon and deservedly demolished.

The Raleigh Inn, in Third Street, showed the story of the servant throwing water over the nobleman at the sight of smoke issuing from his mouth. This was a favorite tale of the day, and the portrayal of it may be seen in many an old-time picturebook for children.

On Thirteenth Street, near Locust, was a sign copied from a London one : —

> "I William McDermott lives here,
> I sells good porter, ale, and beer,
> I've made my sign a little wider
> To let you know I sell good cider."

On the Germantown road the Woodman Tavern had a sign-board with a woodman, axe, and the following lines : —

> "In Freedom's happy land
> My task of duty done,
> In Mirth's light-hearted band
> Why not the lowly woodman one?"

The Yellow Cottage was a well-known Philadelphia tavern, half citified, half countrified. Its sign read : —

> "Rove not from sign to sign, but stop in here,
> Where naught exceeds the prospect but the beer."

These lines were a paraphrase of the witty and celebrated sign, said to have been written by Dean Swift for a barber who kept a public house : —

> " Rove not from pole to pole, but stop in here,
> Where naught excels the shaving but the beer."

Sir Walter Scott, in his *Fortunes of Nigel*, gives this version as a chapter motto : —

> " Rove not from pole to pole — the man lives here,
> Whose razor's only equalled by his beer."

Entering a large double gate, the passer-by who was seduced by this sign of the Yellow Cottage walked up a grand walk to this cottage, which was surrounded by a brick pavement about five feet wide which was closely bordered in front and sides by lilac bushes and some shrubs called "Washington's bowers." These concealed all the lower story on three sides except the front entrance. If you could pass the bar, you could go out the back entrance to a porch which extended across the back of the house. Here card-playing, dominos, etc., constantly went on; thence down a sloping field, at the

Sign-board of William Pitt Tavern.

end of the field, was an exit. On one side of this
field was a stable, chicken-house, and pens which
always held for view a fat hog or ox or some unusual natural object. Shooting parties were held
here ; quoit-playing, axe-throwing, weight-lifting,
etc. ; and it had also a charming view of the river.

Biblical names were not common on tavern sign-
boards. " Adam and Eveses Garden " in Philadelphia was not a Garden of Eden. This was and is a
common title in England. Noah's Ark seems somewhat inappropriate. The Angel had originally a
religious significance. The Bible and Peacock seems
less appropriate than the Bible and Key, for divina-
tion by Bible and key has ever been as universal in
America as in England.

In Philadelphia, on Shippen Street, between
Third and Fourth, was a tavern sign representing
a sailor and a woman, separated by these two lines : —

> " The sea-worn sailor here will find
>   The porter good, the treatment kind."

No doubt thirsty tars found this sign most
attractive ; more so, I am sure, than the pretentious
sign of Lebanon Tavern, corner of Tenth and
South streets. This sign was painted by the artist
Pratt. On one side was Neptune in his chariot,
surrounded by Tritons ; underneath the lines : —

> " Neptune with his triumphant host
>   Commands the ocean to be silent,
>   Smooths the surface of its waters,
>   And universal calm succeeds."

On the other side a marine view of ships, etc
with the lines : —

> " Now calm at sea and peace on land
> Have blest our Continental stores,
> Our fleets are ready, at command,
> To sway and curb contending powers."

As the sign purveyor dropped easily into verse,
albeit of the blankest type, these
lines surmounted the door : —

> " Of the waters of Lebanon
>   Good cheer, good chocolate, and tea,
> With kind entertainment
>   By John Kennedy."

Chocolate and tea seem but
dull bait to lure the sailor of that
day. The Three Jolly Sailors
showed their cheerful faces on a
sign-board appropriately found
on Water Street. One of the
tars was busy strapping a block,
and the legend below read : —

> " Brother Sailor ! please to stop
> And lend a hand to strap this block;
> For if you do not stop or call,
> I cannot strap this block at all."

Sign-board of Doolittle Tavern.

In Castleford, England, the Three Jolly Sailors
has a different rhyme : —

> " Coil up your ropes and anchor here,
>   Till better weather does appear."

In Boston the Ship in Distress was a copy of a famous sign-board which hung in Brighton, England, a century ago.   Both had the appealing lines :—

"With sorrows I am compassed round,
  Pray lend a hand, my ship's aground."

Tippling-houses in both Philadelphia and Boston had a sign-board painted with a tree, a bird, a ship, and a can of beer, and these quaint lines, an excellent tavern rhyme :—

"This is the tree that never grew,
  This is the bird that never flew,
  This is the ship that never sailed,
  This is the mug that never failed."

Other Philadelphia sign-boards of especial allurement to sailors were "The Wounded Tar," "The Top-Gallant," "The Brig and Snow," "The Jolly Sailors," "The Two Sloops," "The Boatswain and Call," and "The Dolphin."   The sign-board of the Poore Tavern (page 405) shows a ship under full sail.

In a small Philadelphia alley running from Spruce Street to Lock Street, was a sign-board lettered "A Man Full of Trouble."   It bore also a picture of a man on whose arm a woman was leaning, and a monkey was perched on his shoulder, and a bird, apparently a parrot, stood on his hand.   The woman carried a bandbox, on the top of which sat a cat. This sign has a long history.   It was copied from the famous sign-board of an old ale-house still in Oxford Street, London ; (it is here shown, opposite

this page).   It is said to have been painted by
Hogarth; at any rate, it is valued enough to be
specified in the lease of the premises as one of the fix-
tures.   The name by which it is known in London
is The Man Loaded with Mischief.   The bird is
a magpie, and the woman holds a glass of gin in her
hand.   In the background at one side is a pot-
house, at the other a pawnbroker's shop.   The
engraving of this sign is signed " Drawn by Experience, Engraved by Sorrow," and the rhyme : —

> " A monkey, a magpie, and a wife
> Is the true emblem of strife."

A similar sign is in Norwich, another in Blew-
bury, England.   One inn is called The Mischief
Inn, the other The Load of Mischief.   Still
another, at Cambridge, England, showed the man
and woman fastened together with a chain and pad-
lock.   A kindred French sign-board is called *Le trio
de Malice* (the trio being a cat, woman, and monkey).

An old Philadelphia tavern on Sixth Street, below
Catherine Street, had the curious name, The Four
Alls.   The meaning was explained by the painting
on the sign, which was a very large one.   It represented a palace, on the steps of which stood a
king, an officer in uniform, a clergyman in gown and
bands, and a laborer in plain dress.   The satirical
inscription read : —

> " 1.   King — I govern All.
>   2.   General — I fight for All.
>   3.   Minister — I pray for All.
>   4.   Laborer — And I pay for All."

A Man Loaded with Mischief.

This is an old historic sign, which may still be seen in the streets of Malta.   In Holland, two hundred years ago, there were four figures, — a soldier, parson, lawyer, and farmer.   The three said their " All " just as in the Philadelphia sign-board, but the farmer answered: —

> " Of gy vecht, of gy bidt, of gy pleyt,
> Ik bin de boer die de eyeren layt."

"You may fight, you may pay, you may plead, but I am the farmer who lays the eggs," — that is, finds the money for it all.   Sometimes the English sign-painters changed the lettering to The Four Awls.   There are several epigrams using the word "all"; one, an address to Janus I., is in the Ashmolean Mss.   It begins: —

> " The Lords craved all,
> The Queen granted all,
> The Ladies of Honour ruled all," etc.

A famous old English sign was "The Man Making His Way Through the World."   The design was a terrestrial globe with the head and shoulders of a naked man breaking out like a chick out of an egg-shell; his nakedness betokened extreme poverty.   In Holland a similar sign reads, "Thus far have I got through the World." One in England shows the head coming out in Russia, while the feet stick out at South America. The man says, "Help me through this World." This sign is sometimes called the Struggling Man. It was displayed in front of a well-known Phila-

delphia inn, and also on one at the South End in
Boston. The story was told by a Revolutionary
officer that during that war a forlorn regiment of
Continentals halted after a weary march from
Providence, in front
of the Boston tavern
and the Struggling
Man. The soldiers
were broken with fa-
tigue, covered with
mud, and ravenous
for food and drink.
One glared angrily
at the sign-board and
at once roared out
with derision: "'List,
durn ye! 'List, and
you'll get through this
world fast enough!"

Sign-board of Walker's Tavern.

Both in Philadel-
phia and Boston was
found the sign known
as the Good Woman,
the Quiet Woman, or
the Silent Woman,
which was a woman
without a head. The
sign, originally intended to refer to some saint who
had met death by losing her head, was naturally
too tempting and apparent a joke to be overlooked.
New Chelmsford in England had until recently a
sign-board with the Good Woman on one side and

King Henry VIII. on the other.   In this case
the Good Woman may have been Anne Boleyn.

A popular Philadelphia inn was the one which
bore the sign of the " Golden Lion," standing on
its hind legs.   Lions fell into disrepute at the time
of the Revolution, and the gallant animal that was
a lion in its youth became the Yellow Cat in
middle and old age.   It was a vastly popular cat,
however, vending beer and porter of highest repute.
It was kept in ancient fashion unchanged until its
antiquity made it an object alike of dignity and
interest — in fact, until our own day.   With its
worn and sanded floor, tables unpainted, and
snowy with daily scrubbing ; with tallow candles
when gas lighted every " saloon " in the city ; with
the old-time bar fenced up to the ceiling with rails,
it had an old age as golden as its youth.   Susan,
an ancient maiden of prehistoric age, fetched up
the beer in old pewter mugs on a pewter platter,
and presented a pretzel with each mug.

The great variety of tavern-signs in Philadelphia
was noted even by Englishmen, who were certainly
acquainted with variety and number at home.   The
Englishman Palmer wrote during his visit in
1818 : —

" We observed several curious tavern signs in Philadelphia and on the roadside, among others Noah's Ark ; a
variety of Apostles ; Bunyan's Pilgrim ; a cock on a lion's
back, crowing, with Liberty issuing from his beak ; naval
engagements in which the British are in a desperate situation ; the most common signs are eagles, heads of public
characters, Indian Kings, &c."

There had been so many sign-boards used by business firms in Philadelphia, that they had been declared public nuisances, and in 1770 all sign-boards, save those of innkeepers, had been ordered to be taken down and removed.

From a famous old hostelry in Dedham, swung from the years 1658 to 1730 the sign-board of Lieutenant Joshua Fisher, surveyor, apothecary, innholder, and officer of " ye trayne band," and his son and successor, Captain Fisher — also Joshua. About 1735 one of the latter's daughters married Dr. Nathaniel Ames, who had already started that remarkable series of annual publications, familiar now to antiquaries, and once to all New England householders, as *Ames' Almanack*. The first of these interesting almanacs had appeared in 1726, when Ames was only seventeen years old, but he was assisted by his astronomer father. After the death successively of his wife and infant child, the doctor entered into a famous lawsuit with the family of his sisters-in-law for the tenure of the land and inn ; and the turning-point of the suit hung upon the settlement of the term " next of kin."

By ancient common law and English law real property never ascended, that is, was never inherited by a father or mother from a child; but in absence of husband, wife, or lineal descendant passed on to the " next of kin," which might be a distant cousin. By general interpretation the Province Laws substituted the so-called civilian method of counting kinship, by which the father could inherit.

Twice defeated in the courts, Dr. Ames boldly

pushed his case in 1748 before the "Superior Court of Judicature, etc., of the Province of Massachusetts Bay," himself preparing unaided both case and argument, and he triumphed.   By the Province Laws he was given full possession of the property inherited by his infant child from the mother — thus the inn became Ames Tavern.

Nervous in temperament, excited by his victory, indignant at the injustice and loss to which he had been subjected, he was loudly intolerant of the law's delay, and especially of the failure of Chief Justice Dudley and

Drawing for Ames' Sign-board.

his associate Lynde, to unite with the three other judges, Saltonstall, Sewall, and Cushing, in the verdict; and in anger and derision he had painted for him and his tavern a new and famous sign, and he hung it in front of the tavern in caricature of the court.

The sign is gone long ago ; but in that entertaining book, *The Almanacks of Nathaniel Ames 1726–1775*, the author, Sam Briggs, gives an illustration of the painting from a drawing found among Dr. Ames' papers after his death, a copy of which is shown on the foregoing page.   On the original sketch these words are written : —

"Sir : — I wish could have some talk on ye above subject, being the bearer waits for an answer shal only observe Mr Greenwood thinks y^t can not be done under £40 Old Tenor."

This was a good price to pay to lampoon the court, for the sign represented the whole court sitting in state in big wigs with an open book before them entitled *Province Laws*.   The dissenting judges, Dudley and Lynde, were painted with their backs turned to the book.   The court, hearing of the offending sign-board, sent the sheriff from Boston to bring it before them.   Dr. Ames was in Boston at the time, heard of the order, rode with speed to Dedham in advance of the sheriff, removed the sign, and it is said had allowance of time sufficient to put up a board for the reception of the officer with this legend, " A wicked and adulterous generation seeketh after a sign, but there shall no sign be given it."

The old road house, after this episode in its history, became more famous than ever before ; and The Almanac was a convenient method of its advertisement, as it was of its distance from other taverns. In the issue of 1751 is this notice : —

" ADVERTISEMENT.

" These are to signify to all Persons that travel the great Post-Road South West from Boston That I keep a house of Public Entertainment Eleven Miles from Boston at the sign of the Sun. If they want Refreshment and see Cause to be my Guests, they shall be well entertained at a reasonable rate.

N. Ames."

Here lived the almanac-maker for fifteen years; here were born by a second wife his famous sons, Dr. Nathaniel Ames and Hon. Fisher Ames. Here in 1774 his successor in matrimony and tavern-keeping, one Richard Woodward, kept open house in September, 1774, for the famous Suffolk Convention, where was chosen the committee that drafted the first resolutions in favor of trying the issue with Great Britain with the sword. My great-grandfather was a member of this convention at Ames Tavern, and it has always seemed to me that this was the birthplace of the War for Independence. During the Revolution, as in the French and Indian War, the tavern doors swung open with constant excitement and interest. Washington, Lafayette, Hancock, Adams, and scores of other patriots sat and drank within its walls. It stood through another war, that of 1812, and in 1817 its historic walls were levelled in the dust.

The tavern sign-board was not necessarily or universally one of the elaborate emblems I have described. Often it was only a board painted legibly with the tavern name. It might be attached

Buckhorn Tavern.

to a wooden arm projecting from the tavern or a post; it might be hung from a near-by tree. Often a wrought-iron arm, shaped like a fire crane, held the sign-board. The ponderous wooden sign of the Barre Hotel hung from a substantial frame erected on the green in front of the tavern. Two upright poles about twenty feet long were set five feet apart, with a weather-vane on top of each pole. A bar stretched from pole to pole and held the sign-board. A drawing of it from an old print is shown on page 280.

Rarely signs were hung from a beam stretched across the road on upright posts. It is said there are twenty-five such still remaining and now in use in England. A friend saw one at the village of Barley in Herts, the Fox and Hounds. The figures were cut out of plank and nailed to the cross-beam, the fox escaping into the thatch of the inn with hound in full cry and huntsmen following. Silhouetted against the sky, it showed well its inequality of outline. A similar sign of a livery stable in Baltimore shows a row of galloping horses.

Sometimes animals' heads or skins were nailed on a board and used as a sign. Ox horns and deer horns were set over the door. The Buck Horn Tavern with its pair of branching buck horns is shown on the opposite page. This tavern stood on Broadway and Twenty-second Street, New York.

The proverb " Good wine needs no bush " refers to the ancient sign for a tavern, a green bush set on a pole or nailed to the tavern door. This was obsolete, even in colonial days ; but in Western mining camps and towns in modern days this emblem has been used to point out the barroom or grocery whiskey barrel. The name " Green Bush " was never a favorite in America. There was a Green Bush Tavern in Barrington, Rhode Island, with a sign-board painted with a green tree.

CHAPTER VIII

THE TAVERN IN WAR

THE tavern has ever played an important part in social, political, and military life, has helped to make history. From the earliest days when men gathered to talk over the terrors of Indian warfare; through the renewal of these fears in the French and Indian War; before and after the glories of Louisburg; and through all the anxious but steadfast years preceding and during the Revolution, these gatherings were held in the ordinaries or taverns. What a scene took place in the Brookfield tavern, the town being then called Quawbaug! The only ordinary, that of Goodman Ayers, was a garrison house as well as tavern, and the sturdy landlord was commander of the trainband. When the outbreak called King Philip's War took place, things looked black for Quawbaug. Hostile and treacherous Indians set upon the little frontier settlement, and the frightened families retreated from their scarcely cleared farms to the tavern. Many of the men were killed and wounded at the beginning of the fray, but there were eighty-two persons, men, women, and children, shut up within the tavern walls, and soon there were four more, for two women gave birth to twins. The Indians, "like so many wild bulls," says a witness, shot into the house, piled up hay and wood against the walls, and set it on fire. But the men sallied out and quenched the flames. The next night the savages renewed their attack.

"They used several stratagems to fire us, namely, by wild-fire on cotton and linen rags with brimstone in them, which rags they tied to the piles of their arrows sharp for the purpose and shot them to the roof of our house after they had set them on fire, which would have much endangered in the burning thereof, had we not used means by cutting holes through the roof and otherwise to beat the said arrows down, and God being pleased to prosper our endeavours therein."

Again they piled hay and flax against the house and fired it; again the brave Englishmen went forth and put out the flames. Then the wily Indians loaded a cart with inflammable material and thrust it down the hill to the tavern. But the Lord sent a rain for the salvation of His people, and when all were exhausted with the smoke, the August heat, the fumes of brimstone, and the burning powder, relief came in a body of men from Groton and one brought by a brave young man who had made his way by stealth from the besieged tavern to Boston. Many of the old garrison houses of New England had, as taverns, a peaceful end of their days.

A centre of events, a centre of alarms, the tavern in many a large city saw the most thrilling acts in our Revolutionary struggle which took place off the battlefields.   The tavern was the rendezvous for patriotic bands who listened to the stirring words of American rebels, and mixed dark treason to King George with every bowl of punch they drank.   The story of our War for Independence could not be dissociated from the old taverns, they are a part of our national history ; and those which still stand are among our most interesting Revolutionary relics.

John Adams left us a good contemporaneous picture of the first notes of dissatisfaction such as were heard in every tavern, in every town, in the years which were leading up to the Revolution. He wrote : —

"Within the course of the year, before the meeting of Congress in 1774, on a journey to some of our circuit courts in Massachusetts, I stopped one night at a tavern in Shrewsbury about forty miles from Boston, and as I was cold and wet, I sat down at a good fire in the bar-room to dry my great-coat and saddle-bags, till a fire could be made in my chamber.   There presently came in, one after another, half a dozen, or half a score substantial yeomen of the neighborhood, who, sitting down to the fire after lighting their pipes, began a lively conversation on politics.   As I believed I was unknown to all of them, I sat in total silence to hear them.   One said, 'The people of Boston are distracted.'   Another answered, 'No wonder the people of Boston are distracted.   Oppression will make wise men mad.'   A third said, 'What would you say if a fellow should come to your house and tell you he was come to take a list of your cattle, that Parliament might tax you for them at so much a head ?   And how should you feel if he was to go and break open your barn or take down

Old North Bridge. Concord Mass.

your oxen, cows, horses, and sheep?' 'What should I say?' replied the first, 'I would knock him in the head.' 'Well,' said a fourth, 'if Parliament can take away Mr. Hancock's wharf and Mr. Rowe's wharf, they can take away your barn and my house.' After much more reasoning in this style, a fifth, who had as yet been silent, broke out: 'Well, it's high time for us to rebel; we must rebel some time or other, and we had better rebel now than at any time to come. If we put it off for ten or twenty years, and let them go on as they have begun, they will get a strong party among us, and plague us a great deal more than they can now.'"

These discussions soon brought decisions, and by 1768 the Sons of Liberty were organized and were holding their meetings, explaining conditions, and advocating union and action. They adopted the name given by Colonel Barré to the enemies of passive obedience in America. Soon scores of towns in the colonies had their liberty trees or liberty poles.

These patriots grew amazingly bold in proclaiming their dissatisfaction with the Crown and their allegiance to their new nation. The landlord of the tavern at York, Maine, speedily set up a sign-board bearing a portrait of Pitt and the words, "Entertainment for the Sons of Liberty." Young women formed into companies called Daughters of Liberty, pledged to wear homespun and drink no tea. I have told the story of feminine revolt at length in my book *Colonial Dames and Goodwives*. John Adams glowed with enthusiasm when he heard two Worcester girls sing the "New Liberty Song," in a

Worcester tavern. In 1768 a Liberty Tree was
dedicated in Providence, Rhode Island. It was a
vast elm which stood in the dooryard of the Olney
Tavern on Constitution Hill. On a platform built
in its branches about twenty feet from the ground,
stood the orator of the day, and in an eloquent dis-
course dedicated the tree to the cause of Liberty.

Boston Liberty Tree and Tavern.

In the trying years that followed, the wise fathers
and young enthusiasts of Providence gathered under
its branches for counsel. The most famous of these
trees of patriotism was the Liberty Tree of Boston.
It stood near a tavern of the same name at the junction of Essex and Washington streets, then known
as Hanover Square. The name was given in 1765
at a patriotic celebration in honor of the expected
repeal of the Stamp Act. Even before that time

effigies of Lord Oliver and a boot for Lord Bute,
placards and mottoes had hung from its branches.
A metal plate was soon attached to it, bearing this
legend, "This tree was planted in 1646 and pruned
by order of the Sons of Liberty February 14, 1766."
Under the tree and at the tavern met all patriot
bands, until the tree was cut down by the roistering
British soldiers and supplied them with fourteen
cords of firewood.   The tavern stood till 1833.   A
picture of the Boston Liberty Tree and Tavern of
the same name is shown on the opposite page.   It
is from an old drawing.

The fourteenth of August, 1769, was a merry
day in Boston and vicinity.   The Sons of Liberty,
after assembling at the Liberty Tree in Boston, all
adjourned for dinner at the Liberty Tree Tavern,
or Robinson's Tavern in Dorchester.   Tables were
spread in an adjoining field under a tent, and over
three hundred people sat down to an abundant feast,
which included three barbecued pigs.   Speeches and
songs inspired and livened the diners.   The last
toast given was, "Strong halters, firm blocks, and
sharp axes to all such as deserve them."   At five
o'clock the Boston Sons, headed by John Hancock
in his chariot, started for home.   Although fourteen
toasts were given in Boston and forty-five in Dorchester, John Adams says in his Diary that "to the
honor of the Sons I did not see one person intoxi-
cated or near it."

The tavern in Portsmouth, New Hampshire,
known by the sign of Earl of Halifax, was regarded
by Portsmouth patriots as a hotbed of Tories.   It

had always been the resort of Government officials ; and in 1775, the meeting of these laced and ruffled gentlemen became most obnoxious to the Sons of Liberty, and soon a mob gathered in front of the tavern, and the irate landlord heard the blows of an axe cutting down his Earl of Halifax sign-post. Seizing an axe he thrust it into the hands of one of his powerful negro slaves, telling him to go and threaten the chopper of the sign-post. Excited by the riotous scene, the black man, without a word, at once dealt a powerful blow upon the head of a man named Noble, who was wielding the encroaching axe. Noble lived

Stavers Inn.

forty years after this blow, but never had his reason. This terrible assault of course enraged the mob, and a general assault was made on the tavern ; windows and doors were broken ; Landlord Stavers fled on horseback, and the terrified black man was found in a cistern in the tavern cellar, up to his chin in water.   When Stavers returned, he was seized by

the Committee of Safety and thrust into Exeter
jail. He took the oath of allegiance and returned
to his battered house. He would not reglaze the
broken windows, but boarded them up, and it is
said that many a distinguished group of officers
feasted in rooms without a pane of glass in the
windows.

Popular opinion was against the Earl of Halifax,
however, and when the old sign-board was touched
up, the name of William Pitt, the friend of America,
appeared on the sign.

The portion of the old Earl of Halifax or Stavers
Inn which is still standing is shown in its forlorn old
age on the opposite page.

Mr. George Davenport, of Boston, a lineal descendant of old William Davenport, owns one of the most
interesting tavern bills I have ever seen. It is of
the old Wolfe Tavern at Newburyport. To those
who can read between the lines it reveals means
and methods which were calculated to arouse enthusiasm and create public sentiment during the
exciting days of the Stamp Act. The bill and its
items read thus : —

" Dr. Messrs. Joseph Stanwood & Others of the Town of
Newburyport for Sunday expences at My House on Thirs-
day, Septr. 26th, A.D. 1765. At the Grate Uneasiness and
Tumult on Occasion of the Stamp Act.

To William Davenport   Old Tenor
To 3 Double Bowls punch by Capt. Robud's
    Order £3, 7, 6
To 7 Double Bowls of punch   . . 7, 7, 6

To Double Bowl of Egg Toddy   .   .   14,
To Double Punch 22/6 Single bowl 11/3   1, 13, 9
To Double Bowl Punch 22/6 Double bowl
    toddy 12/ 1, 14, 6
To Bowl Punch 11/3 Bowl Toddy 6/   17, 3
To Double Bowl Toddy 12/ bowl punch
    11/3   .   .   .   .   .   1, 3, 3
To Double Bowl punch 22/6 Nip Toddy
    3/ 1, 5, 6
To Mug Flip 5/ To a Thrible Bowl Punch
    33/9   .   .   .   .   .   1, 18, 9
To Double Bowl Punch 22/6 To a Thrible
    Bowl Ditto 33/9   .   .   .   2, 16, 3
To Double Bowl Punch 22/6   .   .   1, 2, 6
To a Double Bowl Punch 22/6   .   .   1, 2, 6
To Thrible Bowl Punch 33/9 Double Bowl
    Ditto 22/6   .   .   .   .   2, 16, 3
To Double Bowl Punch 22/6 Bowl Ditto
    11/3   .   .   .   .   .   1, 13, 9
To Double Bowl Punch 22/6 To Double
    Ditto 22/6 Bowl   .   .   .   2, 5
To 6 Lemons 15/ To Bowl of Punch
    11/3   .   .   .   .   .   1, 6, 3
To 2 Double Bowls Punch   .   .   .   2, 5
To Double Bowle Punch 22/6 bowl Punch
    11/3   .   .   .   .   .   1, 13, 9
To 2 Double Bowles punch 1/5 To bowl
    punch 11/3   .   .   .   .   2, 16, 3
To bowl Punch 11/3 To bowl punch
    11/3   .   .   .   .   .   1, 2, 6
To the Suppers which were cooked Hot   2, 5
To 8 Double Bowles Punch after Supper   9
To Double Bowl Toddy 12/ Bowl Punch
    11/3   .   .   .   .   .   1, 2, 6
To Bowl Egg Toddy 7/   .   .   .   7

Prince Stetson & Co.

RESPECTFULLY INFORM THE PUBLIC,

That they have put in complete repair that well known

TAVERN, *Formerly kept by Mr DAVENPORT,*

SIGN OF

JAMES WOLFE Esq^R.

State Street,

NEWBURYPORT.

Where those who favour them with their custom
shall experience every convenience and
attention which they can command.

Handbill of Wolfe Tavern.

To 6 pintes and 1/2 of Spirits @ 10/
    per pint 3, 5
To a Breakfast of Coffee for Sd Company   2, 5
                                 59, 17, 3
            Lawful Money   7, 19, 7½
Newbury Port 28 Sept. 1765.
    Errors excepted   William Davenport."

There was also a credit account of eleven pounds received in various sums from Captain Robud, Richard Farrow, and one Celeby.

It is impossible to do more than to name, almost at haphazard, a few of the taverns that had some share in scenes of Revolutionary struggle. Many served as court-rooms when court-martials were held; others were seized for military prisons; others were fired upon; others served as barracks; some as officers' headquarters; others held secret meetings of patriots; many were used as hospitals.

Many an old tavern is still standing which saw these scenes in the Revolutionary War. A splendid group of these hale and hearty old veterans is found in the rural towns near Boston. At the Wright Tavern, in Concord (shown on page 417), lodged Major Pitcairn, the British commander, and in the parlor on the morning before the battle of Concord, he stirred his glass of brandy with his bloody finger, saying he would thus stir the rebel's blood before night. The Monroe Tavern, of Lexington (facing page 406), was the headquarters of Lord Percy on the famous 19th of April, 1775. The Buckman Tavern, of the same town (page 23), was the rallying place of the Minute Men on April 18th,

and contains many a bullet hole made by the shots
of British soldiers. The Cooper Tavern (page 68)
and the Russel Tavern (page 379), both of Arlington, were also scenes of activity and participation in
the war. The Wayside Inn of Sudbury (page 372)
and the Black
Horse Tavern of
Winchester were
the scenes of the
reassembling of the
soldiers after the
battle of Lexing-
ton.

Sign-board of Wolfe Tavern.

On the south
side of Faneuil
Hall Square in Bos-
ton, a narrow pas-
sageway leads into
the gloomy recesses
of a yard or court
of irregular shape;
this is Corn Court,
and in the middle
of this court stands,
overshadowed by
tall modern neighbors, the oldest inn in Boston. It
has been raised and added to, and disfigured with
vast painted signs, and hideous fire escapes, but
within still retains its taproom and ancient appearance. As early as 1634, Samuel Cole had an ordinary on this spot, and in 1636, Governor Vane
entertained there Miantonomah and his twenty

warriors. This building, built nearly two centuries ago, was given the name of Hancock in 1780, when he became governor. In 1794, Talleyrand was a guest at this old hostelry, and Louis Philippe in 1797. Washington, Franklin, and scores of other patriots have tarried within its walls; and in its tap-room were held meetings of the historic Boston Tea-party.

The Green Dragon Inn was one of the most famous of historic taverns. A representation of it from an old print is shown on page 187. The metal dragon which gave the name projected from the wall on an iron rod.

Warren was the first Grand Master of the first Grand Lodge of Masons that held its meetings at this inn; and other patriots came to the inn to confer with him on the troublous times. The inn was a famous resort for the sturdy mechanics of the North End. Paul Revere wrote: —

"In the fall of 1774 and winter of 1775, I was one of upwards of thirty men, chiefly mechanics, who formed ourselves with a Committee for the purpose of watching the movements of the British soldiers and gaining every intelligence of the movements of the Tories. We held our meetings at the Green Dragon Tavern. This committee were astonished to find all their secrets known to General Gage, although every time they met every member swore not to reveal their transactions even to Hancock, Adams, Otis, Warren or Church."

The latter, Dr. Church, proved to be the traitor. The mass meeting of these mechanics and their friends held in this inn when the question of the adoption of the Federal Constitution was being considered was deemed by Samuel Adams one of the most important factors of its acceptance. Daniel Webster styled the Green Dragon the Headquarters of the Revolution. During the war it was used as a hospital.

Hancock Tavern.

It is pleasant to note how many old taverns in New England, though no longer public hostelries, still are occupied by descendants of the original owners. Such is the home of Hon. John Winn in Burlington, Massachusetts. It stands on the road to Lowell by way of Woburn, about eleven miles out of Boston. The house was used at the time of the battle of Bunker Hill as a storage-place for the valuables of Boston and Charlestown families. The present home of the Winns was built in 1734 upon the exact site of the house built in 1640 by the first Edward Winn, the emigrant. In it the first white child was born in the town of Woburn, December 5, 1641.

The tavern was kept in Revolutionary days by Lieutenant Joseph Winn, who marched off to join the Lexington farmers on April 19, 1775, at two o'clock in the morning, when the alarm came "to every Middlesex village and farm" to gather against the redcoats. He came home late that night, and fought again at Bunker Hill.

The tavern sign bore the coat of arms of the Winns; it was — not to use strict heraldic terms — three spread eagles on a shield. As it was not painted with any too strict obedience to the rules of heraldry or art, nor was it hung in a community that had any very profound knowledge or reverence on either subject, the three noble birds soon received a comparatively degraded title, and the sign-board and tavern were known as the Three Broiled Chickens.

A building in New York which was owned by the De Lanceys before it became a public house is still standing on the southeast corner of Broad and Pearl streets; its name is well known to-day, Fraunces' Tavern. This name came from the stewardship of Samuel Fraunces, "Black Sam," a soldier of the American Revolution. The tavern originally bore a sign with the device of the head of Queen Charlotte, and was known as the Queen's Head, but in Revolutionary times Black Sam was a patriot, and in his house were held many patriotic and public meetings. The most famous of these meetings, one which has given the name of Washington's Headquarters to the tavern, was held in the Long Room on December 4, 1783 : whereat Washington sadly bade farewell to his fellow-officers who had fought with him in the War for Independence.

Sam Fraunces.

In this room, ten days previously, had been celebrated the evacuation of the city of New York by the British, by a dinner given to General Washington by Governor Clinton, at which the significant thirteen toasts were drunk to the new nation. Black Sam was a public benefactor as well as a patriot. He established a course of lectures on natural philosophy, and opened an exhibition of wax figures, seventy in all, for the amusement of New Yorkers. His story, and that of the tavern bearing his name, have been told at length many times in print.

Another interesting Revolutionary inn in New York was the Golden Hill Inn. The general estimate of the date of its building is 1694; then 122 William Street was a golden grainfield, on one

corner of the Damon Farm.   After three-quarters
of a century of good hospitality it was chosen as
the headquarters of the Sons of Liberty in New
York, and within its walls gathered the committee
in 1769, to protest against Lieutenant-governor
Colden's dictum that the colonists must pay for
supplies for the British soldiers.   The result was a
call for a meeting of the citizens and the governor's
angry offer of a reward for knowledge of the place
of meeting.   The cutting down of the liberty pole
on the night of January 17, 1770, and the seizure
of four red-coats by the patriots ended in a fight in
the inn garden and the death of one patriot.   A
century of stirring life followed until 1896, when
the old tavern sadly closed its doors under the
pressure of the Raines Law.

The Keeler Tavern was a famous hostelry for
travellers between New York and Boston.   Its old
sign-board is shown on page 205.   During the
Revolution, landlord Keeler was well known to be
a patriot, and was suspected of manufacturing car-
tridges in his tavern.   The British poured a special
fire upon the building, and one cannon ball lodged
in a timber on the north side of the house still
is to be seen by drawing aside the shingle that
usually conceals it.   A companion cannon ball
whistled so close to a man who was climbing the
stairs of the house that he tumbled down backward
screaming, "I'm a dead man," until his friends with
difficulty silenced him, and assured him he was
living.   A son of the landlord, Jeremiah Keeler,
enlisted in the Continental army when but seven-

teen ; he became a sergeant, and was the first man to scale the English breastworks at Yorktown. He was presented with a sword by his commanding officer, Lafayette, and it is still preserved.

When Lafayette made his triumphal progress through the United States in 1824, he visited Ridgefield and the tavern to see Jeremiah Keeler, and a big ball was given in the tavern in his honor. Jerome Bonaparte and his beautiful Baltimore bride stopped there in 1804. Oliver Wolcott and Timothy Pickering were other sojourners under its roof. Peter Parley gave to the Keeler Tavern the palm for good cooking.

The old Conkey Tavern at Prescott, Massachusetts, saw the gathering of a very futile but picturesque windstorm of Revolutionary grievance. It was built in 1758 by William Conkey, on a lovely but lonely valley midway between the east and west hills of Pelham. The Swift River running through this valley was made the boundary in the town division in 1822, which made eastern Pelham into Prescott. Captain Daniel Shays, the leader of Shays' Rebellion, lived half a mile from the tavern on the Centre Range Road. In the cheerful rooms of this tavern, Shays, aided by the well-stocked tavern-bar, incited the debt-burdened farmers to rebel against their state government. Here he drilled his "floodwood," and from hence he led them forth to Springfield, and on January 25, 1787, was promptly repulsed by the state militia under General Lincoln. Eleven hundred men trooped back to Pelham, and after four days of what must have proved scant and

Green Dragon Tavern.

cold fare in those barren winter hilltops, again sallied out to Petersham. Here he was again routed by Lincoln, who, with his men, had marched thirty miles without halt, from eight o'clock at night to nine the following morning through a blinding, northeast New England snowstorm. A hundred and fifty of Shays' men were captured, but their valiant and wordy leader escaped.

When the photograph (shown opposite page 188) was taken, in 1883, the old timbers within the house were sound and firm, and the beams overhead still bore the marks of the muskets of Shays' impatient men. It was a characteristic " deserted home " of New England.

Nothing could more fully picture Whittier's lines : —

"Against the wooded hills it stands,
    Ghost of a dead house ; staring through
Its broken lights on wasted lands
    Where old-time harvests grew.

"Unploughed, unsown, by scythe unshorn,
    The poor forsaken farm-fields lie,
Once rich and rife with golden corn
    And pale-green breadths of rye.

"So sad, so drear ; it seems almost
    Some haunting Presence makes its sign,
That down some shadowy lane some ghost
    Might drive his spectral kine.''

Since then the old tavern has fallen down, a sad ruin, like many another on New England hills, in a country as wild and lonely, probably far lonelier, than in the days of the Revolution and Shays' Rebellion. The sign-board (page 190) is still preserved.

Eighteenth-century taverns had a special function which had a bearing on their war relations; they were "improved" as recruiting offices. During the years 1742 to 1748, and from 1756 to 1763, while England was at war with France, the "listing" was brisk. Here is a typical advertisement dated 1759 : —

"All able-bodied fit Men that have an Inclination to serve his Majesty King George the Second, in the First Independent Company of Rangers, now in the Province of *Nova Scotia* commanded by *Joseph Gorham, Esq.* ; shall, on enlisting, receive good Pay and Cloathing, a large Bounty, with a Crown to drink the King's Health. And by repairing to the Sign of the Bear in King-Street, *Boston*, and to

Conkey Tavern.

Mr. *Cornelius Crocker*, Innholder in *Barnstable*, may hear the particular Encouragement, and many Advantages accruing to a Soldier, in the Course of the Duty of that Company, too long to insert here; and further may depend on being discharged at the expiration of the Time entertain'd for, and to have every other Encouragement punctually compli'd with."

In the " French War of 1744," the Governor of Jamaica sent his "leftenants" to Philadelphia to fill up his regiments. It was worth " listing " at the Widow Roberts' Coffee-house in those days, when every " sojer " got six shillings a week extra, and his family carried free to Antigua if he wished it, and land to settle on in that glorious country when war was over. Brisk and cheerful was the enrolment, and I trust all lived happy ever after in the tropic land, so far away in miles and environment from the Quaker town of their youth.

It was pleasant work, also, for "gentlemen sailors " in 1744. The colonies whisked out on the high seas that year a hundred and thirteen full-manned privateers. Wealthy merchants gathered around the inn tables to join fortunes in these ventures ; plans were quickly matured ; and the articles of agreement signed by these rich ship-owners were quickly followed by articles of agreement to be signed by the seamen. Oh, what prizes these cruisers brought into port ! There are no items in the newspapers of that day under the head of Philadelphia and New York news save lists of prizes. When these half-pirates came in, cannon were fired, the whole town turned out, and the taverns were

filled with rejoicings. The names of the ships and
their captains were household words. The captured cargoes were carried ashore; inventories were
posted in the taprooms, and often the goods were
sold within the welcoming tavern doors.

Sign-board of Conkey Tavern.

It has been said that taverns bearing names of
ships, maritime phrases, and seafaring titles were
usually chosen as shipping offices for the enlistment
of privateersmen and marines on men-of-war. It is
more probable that the most popular tavern in any
locality frequented by sailors and seamen was the
one chosen, whatever its name. In the *Boston Post
Boy* of June, 1762, is the following notice : —

"NOW BOUND ON A CRUIZE OF SIX MONTHS

Against His Majesties enemies, The Brigantine *Tartar*,
a Prime Sailor mounting Fourteen Six Pounders, Twenty

Culverines, and will carry One Hundred and Twenty Men. Commanded by William Augustus Peck.   All

Gentlemen Seamen

and able bodied Landsmen who have a mind to make their Fortunes, and are inclined to take a Cruize in this said Vessel, by applying at this King's Head Tavern at the North End, may view the Articles which are more advantageous to the Ship's Company than were ever before offered in this Place."

To those who know the condition of Jack Tar aboard ship a century ago, and the attitude which Captain Peck doubtless assumed to his seamen the moment the *Tartar* was started on this "Cruize," there is a sarcastic pleasantry in the term Gentlemen Seamen used by him in common with other captains ashore, that might be swallowed in a taproom with bowls of grog and flip, but would never go down smoothly on shipboard.

Gentlemen sailors were frequently impressed in a very different manner.   The press-gang was one of the peculiar institutions of Great Britain, and its aggressive outrages formed one of the causes of "Madison's War," as old people liked to term the War of 1812.   The *Virginia Gazette* of the first of October, 1767, tells of a far different scene from that indicated by the plausible words of Captain Peck; one in which a Norfolk tavern took a part : —

" It appears that Captain Morgan of the Hornet, Sloop of War, concerted a bloody riotous Plan, to impress Seamen, at Norfolk, Virginia, for which Purpose his Tender was equipped with Guns and Men, and under cover of the Night, said Morgan landed at a public wharff, having first made proper Dispositions either for an Attack or Retreat; then went to a Tavern, and took a chearful Glass, after which they went to work and took every Person they met with and knock'd all down that resisted; and dragg'd them

Naval Pitcher.

on board the Tender but the Town soon took the Alarm, and being headed by Paul Loyal, Esq., a Magistrate, they endeavor'd to convince Captain Morgan of his Error; but being deaf to all they said he ordered the People in the Tender to fire on the Inhabitants, but they refused to obey their Commander's orders and he was soon oblig'd to fly, leaving some of his Hornets behind, who were sent to Gaol."

It is astonishing to read of such ruffianly kid-
nappings under the protection of the British Government, and to know that seamen and sailors who
had been so treated would assist in such outrages on
others.   It is only one of the many proofs that we
meet everywhere in history of the thick-skinned
indifference and cruelty of nearly all of the human
race a century ago.

It was far worse in these matters in England than
in the colonies.   Mr. Ashton tells us that in one
night over two thousand one hundred men were
pressed in London alone.   Riot and bloodshed
accompanied those infamous raids; sometimes a
whole town turned out to resist the officers and
ship's men.

CHAPTER IX

THE TAVERN PANORAMA

WE have to-day scores of places of amusement, and means of amusement, where in earlier days all diversions centred at the tavern. The furnishing of food and shelter to travellers and to horses, and of liquid comfort to neighbors, was not the only function of the tavern, nor the meeting for cheerful interchange of news and sentiment. Whatever there was of novelty in entertainment or instruction, was delivered at the tavern, and it served as the gathering place for folk on scores of duties or pleasures bent. There was in fact a constant panorama passing within the walls and before the doors of an old tavern, not only in the shape of distinguished, picturesque, and unwonted guests, but through the variety of uses to which the tavern was put. It would be impossible to enumerate them all. Many of the chapters of this book indicate some of them. We can simply glance at a few more of the most common and of the most interesting ones.

Though guests of colonial days are often named as having visited the old taverns which still linger intact, the names of importance which are most

frequently heard are those of Revolutionary heroes
and visitors, those of Franklin, Washington, and
Lafayette being most proudly enumerated. Franklin was a great local traveller. His post-office affairs
took him frequently along the road. He was fond
of visiting, and people were naturally fond of having
him visit them. He was such a welcome guest that
he need not have entered a tavern from Maine to
Georgia. Washington made several trips through
the states, one of much ceremony. He gives the
names of the taverns at which he stopped.

I have been in tavern-rooms honored a century
ago by the sleeping presence of Washington, but
I have never slept in them. I would rather look at
them than sleep in them; and I have moralized over
the simplicity and lack of luxury which was the best
that the tavern could offer, even to that great man.

Lafayette was made welcome in many private
houses in his tour in 1824, but he also was a
tavern guest. His journal is preserved in Paris,
untranslated. In it he tells of seeing the well-known
Landing of Lafayette plates and dishes for the first
time at a tavern in a small town in western New
York.

All the statesmen of the South stopped at taverns on the old National road: Harrison, Hous-
ton, Taylor, Polk, and Allen. Homespun Davy
Crockett, popular General Jackson, stately Henry
Clay, furnished a show for the country by-standers
to gape at. In the Northern states Daniel Webster
was the god whose coming was adored. A halo of
glory shed by his presence still hangs round many

Washington Tavern, North Wilbraham, Massachusetts.

a tavern room, and well it may, for he was a giant among men.

To show the variety of the tavern panorama let me quote what Edwin Lasseter Bynner wrote of the inns of Boston : —

"They were the centres of so much of its life and affairs, the resort at once of judge and jury, of the clergy and the laity, of the politician and the merchant; where the selectmen came to talk over the affairs of the town, and higher officials to discuss the higher interests of the province; where royal governors and distinguished strangers were entertained alike with the humblest wayfarer and the meanest citizen; where were held the carousals of roistering red-coat officers, and the midnight plottings of muttering stern-lipped patriots; where, in fine, the swaggering

ensign of the royal army, the frowning Puritan, the obnoxious Quaker, the Huguenot refugee, and the savage Indian
chief from the neighboring forest might perchance jostle
each other in the common taproom."

Naturally the tavern proved the exhibition place
and temporary lodging-place of all secular shows
which could not be housed in the meeting-house.
It contained the second assembly room in size, and
often the only other large room in town save that
devoted to religious gatherings. Hence, when in
Salem in 1781 "the Sentimentalists and all Volon-
tiers who are pleased to encourage the extensive
Propogation of Polite Literature" were invited to
attend a book auction by a "Provedore and Professor of Auctioneering," this sale of books was held
at Mr. Goodhue's tavern. At the American Coffee-
house in Boston the firm that vendued books within
doors also sold jackasses on the street.

"Monstrous Sights" found at the tavern a congenial temporary home, where discussion of their
appearance was held before the tavern bar, while the
tavern barn restrained and confined the monster if
he chanced to be a wild beast. A moose, a walrus,
a camel, a lion, a leopard, appeared in succession in
Salem taverns, chiefly at the Black Horse. Then
came a wonder of natural history, a Pygarg, said
to be from Russia. We have a description of it:
it had "the likeness of a camel, bear, mule, goat,
and common bullock"; it is spoken of in the book
of Deuteronomy, Chapter XIV. I am not sure
that we would recognize our native American moose
if he were not called by name, in the creature adver-

tised as having "a face like a mouse, ears like an ass, neck and back like a camel, hind-parts like a horse, tail like a rabbit, and feet like a heifer." Cassowaries, learned pigs, learned horses, and rabbits were shown for petty sums. Deformed beasts and persons were exhibited. Pictures, "prospects," statues, elaborate clocks, moving puppets, and many mechanical contrivances could be viewed in the tavern parlor.

"Electrical machines" were the wonder of their day. Solemn professors and gay "fakirs" exhibited them from tavern to tavern. The first lightning-rods also made a great show. Shortly after the invention of balloons, came their advent as popular shows in many towns. They often ascended from the green in front of the tavern. They bore many pompous names,—"Archimedial Phaetons," "Vertical Aerial Coaches," "Patent Fœderal Balloons." The public was assured that "persons of timid nature" would find nothing to terrify them in the ascent. They were not only recommended as engines of amusement and wonder, but were urged upon "Invaletudinarians" as hygienic factors, in that they caused in the ascent the "sudden revulsion of the blood and humours" of aeronautic travellers.

The Bunch of Grapes housed Mr. Douglas when he delivered his famous lecture on "Heads, Coats of Arms, Wigs, Ladies' Head Dresses," etc.; it was an office for John Hurd, an early insurance broker, chiefly for marine risks. Nearly all the first insurance offices were in taverns.

Black Horse Tavern, Salem, Massachusetts.

One intelligent chronicler relates : —

"The taverns of Boston were the original business Exchanges; they combined the Counting House, the Exchange-office, the Reading-room, and the Bank: each represented a locality. To the Lamb Tavern, called by the sailors 'sheep's baby,' people went 'to see a man from Dedham'— it was the resort of all from Norfolk County. The old Eastern Stage House in Ann Street was frequented by 'down Easters,' captains of vessels, formerly from the Penobscot and Kennebec; there were to be seen groups of sturdy men seated round an enormous fire-place, chalking down the price of bark and lumber, and shippers bringing in a vagrant tarpaulin to 'sign the articles.' To the Exchange Coffee-House resorted the nabobs of Essex County; here those aristocratic eastern towns, Newburyport and Portsmouth, were represented by ship owners and ship builders, merchants of the first class."

The first attempt at the production of plays in New England was a signal for prompt and vital opposition. Little plays called drolls were exhibited in the taverns and coffee-houses; such plays as *Pickle Herring, Taylor riding to Brentford, Harlequin and Scaramouch.* About 1750 two young English strollers produced what must have been a mightily bald rendering of *Otway's Orphans* in a Boston coffee-house; this was a step too far in frivolity, and stern Boston magistrates took rigid care there were no more similar offences. Many ingenious ruses were invented and presented to the public to avoid the hated term and conceal the hated fact of play acting. "Histrionic academies" were a sneaking introduction of plays. In 1762 a clever but sanctimonious manager succeeded in crowding his company and his play into a Newport tavern. Here is his truckling play-bill : —

"KINGS ARMS TAVERN NEWPORT RHODE ISLAND

On Monday, June 10th, at the Public Room of the Above Inn will be delivered a series of

Moral Dialogues

In Five Parts

Depicting the evil effects of jealousy and other bad passions and Proving that happiness can only spring from the pursuit of Virtue.

MR. DOUGLASS — Will represent a noble magnanimous Moor called Othello, who loves a young lady named Desdemona, and, after he marries her, harbours (as in too many cases) the dreadful passion of jealousy.

> *Of jealousy, our being's bane*
> *Mark the small cause and the most dreadful pain.*

MR. ALLYN — Will depict the character of a specious villain, in the regiment of Othello, who is so base as to hate his commander on mere suspicion and to impose on his best friend. Of such characters, it is to be feared, there are thousands in the world, and the one in question may present to us a salutary warning.

> *The man that wrongs his master and his friend*
> *What can he come to but a shameful end?*

MR. HALLAM — Will delineate a young and thoughtless officer who is traduced by Mr. Allyn and, getting drunk, loses his situation and his general's esteem. All young men whatsoever take example from Cassio.

> *The ill effects of drinking would you see?*
> *Be warned and fly from evil company.*

MR. MORRIS — Will represent an old gentleman, the father of Desdemona, who is not cruel or covetous, but is foolish enough to dislike the noble Moor, his son-in-law, because his face is not white, forgetting that we all spring from one root. Such prejudices are very numerous and very wrong.

> *Fathers beware what sense and love ye lack!*
> *'Tis crime, not colour, that makes the being black.*

Mr. Quelch — Will depict a fool who wishes to become a knave, and, trusting to one, gets killed by one. Such is the friendship of rogues! Take heed!

Where fools would become, how often you'll
Perceive the knave not wiser than the fool.

Mrs. Morris — Will represent a young and virtuous wife, who being wrongfully suspected, gets smothered (in an adjoining room) by her husband.

Reader, attend, and ere thou goest hence
Let fall a tear to helpless innocence.

Mrs. Douglass — Will be her faithful attendant who will hold out a good example to all servants male and female, and to all people in subjection.

Obedience and gratitude
Are things as rare as they are good.

Various other Dialogues, too numerous to mention here, will be delivered at night, all adapted to the mind and manners. The whole will be repeated on Wednesday and on Saturday. Tickets, six shillings each, to be had within. Commencement at 7. Conclusion at half-past ten : in order that every Spectator may go home at a sober hour and reflect upon what he has seen, before he retired to rest.

God save the King
Long may he sway.
East, north, and south
And fair America.''

We can see the little public room of the tavern with its rows of chairs and benches at one end and the group of starveling actors at the other, who

never played a greater farce than when they set up
as being solely ministers of piety and virtue.

"Consorts" of music were given in the taverns,
and, most exciting of all, lotteries were drawn there.
This licensed and highly approved form of gam-
bling had the sanction of
the law and the participation of every community.
Churches had lotteries "for
promoting public worship
and the advancement of
religion." Colleges and
schools thus increased their
endowments. Towns and
states raised money to pay
the public debt by means
of lotteries.

It was asserted that
"the interests of litera-
ture and learning were
supported, the arts and
sciences were encouraged,
religion was extended, the
wastes of war were repaired,
inundation prevented,

Stickney Tavern.

travel increased, and the burthen of taxes lessened
by lotteries." Many private lotteries were drawn
at the taverns, which were thronged at that time
with excited ticket-owners.

Lodges of Freemasons in America, following the
custom which prevailed in England, met at the
taverns. In Philadelphia they met at Peg Mullen's

Beefsteak House.   The lodges were often known by the names of the taverns at which the meetings were held.   One Boston lodge met at the Royal Exchange Tavern, and hence was known by its name.   That hostelry was, however, so popular with the visiting public that sometimes the brethren had to suspend their meetings for want of room. In December, 1749, the Masons of Boston celebrated the feast of St. John, and appeared in procession on the streets.   This excited the greatest curiosity and ridicule.   Joseph Green wrote a poem in which the chief object of his wit was Luke Vardy, the keeper of the Royal Exchange : —

> " Where's honest Luke, that cook from London ?
> For without Luke the Lodge is undone.
> 'Twas he who oft dispell'd their sadness,
> And filled the *Brethren's* hearts with gladness.
> *Luke* in return is made a brother
> As good and true as any other.
> And still, though broke with age and wine,
> Preserves the *token* and the *sign*."

Massachusetts Grand Lodge organized at Green Dragon, and the first lodge of all, St. John's Lodge, met in 1733 at the Bunch of Grapes in King (now State) Street.   One of the three bunches of grapes that formed the original, tavern sign still hangs in front of the lodge room of St. John's Lodge in Masonic Temple, Boston.   This tavern had an early and lasting reputation as " the best punch-house in Boston."   In Revolutionary days it became the headquarters of High Whigs, and a scarlet coat was an inflammatory signal in that taproom. The "Whig Tavern" was a proper centre for popular gatherings after the evacuation of Boston ; General Stark's victory at Bennington was celebrated there "to high taste," says a participant. The firing of cannon, discharge of rockets, playing of fifes and drums, made satisfactory noise. "The gentlemen had ample liquor within doors, and two barrels of grog were distributed to outsiders on the streets—all "with the greatest propriety." When General Stark arrived, a few weeks later, there was equal rejoicing. The glories of the entertainment of Washington and a series of gallant soldiers and distinguished travellers do not, perhaps, reflect the honor upon the old tavern that comes from its having been the scene of a most significant fact in our history. It was the gathering place and place of organization of the Ohio Company — the first concerted movement of New England toward the Great West.

Sign-board of Keeler's Tavern.

The famous Craft's Tavern in the little town of Walpole, New Hampshire, kept by Major Asa Bullard, was the gathering place in 1796 of one of the most brilliant groups of writers ever engaged in a literary undertaking in this country. It was called the Literary Club of Walpole, and is a landmark in the literary life of New England. In this rustic New Hampshire tavern this Club might repeat Beaumont's lines to Jonson beginning : —

"What things have we seen
Done at the Mermaid, heard words that have been
So nimble, and so full of subtle flame."

The head of this Yankee collection of wits was
the Lay Preacher, Joseph Dennie, who, at the death

Plate, Nahant Hotel.

of the novelist, Charles Brockden Brown, was
the only man in the United States who made a
profession of literature.   He was born in Boston,
studied law in Charlestown, New Hampshire, then
an important and bustling town, went to Walpole,

and became conductor of the *New Hampshire Journal and Farmer's Museum*. For this newspaper and
in this Craft's Tavern he wrote his famous *Lay
Sermons* which were read from Maine to Georgia.
In the talented tavern circle was Royall Tyler,
author of the play *The Contrast* and the novel *The
Algerine Captive*. He became Chief Justice of Vermont. Another contributor was David Everett,
author of the well-known juvenile spouting-piece,
beginning:—

> "You'd scarce expect one of my age
> To speak in public on the stage."

Still another, Thomas G. Fessenden, wrote *Ter-
rible Tractoration*. It was a day of pseudonyms;
Fessenden wrote as Simon Spunky and Christopher
Caustic; Everett called himself Peter Peveril; Isaac
Story was Peter Quinn; Dennie was Oliver Old-
school; Tyler was Colon and Spondee.

A day of great sport at the tavern was when there
was a turkey-shoot; these often took place on
Thanksgiving Day. Notices such as this were frequently found in the autumnal newspapers : —

"SHARP–SHOOTING.

" Thos. D. Ponsland informs his Friends and the Friends
of *Sport* that he will on Friday, 7th day of December next,
set up for SHOOTING a number of

FINE FAT TURKEYS

and invites all *Gunners* and others who would wish to
recreate themselves to call on the day after Thanksgiving

at the Old Bakers' Tavern, Upp. Parish Beverly, where every accommodation would be afforded."

In the *Boston Evening Post* of January 11, 1773, notice was given that "a Bear and Number of Turkeys" would be set up as a mark at the Punch Bowl Tavern in Brookline.

Captain Basil Hall, travelling in America in 1827, was much surprised at the account of one of these turkey-shoots, which he thus fully describes: —

"At a country inn bearing the English name of Andover, close to the Indian river Shawsheen, I observed the following printed bill stuck up in the bar.

SPORTSMEN ATTEND

300 FOWLS

will be set up for the sportsmen at the Subscriber's Hotel in Tewksbury, on Friday the 12 October, inst. at 8 A.M.

Gentlemen of Tewksbury,
Lowell and vicinity are invited to attend.

WILLIAM HARDY.

"This placard was utterly unintelligible to me; and the Landlord laughed at my curiosity but good humouredly enlightened my ignorance by explaining that these shooting matches were so common in America, that he had no doubt I would fall in with them often. I regretted very much having passed one day too late for this transatlantic battle. It appears that these birds were literally barn door fowls, placed at certain distances, and fired at by any one who chooses to pay the allotted sum for a shot. If he kills the bird, he is allowed to carry it off; otherwise, like a true sportsman, he has the amusement for his money. Cocks and hens being small birds, are placed at the distance of 165 feet; and for every shot with ball the sportsman has to pay four cents. Turkeys are placed at twice the distance, or 110 yards, if a common musket be used; but at 165 yards if the weapon be a rifle. In both those cases the price per shot is from six to ten cents."

There were other sports offered at the taverns, as shown by an advertisement in the *Essex Register* of June, 1806 : —

"SPORTSMEN ATTEND.

The Gentlemen *Sportsmen* of this town and Vicinity are informed that a Grand Combat will take place between the Urus Zebu and Spanish Bull on 4th of July if fair weather. If not the next fair day at the Half Way House on the *Salem Turnpike*. No danger need be apprehended during the performance, as the Circus is very convenient. After the performance there will be a Grand Fox Chase on the Marshes near the Circus to start precisely at 6 o'clock."

A woman tavern-keeper on Boston Neck, Sally Barton, of the George, also had bull-baiting as one of the attractions of her home. In 1763, the keeper of the DeLancey Arms in New York had a bull-baiting. The English officers stationed in America brought over this fashion. In the year 1774, there was a bull-baiting held every day for many months on what is now a quiet street near my home. Landlord Loosely, — most appropriately named, — of the King's Head Tavern, took charge of these bull-baitings and advertised for good active bulls and strong dogs. One advertisement, in rhyme, begins : —

"This notice gives to all who covet
Baiting the bull, and dearly love it."

Fox-hunting, too, was beloved of the British visitors, and of Southern planters as well. The Middle and Southern states saw frequent meets of mounted gentlemen with hounds, usually at the tavern, to which they returned after the day's run to end with suitable jollity.

The old English " drift of the forest " became in America a wolf-rout or wolf-drive. Then circles of men and boys were formed to drive in toward the centre of the ring and kill squirrels and hares which pestered the farmers. Then came shooting matches in which every living wild creature was a prey. The extent to which these devastating hunting parties could be carried is shown by an article in a Bedford County (Pennsylvania) newspaper. On Friday, December 4, 1818, about seven hundred men from neighboring townships formed such a party. The signal was first given on French Town Mountain, and the circle of forty miles of horn blowing to horn was completed in fifteen minutes. The hunters progressed to a centre in Wysox township, using guns as long as they could with safety, then bayonets, clubs, poles, pitchforks, etc. Five bears, nine wolves, and fourteen foxes were killed, and three hundred deer — it makes one's heart ache. It was estimated that more than double the number

escaped.   The expedition closed with great mirth
at the tavern.

I find through many legal reports and accounts
of trials and arrests, that upper rooms in the taverns
were frequently used as lockups or temporary jails.
Mr. S. L. Frey,
of Palatine Bridge,
in his charming ac-
count of olden days
in that town, tells an
amusing episode of
tavern life connected
with this custom.
Near the village
schoolhouse lived a
man named Fisk —
a quiet citizen,
friendly to the boys,
but given, however,
to frequent disap-
pearances, and a
profound reticence
as to his means of
livelihood which was
naturally a distinct

Sign-board of Wolfe Tavern, Brooklyn,
Connecticut.

grievance and indeed an injustice to every respect-
ably inquisitive neighbor.   The boys noted that he
was a great lover of horses, and seemed to have a
constant succession of new ones in his stable, and
that these newcomers vanished in as silent and
unaccountable a manner as they had arrived.

One morning the scholars were excited and delighted to learn that the band of horse thieves that had for years ravaged the valley had at last been ferreted out, the two leaders captured and safely lodged during the night in the village jail, namely, a doubly locked and outside bolted room in Uncle Jesse Vincent's tavern.   And the climax of all the excitement and pleasure was the fact that Neighbor Fisk was the leader of the gang.

Court was called in the tavern parlor at noon. The sheriff and his officers, lawyers from neighboring towns, all importance and pomposity, all the men and all the boys from miles around were waiting eagerly to see once more the mysterious Fisk, when a loud shout came from the men who had gone to lead forth the prisoners that both had escaped.   Of course they had!   An open window, a leanto roof, a trellis and a high fence, — no decent prisoner could help escaping.

But they had been startled in their plans, and hurried while exchanging clothes, and it was plain from the garments left behind that one man had vanished clad only in his shirt, stockings, and shoes. The dire confusion of the first mortifying discovery soon changed to organized plans of pursuit, and the chase turned to a great piece of woodland behind the tavern.   Oak and hickory with undergrowth of witchhazel — a prime place for partridges and gray squirrels — led back from the river to the hills and a deep gorge filled with solemn pines and hemlocks.

The rampant boys were snubbed early in the day by the sheriff and told to keep back; and one tall boy — "mad" at the insult — conceived the plan of personating the thief. He was a famous runner, the best in the school. He hid his coat in a hollow log, pulled his shirt over his trousers, Chinaman fashion, worked his way around on the edge of the hunting party, and was soon "discovered" by his boy friends, whose shouts of "Stop thief!" "Here he is!" brought the whole army of searchers after him. Oh! what a hunt followed. All were on foot, for no horses could pass through the heavy undergrowth; the white flag of the pursued fluttered in and out far in front into the swamp, under the bushes. Talk of hare and hounds! no game was ever run like that. The fleet young horse thief in front easily distanced the puffing sheriffs in the rear, and at last the pursuit was given over. Fisk escaped, thanks to his friends the boys, but the story of the wrath that was visited on the conspirators when their fun was discovered the next day at the tavern is "another story."

Sittings of courts were often held in the public room of taverns, not only in small towns where assembly rooms were few, but in large cities. From the settlement of Philadelphia till 1759, justices of peace heard and decided causes in the public inns of Philadelphia, and the Common Council had frequent sittings there. In Boston the courts were held in suburban taverns when the smallpox scourged the town. In Postlethwaite's Tavern (shown on page 214) the first courts of Lancaster County, Pennsylvania, were held in 1729, and propositions were made to make it the county seat;

but the present site of the city of Lancaster was
finally chosen, though Landlord Postlethwaite made
strenuous endeavors to retain his tavern as a
centre.

Our ancestors found in criminals and all the
accompaniments of crime their chief source of diver-

Postlethwaite's Tavern, 1729.

sion.   They did not believe in lonely captivity but
in public obloquy for criminals.   The only exciting
and stirring emotions which entered their lives came
through the recounting of crimes and offences, and
the sight of the punishment of these crimes and
offences; rising of course to the highest point of
excitement in witnessing the public executions of

criminals. The bilboes were the first engine of punishment in Boston, and were used until 1639, and perhaps much later. The drinkers of a cup of sack at the Boston ordinary had much diversion in seeing James Woodward, who had had too much sack at the Cambridge ordinary, "laid by the heels" on the ground with a great bar of iron fastened and locked to his legs with sliding shackles and a bolt. Still more satisfaction had all honest Puritans when Thomas Morton, of Merrymount, that amusing old debauchee and roisterer, was "clapt into the bilbowes," where "the harmless salvages" gathered around and stared at him like "poor silly lambes."

The stocks soon superseded the bilboes and were near neighbors and amusement purveyors to the tavern. Towns were forced by law to set up "good sufficient stocks." Warwick, Rhode Island, ordered that "John Lowe should erect the public stocks and whipping-post near David Arnold's Tavern, and procure iron and timber for the same." The stocks were simple to make; a heavy timber or plank had on the upper edge two half-circle holes which met two similar notches or holes in a movable upper timber. When this was in place these notches formed round holes to enclose the legs of the prisoner, who could then be locked in.

The whipping-post, a good sound British institution, was promptly set up in every town, and the sound of the cat often entered the tavern windows. I can imagine all the young folk thronging to witness the whipping of some ardent young swain who had dared to make love to some fair damsel without the consent of her parents. There was no room for the escape of any man who thus "inveagled" a girl; the New Haven colony specified that any tempting without the parents' sanction could not be done by "speech, writing, message, company-keeping, unnecessary familiarity, disorderly night meetings, sinful dalliance, gifts, or (as a wholesale blow to lovers' inventions) in any other way."

But sly Puritan maids found that even the "any other way" of Puritan law-makers could be circumvented. Jacob Murline, in Hartford, on May-day in 1660, without asking any permission of Goodman Tuttle, had some very boisterous love-making with Sarah Tuttle, his daughter. It began by Jacob's seizing Sarah's gloves and demanding the mediæval forfeit — a kiss. "Whereupon," writes the scandalized Puritan chronicler, "they sat down together, his arm being about her, and her arm upon his shoulder or about his neck, and hee kissed her and shee kissed him, or they kissed one another, continuing in this posture about half an hour." The angry father, on hearing of this, haled Jacob into court and sued him for damages in "inveagling" his daughter's affections. There were plenty of witnesses of the kissing, and Jacob seemed doomed to heavy fines and the cat-o'-nine-tails, when crafty Sarah informed the Court that Jacob did not inveigle her, that she wished him to kiss her — in fact, that she enticed him. The baffled Court therefore had to fine Sarah, and of course Sarah's father had to pay the fine; but the magistrate called her justly a

" Bould Virgin," and lectured her severely. To all this she gave the demure answer "that she hoped God would help her to Carry it Better for time to come," which would seem to be somewhat super-fluous, since she had, without any help, seemed to do about as well for herself as any girl could wish to under the cir-cumstances.

For some years the Quakers never were absent from the whip-ping-post. They were trying enough, preach-ing everywhere, and on all occa-sions, yet never willing to keep silent when the Puritan preacher held forth; not willing, even, to keep away from the Puritan meet-

Sign-board of Pembroke Tavern.

ing. They interrupted these meetings in most offensive ways, and were promptly whipped. One poor Quakeress, Lydia Wardwell, "a young tender chaste person," but almost demented with religious excitement, was taken forcibly from the Ipswich meeting-house and "tyed to the fence-post of the Tavern," and then sorely lashed.

The pillory sometimes took the place of the stocks. In enduring this punishment the culprit stood on a sort of bench, and his head and hands were confined in holes cut in a hinged or divisible board. Lecture day was often chosen as the day of punishment; as Hawthorne said, "it was a day of public shame, the day on which transgressors received their reward of ignominy." Thus Nicholas Olmstead, sentenced to the pillory in Hartford "next Lecture day," was "sett on a lytle before the beginning and to stay on a lytle after the end." In Maryland offenders were "nayled by both eares to the Pillory, 3 Nailes in each Eare, and the Nailes to be slit out." Samuel Breck says that in 1771, in Boston, men and women were constantly seen pilloried, exposed to insults and jeers, and pelted with filth and garbage.

The 18th of September, 1755, was a great day in Cambridge, Massachusetts. A negro woman named Phyllis was then and there burned to death — in punishment for her share in the murder of her master. The diary of a Boston gentleman still exists which shows us how he passed the day; cheerfully drinking punch from tavern to tavern, and cheerfully watching the hanging of the man-murderer and the burning of the woman. The day's record ends: "Went home, went to bed and slept and woke up very finely refreshed." Criminals were preached at in public, read their dying confessions in public, were carted through the streets in open tumbrils, and were hanged in public. On all those occasions the taverns flowed with good cheer and merry meetings, for people came for many miles to witness the interesting sight, and many were the happy reunions of friends.

Another bustling busy day at the tavern was when "vandues" were held within its walls. Due notice of these "vandues" had been given by posters displayed in the tavern and village store, and occasionally by scant newspaper advertisements. These auction sales were rarely of mixed merchandise, but were of some special goods, such as India cotton stuffs, foreign books, or boots and shoes. Criminals and paupers were also sold for terms of service; usually the former were some of the varied tribe of sneak-thieves which wandered through the country. In one case the human "lot" offered for sale was a "prygman" — he had, like Autolycus, stolen the bleaching linen from the grass and hedges.

Another was an habitual fruit and vegetable thief (and he must have been an extraordinary one to have been noted in a country where fruit and vegetables on every farm were so freely shared with all passers-by). Another, an Indian, stole from the lobster and eel pots of his honest white neighbors. A sheep thief, sold at public auction in Clifford's Tavern in Dunbarton, New Hampshire, took part in an interesting prologue, as well as in the main performance, in the shape of a whipping of thirteen stripes administered to him by the vigorous sheriff. Nevertheless, he found a purchaser, who took his subdued and sore servant home to his farm and set

him to breaking and hatchelling flax.   The convict
fell to work as cheerfully and assiduously as any
honest laborer, but when he had cleaned as much
flax as he could carry, he added an unexpected
epilogue to this
New England
comedy by de-
parting with his
dressed flax for
parts unknown;
thus proving
that he laughs
best who laughs
last.   Though
it would seem
that the select-
men of the
town, who had
been amply paid
" damages and
costs " through
his sale, and
who had also
effectually ban-
ished a rogue
from their town-

Map Pitcher.

ship, might join with him in a mirthful chorus.

The sale of paupers at the tavern was much more
frequent than of criminals.   It was an exhibition
of curious contrasts : the prosperous and thirsty
townsmen drinking at the tavern bar, and the forlorn group of homeless, friendless creatures, usually

young children and aged folk, waiting to be sold to
the lowest bidder for a term of feeble service and
meagre keep. The children were known after the
sale as " bound boys " and " bound girls," and much
sympathy has been expended in modern books over
the hardness of their lives, and many pathetic
stories written of them. This method was, however, as good a solution of the problem of infant
pauperism as we have yet discovered. The children were removed from vicious associations in
almshouses, and isolated in homes where they had
to work just as the daughters and sons of the
household worked. In many cases they entered
childless homes, and grew to be the prop and happiness of their adopted parents, and the heirs of
their little savings. The auction at the tavern was
frankly brutal, but the end accomplished was so
satisfactory that the custom has within a few years
been resumed by the more advanced and thoughtful guardians of paupers in many New England
towns. As for the auction sale of aged and infirm
paupers, it is not wholly a thing of the past. In
Lackawanna township in Pike County, Pennsylvania, paupers still are sold to the lowest bidder.
A year ago, in 1899, at Rowland Station in that
township the signs were posted, " A Woman for
Sale," and as of old the " vandue " was held at a
tavern, one called Rutan's Hotel. The bar-room
was crowded, and Mrs. Elmira Quick, seventy-
seven years old, was put up " to be sold to the
lowest bidder for keep for a year." The bidding
was spirited and ran quickly down from four dol-

lars a week.   A backwoodsman had just offered t)
take her for a dollar and a half a week, when Mrs
Quick firmly bid a dollar and a quarter.   The
Overseer of the Poor hesitated, but Mrs. Quick
stated she could maintain herself on that amount —
sixteen cents a day — and no one made an offer to
take her for less ; so he was forced to conclude the
bargain and draw up the sale-papers.   Let me add
that this woman has three sons and a daughter living — and these are our good *new* times.

CHAPTER X

FROM PATH TO TURNPIKE

THE first roads in New England are called in the early court-records "trodden paths." They were narrow worn lines, scarce two feet wide, lightly trodden over pine needles and fallen leaves among the tree trunks by the soft moccasined foot of the tawny savages as they walked silently in Indian file through the forests. These paths were soon deepened and worn bare by the heavy hobnailed shoes of the white settlers, others were formed by the slow tread of domestic cattle, the best of all path makers, as they wound around the hillsides to pasture or drinking place. Then a scarcely broader bridle-path for horses, perhaps with blazed trees as guide-posts, widened slowly to travelled roads and uneven cart-ways. These roads followed and still wind to-day in the very lines of the foot-path and the cattle-track.

The early colonists walked as did their predecessors, the Indians, on their own stout legs, when they travelled by land. We find even the governors of the colonies walking off sturdily into the forests ; crossing the rivers and brooks on fallen trees ; and sometimes being carried across "pick-a-back" by

vigorous Indian guides.   We have one record of
Governor Winthrop in that dependent and rather
un-governor-like attitude, and it is well to think of
this picture of him as affording a glimpse of one of
the human sides of his life, to balance the prevail-
ing Chinese worship and idealization of him and our
other ancestors.

The earliest trail or path was the old Plymouth
or Coast Path, which connected the capitols of two
colonies, Boston and Plymouth.   It ran through
old Braintree, and its permanence was established by
an action of the General Court in 1639.   The Old
Connecticut Path started from Cambridge, ran
through Marlborough, Grafton, Oxford, and on to
Springfield and Albany.   The New Connecticut
Path or Road started also from Cambridge, thence
to Grafton, then to Worcester, Brookfield, and on
to Albany.   The Providence Path ran through
Narragansett and Providence Plantations.   The
Nipmuck Trail was made from Norwich.   The
" Kennebunk Road by the Sea" was ordered by
the Massachusetts Commissioners in 1653, sufficient highway " between towns and towns for horse
and foot."   Kittery and York were enjoined to
" make straight and convenient way along East for
Man and Horse."

The most famous of all these paths was the one
known as the Bay Path.   It was in existence in
1673, and doubtless before.   It left the Old Connecticut Path at Wayland, Massachusetts, and ran
through Marlborough to Worcester, then to Oxford,
Charlton, and Brookfield, where jutted off the Had-

ley Path, to Ware, Belchertown, and Hadley, while the Bay Path rejoined the Old Connecticut Path and thus on to Springfield. Holland wrote of the Bay Path in his novel of that title : —

"It was marked by trees a portion of the distance and by slight clearings of brush and thicket for the remainder. No stream was bridged, no hill was graded, and no marsh drained. The path led through woods which bore the mark of centuries, over barren hills which had been licked by the Indian hounds of fire, and along the banks of streams that the seine had never dragged. A powerful interest was attached to the Bay Path. It was the channel through which laws were communicated, through which flowed news from distant friends, and through which came long, loving letters and messages. That rough thread of soil, chipped by the blades of a hundred streams, was a trail that radiated at each terminus into a thousand fibres of love, and interest, and hope, and memory. Every rod had been prayed over by friends on the journey and friends at home."

Born in a home almost by the wayside of the old Bay Path, I feel deeply the inexplicable charm which attaches itself to these old paths or trails. I have ridden hundreds of miles on these various Indian paths, and I ever love to trace the roadway where it is now the broad, travelled road, and where it turns aside in an overgrown and narrow lane which is to-day almost as neglected and wild as the old path. There still seems to cling to it something of the human interest ever found in a foot-path, the intangible attraction which makes even the simplest foot-path across a pasture, or up a wooded hill, full of charm, of suggestion, of sentiment.

It is interesting to see how quickly the colonists acquired horses. Before John Winthrop died Massachusetts had a cavalry corps. Restrictive measures were enjoined by the magistrates to improve the breed and limit the number of horses. These horses were poor and scrubby and small, but before 1635 a cargo of Flemish draft horses was imported. A characteristic American breed, the Narragansett Pacers, was reared in Rhode Island. They were famous saddle-horses, giving ease of motion to the rider, being sure-footed and most tough and enduring. For a century they were raised in large numbers and sold at good prices, but became little valued after trotting-horses were bred and folk drove instead of riding horseback. I saw the last of the Narragansett Pacers. She died about twenty years ago; of an ugly sorrel color, with broad back and short legs and a curious rocking pace, she seemed almost a caricature of a horse, but was, nevertheless, a source of inordinate pride to her owner.

Women rode with as much ease and frequency as men. Young girls rode on side saddles for long journeys. Older women rode behind men on pillions, which were padded cushions which had a sort of platform stirrup. An excellent representation of a pillion is here given in Mr. Henry's charming picture, "Waiting at the Ferry," as well as of an old-time gig used at the end of the eighteenth and in the early part of the nineteenth century.

Horseflesh was so plentiful that "no one walked save a vagabond or a fool." Doubtless our national characteristic of never walking a step when we can

Waiting for the Ferry.

ride dates from the days "when we lived under the King." Driving alone, that is, a man or woman driving for pleasure alone, without a driver or post-boy, is an American fashion. It was carried back to Europe by both the French and English officers who were here in Revolutionary times. The custom was noted with approval by the French in their various books and letters on this country. They also, La Rochefoucauld among them, praised our roads.

Mr. Ernst, an authority upon transportation and postal matters, believes that our roads in the northern provinces, on the whole, were excellent. He says that the actual cost of the roads as contained in Massachusetts records proves that the notion that our New England roads were wretched is not founded on fact. He notes our great use of pleasure carriages as a proof of good roads; in 1753 Massachusetts had about seven such carriages to every thousand persons. The English carriages were very heavy. In America we adopted the light-weight continental carriages — because our roads were good.

The corduroy road was one of the common road improvements made to render the roads passable by carts and stage-wagons. Marshy places and chuck-holes were filled up with saplings and logs from the crowded forests, and whole roads were made of logs which were cut in lengths about ten or twelve feet long, and laid close to each other across the road. Many corduroy roads still remain, and some are veritable antiques; in Canada they still are built. A few years ago I rode many miles over one in a miner's springless cart over the mountains of the Alexandrite range in upper Canada, and I deem it the most trying ordeal I ever experienced.

As soon as there were roads, there were ferries and bridges. Out from Boston to the main were ferries in 1639 to Chelsea and Charlestown. There was a " cart-bridge " built by Boston and Roxbury over Muddy River in 1633. There was a "foot-bridge " also at Scituate, and at Ipswich in 1635. In 1634 a " horse-bridge " was built at Neponset, and others soon followed. These had a railing on one side only. It was a great step when the " Bay " granted fifty pounds to Lynn for a cart-bridge where there had been only a ferry. After King Philip's War, cart-bridges multiplied; there was one in Scituate, one in Bristol, one in Cambridge.

These early bridges of provincial days were but insecure makeshifts in many cases, miserable floating bridges being common across the wide rivers. In England bridges were poor also. We were to be early in fine bridge-building, and to excel in it as we have to this day. We were also in advance of the mother country in laying macadamized roads, in the use of mail-coaches, in modes of steam travel by water, just as we were in using flintlock firearms, and other advanced means of warfare.

The Charles River between Boston and Charlestown was about as wide at the point where the old ferry crossed as was the Thames at London Bridge, and Americans were emulative of that structure. Much talking and planning was done, but no bridge was built across the Charles till after the Revolution. Then Lemuel Cox, a Medford shipwright, planned and built a successful bridge in 1786. It was the longest bridge in the world, and deemed a triumph of engineering. The following year he built the Malden Bridge, then the fine Essex Bridge at Salem. In 1770 Cox went to Ireland and built a bridge nine hundred feet long over the deep Foyle at Londonderry, Ireland. This was another American victory, for the great English engineer, Milne, had pronounced the deed impossible. This bridge was of American oak and pine, and was built by Maine lumbermen and carpenters.

According to the universal " Gust of the Age" — as Dr. Prince said — the aid of the Muses was called in to celebrate the opening of the Charlestown Bridge. This took place on the anniversary of the battle of Bunker Hill, and a vast feast was given. Broadsides were distributed bearing "poems" as long as the bridge. Here are a few specimen verses : —

> " I sing the day in which the BRIDGE
>   Is finished and done.
>   Boston and Charlestown lads rejoice
>   And fire your cannon guns.

> " The BRIDGE is finished now I say
>   Each other bridge outvies
>   For London Bridge compared with ours
>   Appears in dim disguise.

> " Now Boston Charlestown nobly join
>   And roast a fatted Ox
>   On noted Bunker Hill combine
>   To toast our Patriot Cox.

"May North and South and Charlestown all
    Agree with one consent
To love each one like Indian's rum
    On publick good be bent."

A perfect epidemic of bridge-building broke out all over the states. In our pride we wished to exhibit our superiority over the English everywhere. Throughout Maryland, Pennsylvania, and upper Virginia, fine wooden and stone bridges were built. On all the turnpikes the bridges equalled the roads. Many of those bridges still are in use. The oldest suspension bridge in America, the "chain-bridge" at Newburyport, Massachusetts, is still standing. A picture of it here is shown. It is a graceful bridge, and its lovely surroundings add to its charm.

The traveller Melish noted specially, in 1812, the fine Trenton Bridge, "very elegant, nine hundred and seventy feet long, with two carriage ways"; the West Boston Bridge "three thousand feet long, with a causeway three thousand more"; the Schuylkill Bridge, which cost over two hundred thousand dollars.

So bad was the state of English roads at the end of the eighteenth century that it took two days' and three nights' incessant travel to get from Manchester to Glasgow. The crossroads were worse. In many cases when mail-coaches had been granted, the roads were too poor to receive them. The ruts, or rather trenches, were up to the axletrees. When a mail-coach was put on the Holyhead Road in 1808, twenty-two townships were indicted for having their roads in a dangerous condition. This

Old Chain-bridge, Newburyport, Massachusetts.

road had vast sums spent upon it; in the six years succeeding 1825 it had £83,700 for "improvements," and repairs were paid by the tolls. Its condition now is very mean, grass-grown in places, and in ill-repair.

The system of road-making known as macadamizing received its name from Mr. Loudon McAdam, who came to England from America in 1783 at a time when many new roads were being made in Scotland. These roads he studied and in 1816 became road surveyor in Bristol, where he was able to carry his principles into practice. The leading feature of his system was setting a limit in size and weight to the stones to be used on the roads, the weight limit being six ounces; also to prohibit any mixture of clay, earth, or chalk with the stone. Similar roads had been made in Pennsylvania long before they were laid in England, and had been tested; and without doubt McAdam simply followed methods he had seen successfully used in America. Among others the Salem and Boston Turnpike, the Essex Turnpike (between Salem and Andover), and the Newburyport Turnpike, all macadamized roads, were in successful operation before Telford and McAdam had perfected their systems.

McAdam's son, Sir James McAdam, was General Superintendent of Metropolitan Roads in England when, as he expressed it, "the calamity of railways fell upon us." This "calamity" brought these results: coaches ran less frequently, and all horse-carriage decreased, toll receipts diminished.

many turnpike roads became bankrupt and passed into possession of towns and parishes, and are kept in scarcely passable repair.   Many English macadamized roads are only kept in order in half, while the other part of the road bears weeds and grass.

The first American turnpike was not in Pennsylvania, as is usually stated, but in Virginia.   It connected Alexandria (then supposed to be the rising metropolis) with "Sniggers and Vesta's Gaps" — that is, the lower Shenandoah.   This turnpike was started in 1785–86, and Thomas Jefferson pronounced it a success.   In 1787 the Grand Jury of Baltimore reported the state of the country roads as a public grievance, and the Frederick, Reisterstown, and York roads were laid out anew by the county as turnpikes with toll-gates.   In 1804 these roads were granted to corporate companies.   Others soon followed, till all the main roads through Maryland were turnpikes.

The most important early turnpike was the one known as the National Road because it was made by the national government.   It extended at first from Cumberland to Wheeling, and was afterward carried farther.   When first opened it was a hundred and thirty miles long, and cost one and three-quarters millions of dollars.   Proposed in Congress in 1797, an act providing for its construction was passed nine years later, and the first mail-coach carrying the United States mail travelled over it in August, 1818.   It was a splendid road, sixty feet wide, of stone broken to pass through a three-inch ring, then covered with gravel and rolled down with an iron roller. One who saw the constructive work on it wrote : —

" That great contractor, Mordecai Cochran, with his immortal Irish brigade — a thousand strong, with their carts, wheelbarrows, picks, shovels, and blasting-tools, graded the commons and climbed the mountain side, leaving behind them a roadway good enough for an emperor."

Over this National Road journeyed many congressmen to and from Washington ; and the mail contractors, anxious to make a good impression on these senators and representatives, and thus gain fresh privileges and large appropriations, ever kept up a splendid stage line. It was on this line that the phrase "chalking his hat" — or the free pass system—originated. Mr. Reeside, the agent of the road, occasionally ten-

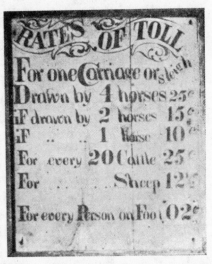

Bridge Toll-board.

dered a free ride to some member of Congress, and devised a hieroglyphic which he marked in chalk on the representative's hat, in order that none of his drivers should be imposed upon by forged passes.

The intent was to extend this road to St. Louis.

From Cumberland to Baltimore the cost of con-struction fell on certain banks in Maryland, which were rechartered on condition that they completed the road.   Instead of being a burden to them, it became a lucrative property, yielding twenty per cent profit for many years.   Not only was this road excellently macadamized, but stone bridges were built for it over rivers and creeks; the dis-tances were indexed by iron mileposts, and the toll-houses were supplied with strong iron gates.

On other turnpikes throughout the country Irish laborers were employed to dig the earth and break the stone.   Until this time Irish immigration had been slight in this country, and in many small com-munities where the new turnpikes passed the first Irish immigrants were stared at as curiosities.

The story of the old Mohawk Turnpike is one of deep interest.   After the Revolution a great movement of removal to the West swept through New England; in the winter of 1795, in three days twelve hundred sleighs passed through Albany bear-ing sturdy New England people as settlers to the Genesee Valley.   Others came on horseback, pros-pecting, — farmers with well-filled saddle bags and pocketbooks.   Among those thrifty New Eng-landers were two young men named Whetmore and Norton, from Litchfield, Connecticut, who noted the bad roads over which all this travel passed; and being surveyors, they planned and eventually carried out a turnpike.   The first charter, granted in 1797, was for the sixteen miles between Albany and Schenectady.   When that was finished, in 1800, the turnpike from Schenectady to Utica, sixty-eight miles long, was begun.   The public readily subscribed to build these roads; the flow of settlers increased; the price of land advanced; everywhere activity prevailed. The turnpike was filled with great trading wagons; there was a tavern at every mile on the road; fifty-two within fifty miles of Albany, but there were not taverns enough to meet the demand caused by the great travel. Eighty or one hundred horses would some-

Megunticook Turnpike.

times be stabled at a single tavern.   All teamsters desired stable-room for their horses; but so crowded were the tavern sheds that many carried sheets of oilcloth to spread over their horses at night in case they could not find shelter.

Common wagons with narrow tires cut grooves in the macadamized road; so the Turnpike Company passed free all wagons with tires six inches broad or wider.

These helped to roll down the road, and by law were not required to turn aside on the road save for wagons with like width of tire.

The New York turnpikes were traversed by a steady procession of these great wagons, marked often in great lettering with the magic words which were in those days equivalent to Eldorado or Golconda — namely, "Ohio,"

PARKER's
Mail Stage,
From Whiteſtown to Canajoharrie.

THE Mail leaves Whiteſtown every Monday and Thurſday, at two o'clock P.M. and proceeds to Old Fort Schuyler the ſame evening; next morning ſtarts at four o'clock, and arrives at Canajoharrie in the evening; exchanges paſſengers with the Albany and Cooperſtown ſtages, and the next day returns to Old Fort Schuyler.

Fare for paſſengers, Two Dollars; way paſſengers, Four Pence per mile; 14lb. baggage gratis; 150wt. rated the ſame as a paſſenger.

Seats may be had by applying at the Poſt-Office, Whiteſtown, at the houſe of the ſubſcriber, Old Fort Schuyler, or at Captain Roof's, Canajoharrie.

JASON PARKER.

Auguſt, 1795.   8ª

or "Genesee Valley." Freight rates from Albany to Utica were a dollar for a hundred and twelve pounds.

In 1793 the old horse-path from Albany over the mountains to the Connecticut River was made wide enough for the passage of a coach. Westward from Albany a coach ran to Whitestone, Oneida County. In 1783 the first regular mail was delivered at Schenectady, nearly a century after its settlement. Soon the "mail-stages" ran as far as Whitestone. An advertisement of one of these clumsy old mail-stages is here shown. We need not wonder at the misspelling in this advertisement of the name of the town, for in 1792 the Postmaster-general advertised for contracts to carry the mail from "Connojorharrie to Kanandarqua."

There were twelve gates on the "pike" between Utica and Schenectady ; at Schenectady, Crane's Village, Caughnawaga (now Fonda), Schenck's Hollow, east of Wagner's Hollow road, Garoga Creek, St. Johnsville, East Creek Bridge, Fink's Ferry, Herkimer, Sterling, Utica. These gates did not swing on hinges, but were portcullises ; a custom in other countries referred to in the beautiful passage in the Psalms, " Lift up your heads, O ye gates," etc.

On every toll-gate was a board with the rates of toll painted thereon. Mr. Rufus A. Grider gives the list of rates on the Schenectady and Utica Turnpike, a distance of sixty-eight miles. They seem to me exceedingly high.

	Cents
"Sheep, per score	8
Hogs, per score	8
Cattle, per score	18
Horses, per score	18

	Cents
Mules, per score	18
Horse and Rider	5
Tied horses, each	5
Sulkies	12½
Chairs	12½
Chariots	25
Coaches	25
Coachers	25
Phaetons	25
Two horse Stages	12½
Four horse Stages	18½
One horse Wagons	9
Two horse Wagons	12½
Three horse Wagons . . .	15½
Four horse Wagons tires under six inches .	75
Five horse Wagons " " " " .	87½
Six horse Wagons " " " " .	1.00
One horse cart	6
Two ox cart	6
Three ox cart	8
Four ox cart	10
Six ox cart	14
One horse sleigh	6
Two horse or ox sleigh	6
Three horse or ox sleigh	8
Four horse or ox sleigh	10
Five horse or ox sleigh	12
Six horse or ox sleigh	14 "

The toll-board which hung for many years on a bridge over the Susquehanna River at Sidney, New York, is shown on page 233.

Sometimes sign-boards were hung on bridges. One is shown on page 239 which hung for many

years on the wooden bridge at Washington's Crossing at Taylorsville, Pennsylvania, on the Bucks
County side. It was painted by Benjamin Hicks,
of Newtown, a copy of Trumbull's picture of Wash-

Bridge Sign-board.

ington crossing the Delaware. It was thrown in the
garret of a store at Taylorsville, and rescued by Mr.
Mercer for the Bucks County Historical Society.

The turnpike charters and toll-rates have revealed
one thing to us, that all single-horse carriages were

two-wheeled, such as the sulky, chair, chaise ; while
four-wheeled carriages always had at least two
horses.

Citizens and travellers deeply resented these tolls,
and ofttimes rose up against the payment. A toll-
keeper in Pelham, Massachusetts, awoke one morning to find his gate gone. A scrawled bit of paper
read : —

> " The man who stopped the boy when going to the mill,
> Will find his gate at the bottom of the hill."

CHAPTER XI

OUR predecessors, the North American Indians, had no horses. An early explorer of
Virginia said that if the country had horses
and kine and were peopled with English, no realm
in Christendom could be compared with it. The
crude means of overland transportation common to
all savages, the carrying of burdens on the back by
various strappings, was the only mode known.

Travel by land in the colonies was for many
years very limited in amount, and equally hazard-
ous and inconvenient. Travel by boat was so greatly
preferred that most of the settlements continued to
be made on the banks of rivers and along the sea-
coast. Even perilous canoes were preferable to the
miseries of land travel.

We were slow in abandoning our water travel and
water transportation. Water lines controlled in the
East till 1800, in the West till 1860, and have now
great revival.

Transportation was wholly done by water. When
horses multiplied, merchandise was drawn short distances in the winter time on crude sledges. Packhorses were in common use in England and on the

Continent, and the scrubby, enduring horses raised
here soon were used as packhorses. Their use
lingered long over the Alleghany Mountains, as it
did on the mountains of the Pacific coast ; in fact
the advance guard of inland commerce in America
has always employed packhorses.

The first appearance of the Conestoga wagon in
history (though the wagons were not then called by
that name) was in 1755, when General Braddock
set out on his ill-fated expedition to western Pennsylvania. There led thither no wagon-road, simply
an Indian trail for packhorses. Braddock insisted
strenuously to the Pennsylvania Assembly upon
obtaining their assistance in widening the trail to a
wagon-road, and also to secure one hundred and
fifty wagons for the army. The cutting of the road
was done, but when returns were made to Braddock at Frederick, Maryland, only twenty-five wagons could be obtained. Franklin said it was a pity
the troops had not been landed in Philadelphia,
since every farmer in the country thereabouts had a
wagon. At Braddock's earnest solicitation, Franklin
issued an ingenious and characteristic advertisement
for one hundred and fifty four-horse wagons, and
fifteen hundred saddle- or packhorses, for the use
of this army. The value of transportation facilities
at the time is proved by Franklin's terms of payment, namely : fifteen shillings a day for each
wagon with four horses and driver, and two shillings a day for horse with saddle or pack. Franklin
agreed that the owners should be fairly compensated
for the loss of these wagons and horses if they were

A Wayside Friend.

not returned, and was eventually nearly ruined by this stipulation.   For the battle at Braddock's Field was disastrous to the English, and the claims of the farmers against Franklin amounted to twenty thousand pounds.   Upon his appeal these claims were paid by the Government under order of General Shirley.   Franklin gathered these wagons and horses in York and Lancaster counties, Pennsylvania, and I doubt if York and Lancaster, England, would have been as good fields at that date.

Braddock's trail became the famous route for crossing the Alleghany Mountains for the principal pioneers who settled southwestern Pennsylvania and western Virginia, and all their effects were carried to their new homes on packhorses.   The only wealth acquired in the wilds by these pioneers was peltry and furs, and each autumn a caravan of packhorses was sent over the mountains bearing the accumulated spoils of the neighborhood, under the charge of a master driver and three or four assistants.   The horses were fitted with pack-saddles, to the hinder part of which was fastened a pair of hobbles made of hickory withes ; and a collar with a bell was on each horse's neck.   The horses' feed of shelled corn was carried in bags destined to be filled with alum salt for the return trip ; and on the journey down, part of this feed was deposited for the use of the return caravan.   Large wallets filled with bread, jerked bear's meat, ham, and cheese furnished food for the drivers.   At night the horses were hobbled and turned out into the woods or pasture, and the bells which had been muffled in the daytime were unfastened, to serve as a guide to the drivers in the morning. The furs were carried to and exchanged first at Baltimore as a market; later the carriers went only to Frederick; then to Hagerstown, Oldtown, and finally to Fort Cumberland. Iron and steel in various forms, and salt, were the things most eagerly desired by the settlers. Each horse could carry two bushels of alum salt, each bushel weighing eighty-four pounds. Not a heavy load, but the horses were scantily fed. Sometimes an iron pot or kettle was tied on either side on top of the salt-bag.

Ginseng, bears' grease, and snakeroot were at a later date collected and added to the furs and hides. The horses marched in single file on a road scarce two feet wide; the foremost horse was led by the master of the caravan, and each successive horse was tethered to the pack-saddle of the one in front. Other men or boys watched the packs and urged on laggard horses.

I do not know the exact mode of lading these packhorses. An English gentlewoman named Celia Fiennes rode on horseback on a side-saddle over many portions of England in the year 1695. She thus describes the packhorses she saw in Devon and Cornwall : —

"Thus harvest is bringing in, on horse backe, with sort of crookes of wood like yokes on either side; two or three on a side stands up in which they stow ye corne, and so tie it with cords; but they cannot so equally poise it but ye going of ye horse is like to cast it down sometimes on ye one side sometimes on ye other, for they load them from ye neck to ye taile, and pretty high, and are forced to support it with their hands so to a horse they have two people women as well as men."

At a later date this packhorse system became that of common carriers. Five hundred horses at a time, after the Revolution, could be seen winding over the mountains. At Lancaster, Harrisburg, Shippensburg, Bedford, Fort Pitt, and other towns were regular packhorse companies. One public carrier at Harris Ferry in 1772 had over two hundred horses and mules. When the road was widened and wagons were introduced, the packhorse drivers considered it an invasion of their rights and fiercely opposed it.

It is interesting to note that the trail of the Indians and the horse-track of these men skilled only in woodcraft were the ones followed in later years by trained engineers in laying out the turnpikes and railroads.

We are prone to pride ourselves in America on many things which we had no part in producing, on some which are in no way distinctive, and on a few which are not in the highest sense to our credit. Of the Conestoga wagon as a perfect vehicle of transportation and as an important historical factor we can honorably and rightfully be proud. It was a truly American product evolved and multiplied to fit, perfectly, existing conditions. Its day of usefulness is past, few ancient specimens exist; and little remains to remind us of it; the derivative word stogey, meaning hard, enduring, tough, is a legacy. Stogeys — shoes — are tough, coarse, leather footwear; and the stogey cigar was a great, heavy, coarse cigar, originally, it is said, a foot long, made to fit the enduring nerves and appetite of the Conestoga teamsters.

This splendid wagon was developed in Pennsylvania by topographical conditions, by the soft soil, by trade requirements, and by native wit. It was the highest type of a commodious freight-carrier by horse power that this or any country has ever known; it was called the Conestoga wagon from the vicinity in which they were first in common use.

These wagons had a boat-shaped body with curved canoe-shaped bottom which fitted them specially for mountain use; for in them freight remained firmly in place at whatever angle the body might be. This wagon body was painted blue or slate-color and had bright vermilion red sideboards. The rear end could be lifted from its sockets; on it hung the feed-trough for the horses. On one side of the body was a small tool-chest with a slanting lid. This held hammer, wrench, hatchet, pincers, and other simple tools. Under the rear axletree were suspended a tar-bucket and water-pail.

In the interesting and extensive museum of old-time articles of domestic use gathered intelligently by the Historical Society of Bucks County, Pennsylvania, are preserved some of the wagon grease-pots or *Tar-lodel*, which formed part of the furniture of the Conestoga wagon. A tree section about a foot long and six inches in diameter was bored and scraped out to make a pot. The outer upper rim was circumscribed with a groove, and fitted with

Conestoga Wagon.

leather thongs, by which it was hung to the axle of the wagon.   Filled with grease and tar it was ever ready for use.   Often a leather *Tar-lodel* took the place of this wooden grease-pot.   The wheels had broad tires, sometimes nearly a foot broad.   The wagon bodies were arched over with six or eight bows, of which the middle ones were the lowest.   These were covered with a strong, pure-white hempen cover corded down strongly at the sides and ends.   These wagons could be loaded up to the top of the bows and carried four to six tons each, — about a ton's weight to each horse.

Sleek, powerful horses of the Conestoga breed were used by prosperous teamsters.   These horses, usually from four to seven in number, were often carefully matched, all dapple-gray or all bay.   From Baltimore ran wagons with twelve horses.   They were so intelligent, so well cared for, so perfectly broken, that they seemed to take pleasure in their work.   The heavy, broad harnesses were costly, of the best leather, trimmed with brass plates ; often each horse had a housing of deerskin or bearskin edged with scarlet fringe, while the headstall was gay with ribbons and ivory rings, and colored worsted rosettes.

Bell-teams were common ; an iron or brass arch was fastened upon the hames, and collar and bells were suspended from it.   Each horse save the saddle-horse had a full set of musical bells tied with gay ribbons ; among these were the curious old ear-bells.   In England these ear-bells dangled two on each side on a strap which passed over the horse's head behind the ears and buckled into the cheeks of the headstall. On the forehead stood up from this strap a stiff tuft or brush (a Russian cockade) of colored horsehair fixed in a brass socket. Even the reins were of high colors, scarlet and orange and green. The driver walking alongside, or seated astride the saddle-horse, governed the perfectly broken and intelligent creatures with a precision and ease that was beautiful to see. A curious adjustable seat called a lazy-board was sometimes hung at the side of the wagon, and afforded a precarious resting place.

These teamsters carried a whip, long and light, which, like everything used by them, was of the finest and best materials. It had a fine squirrel-skin or silk "cracker." This whip was carried under the arm, and the Conestoga horses were guided more by the crack than by the blow.

All chronicles agree that a fully equipped Conestoga wagon in the days when those wagons were in their prime was a truly pleasing sight, giving one that sense of satisfaction which ever comes from the regard of any object, especially a piece of mechanism, which is perfectly fitted for the object it is designed to attain. An American poet writes of them : —

> " The old road blossoms with romance
> Of covered vehicles of every grade
> From ox-cart of most primitive design
> To Conestoga wagons with their fine
> Deep-dusted, six-horse teams in heavy gear,
> High hames and chiming bells — to childish ear
> And eye entrancing as the glittering train
> Of some sun-smitten pageant of old Spain."

The number of these wagons was vast. At one time over three thousand ran constantly back and forward between Philadelphia and other Pennsylvania towns. Sometimes a hundred would follow in close row ; " the leaders of one wagon with their noses in the trough of the wagon ahead." These " Regulars " with fully equipped Conestoga wagons made freighting their constant and only business. Farmers and teamsters who made occasional trips, chiefly during the farmers' dull season — the winter — were called " Militia."

A local poet wrote of them : —

> " Militia-men drove narrow treads,
> Four horses and plain red Dutch beds,
> And always carried grub and feed."

" Grub," food for the driver, and feed for the horses was seldom carried by the Regulars ; but the horses when unharnessed always fed from the long troughs which were hitched to the wagon pole.

All these teamsters carried their own blankets, and many carried also a narrow mattress about two feet wide which they slept upon. This was strapped in a roll in the morning and put into the wagon. Often the teamsters slept on the barroom floor around the fireplace, feet to the fire. Some taverns had bunks with wooden covers around the sides of the room. The teamster spread his lunch on the top or cover of his bunk ; when he had finished he could lift the lid, and he had a coffinlike box to sleep in — but this was an unusual luxury. McGowan's Tavern was a favorite stopping place.

The barroom had a double chimney and fire-
places; fifteen feet of blazing hearth meant comfort, and allured all teamsters. The blood of
battle stained the walls and ceiling, which the landlord never removed to show that he "meant business."

The Conestoga wagons were in constant use in
times of war as well as in peace. They were not
only furnished to Braddock's army, as has been
told, but to the Continental army in the War of
the Revolution. President Reed of Pennsylvania
wrote to General Washington in 1780 that "the
army had been chiefly supplied with horses and
waggons from this state (Pennsylvania) during the
war," and it was also declared that half the supplies
furnished the army came from the same state.
Reed deplored the fact that a further demand for
over one thousand teams was to be made on them,
and said the state could not stand it.

During the War of 1812 these wagons transported arms, ammunition, and supplies to the army
on the frontier. Long lines of these teams could
be seen carrying solace and reënforcements to the
soldiers.

In England a huge, clumsy wagon was used for
common carrier and passenger transportation, until
our own day. It was inferior to the Conestoga
wagon in detail and equipments. Illustrations from
an old print in a child's story-book are given of these
wagons on page 251. Their most marked characteristic was the width of wheel tire. From the middle
colonies the Conestoga wagon found its way to every

The Stage Waggon.

WHILE the old waggoner is stopping to drink, poor Jack the soldier is bidding his wife good bye.—She has come a long way with her children to see him once more : and now is going home again in the waggon. She does not know whether she shall ever see him again.—Jack was obliged to leave his country life, and his good master, and his plough and his comfortable cottage, and his poor wife and little ones to go and be a soldier, and learn to fight, because *other people* would quarrel.

colony and every settlement; nor did its life end in
the Eastern states or with the establishment of railroads.   Renamed the "prairie schooner," it carried
civilization and emigration across the continent to the
Golden Gate.   Till our own day the white tilts could
be seen slowly travelling westward.   The bleaching
bones of these wagons may be still seen in our far
West, and are as distinct relics of that old pioneer
Western life as are the bones of the buffalo.   A few
wagons still remain in Pennsylvania, in Lancaster
County; the one painted by Hovenden in "Westward Ho" is in the collection of the Bucks County
Historical Society.   One toiled slowly and painfully,
in the year 1899, up the green hillsides of Vermont,
bearing two or three old people and a few shattered
household gods — the relics, human and material,
of a family that had "gone West" many years ago.

CHAPTER XII

THE story of the stage-coach begins at a much later date than that of the tavern; but the two allies reached the height of their glory together. No more prosperous calling ever existed than that of landlord of an old-time stage-tavern; no greater symbol of good cheer could be afforded. Though a popular historical novel by one of our popular writers shows us the heroine in a year of the seventeenth century conveyed away from her New England home in a well-equipped stage-coach, there were no stage-coaches at that date in New England, nor were they overfrequent in Old England.

Stow says, in his *Survey of London* (1633): " Of old time, Coaches were not known in this Island but Chariots or Whirlicotes." The whirlicote is described as a cot or bed on wheels, a sort of wheeled litter, and was used as early as the time of Richard II. The first coach made in England by Walter Rippen was for the Earl of Rutland, in 1555. The queen had one the next year, and Queen Elizabeth a state coach eight years later from the same maker. That splendid association

— "The Company of Coach and Harness Makers," was founded by Charles II. in May, 1667.

Venomous diatribes were set in print against coaches, as is usual with all innovations, useful and otherwise. Of them the assertions of Taylor the "Water Poet" are good examples. He said that

English Coach, 1747.

coaches dammed the streets, and aided purse-cutting; that butchers could not pass with their cattle; that market-folk were hindered in bringing victuals to town; that carts and carriers were stopped; that milkmaids were flung in the dirt; that people were "crowded and shrowded up against stalls and stoops" — still coaches continued to be built.

The early English stage-coaches were clumsy machines. One of the year 1747 is shown on the opposite page. With no windows, no seats or railing on top, and an uncomfortable basket rumble behind, they seem crude and inconvenient enough when compared with the dashing mail-coaches which were evolved a century later, and were such a favorite subject with English painters, engravers, and lithographers for many years. Those pictures expressed, as Dickens said, "past coachfulness: pictures of colored prints of coaches starting, arriving, changing horses, coaches in the sunshine, coaches in the snow, coaches in the wind, coaches in the mist and rain, coaches in all circumstances compatible with their triumph and victory, but never in the act of breaking down or overturning."

A copy of one of those prints of an English mail-coach, in the height of its career, is shown opposite page 256.

Stage-wagons were used throughout England as a means of cheaper conveyance. They were intolerably slow and equally clumsy. On page 251 a leaf from an old-time English story-book shows two of these lumbering vehicles, which ill compare with the English mail-coaches.

Coaching days in England have had ample and entertaining record in instructive and reminiscent books, such as: *Brighton and its Coaches*, by William C. A. Blew, 1894; *The Brighton Road, etc.*, by Charles G. Harper, 1892; *Old Coaching Days*, by Stanley Harris, 1882; *Annals of the Road*, by Captain Malet, 1876; *Down the Road, etc.*, by C. T. S.

Birch Reynardson, 1875; *Coaching Days and Coaching Ways*, by W. Outram Tristam, 1888.

We have no similar anecdotic and personal records of American coaching life, though we have the two fine books of modern coaching ways entitled *Driving for Pleasure*, by Francis T. Underhill, and *A Manual of Coaching*, by Fairman Rogers, both most interesting and valuable.

We began early in our history to have coaches. Even Governor Bradstreet in his day rode in a hackney coach. John Winthrop, of Connecticut, had a private coach in 1685; Sir Edmund Andros had one in Boston in 1687. At the funeral of the lieutenant-governor in 1732 in Boston there were plenty of coaches, though there were few in New York; the provincial governors usually had one. Watson, in his *Annals of Philadelphia*, gives a list of all private citizens who kept carriages in that city in 1761 — there were but thirty-eight. There were three coaches, two landaus, eighteen chariots, and fifteen chairs. Eleven years later only eighty-four Philadelphians had private carriages. In 1794, when the city had a population of about fifty thousand, eight hundred and forty-seven carriage-owners appear: among them were found thirty-three coaches and one hundred and fifty-seven coachees.

The testimony of the traveller Bennet, who was in Boston in 1740, is most explicit on the subject of travel and transportation in that city and vicinity : —

"There are several families in Boston that keep a coach and a pair of horses, and some few drive with four horses;

Quicksilver Royal Mail, 1835.

but for chaises and saddle-horses, considering the bulk of the place, they outdo London. They have some nimble, lively horses for the coach, but not any of that beautiful black breed so common in London. Their saddle-horses all pace naturally, and are generally counted sure-footed; but they are not kept in that fine order as in England. The common draught-horses used in carts about the town are very small and poor, and seldom have their fill of anything but labor. The country carts and wagons are generally drawn by oxen, from two to six according to the distance, or the burden they are laden with."

The traveller Weld thus described the peculiarly American carriage called a " coachee " : —

" The body of it is rather longer than a coach, but of the same shape. In the front it is left quite open down to the bottom, and the driver sits on a bench under the roof of the carriage. There are two seats in it for passengers, who sit in it with their faces to the horses. The roof is supported by small props which are placed at the corners. On each side of the door, above the panels, it is quite open ; and, to guard against bad weather, there are curtains which let down from the roof and fasten to buttons on the outside. The light wagons are in the same construction, and are calculated to hold from four to twelve people. The wagon has no doors, but the passengers scramble in the best way they can over the seat of the driver. The wagons are used universally for stage-coaches."

A vehicle often mentioned by Judge Sewall and contemporary writers is a calash. It was a clumsy thing, an open seat set on a low and heavy pair of wheels. A curricle had two horses, a chaise one ; both had what were called whip springs behind and

elbow springs in front.   A whisky was a light body
fixed in shafts which were connected with long hori-
zontal springs by scroll irons.   A French traveller
tells of riding around Boston in a whisky.   The
chair so often named in letters, wills, etc., was not a
sedan-chair, but was much like a chaise without a top.

The French chaise was introduced here by the
Huguenots before the year 1700.   The Yankee
"shay" is simply the fancied singular number of
the French chaise.   We improved upon the French
vehicle, and finally replaced it by our characteristic
carriage, the buggy.

Chariots were a distinctly aristocratic vehicle,
used as in England by persons of wealth, and
deemed a great luxury.   One was advertised in
Boston in 1743 as "a very handsome chariot, fit
for town or country, lined with red coffy, handsomely carved and painted, with a whole front
glass, the seat-cloth embroided with silver, and a
silk fringe round the seat."   It was offered for sale
by John Lucas, a Boston coach-builder, and had
doubtless been built by him.

The ancient chariot shown on page 259, formerly
belonging to John Brown, the founder of Brown
University, is preserved at the old Occupasnetuxet
homestead in Warwick, Rhode Island, securely
stored in one of the carriage houses on the estate, a
highly prized relic of days long ago.   In this ancient
vehicle General Washington rode from place to
place when he made his visit to Rhode Island in
August, 1790, escorted by John Brown, the ances-
tor of its present owners.

"One Hoss Shay."

The body of this old chariot is suspended on heavy thorough-braces attached to heavy iron holders as large as a man's wrist, the forward ones so curved as to allow the forward wheels to pass under them, in order that the chariot may be turned within a short compass. It has but one seat for passengers, which will accommodate two persons ; and an elevated seat for the driver, which is separate from the main body. The wheels are heavy, the hind ones twice the height of the forward ones, the tires of which are attached to the felloes in several distinct pieces.

Washington Chariot.

It is easy to picture the importance attached to buying or owning a wheeled vehicle in a community which rode chiefly on horseback. Contemporary evidence of this is often found, such as these entries in the diary of Rev. Joseph Emerson of Malden. In the winter of 1735 he writes : —

"Some talk about my buying a Shay. How much reason have I to watch and pray and strive against inordinate Affection for the Things of the World."

A week later, however, he proudly recalls the buying of the "Shay" for £27 10s., which must have made a decided hole in his year's salary. His delight in his purchase and possession is somewhat marred by noting that his parishioners smile as he is drawn past them in his magnificence; it is also decidedly taken down by the vehicle being violently overturned, though his wife and he were uninjured. It cost a pretty penny, moreover, to get it repaired. He scarce gets the beloved but sighed-over "Shay" home when he thus notes: —

"Went to the beach with 3 of the Children in my Shay. The beast being frighted when we all were out of the shay, overturned and broke it. I desire — I hope I desire it — that the Lord would teach me suitably to repent this Providence, to make suitable remarks on it, and to be suitably affected with it. Have I done well to get me a Shay? Have I not been too fond & too proud of this convenience? Should I not be more in my study and less fond of driving? Do I not withold more than is meet from charity? &c."

Shortly afterward, as the "beast" continued to be "frighted," he sold his horse and shay to a fellow-preacher, Rev. Mr. Smith, who — I doubt not — went through the same elations, depressions, frightings, and self-scourgings in which the Puritan spirit and horseman's pride so strongly clashed.

On May 13, 1718, Jonathan Wardwell's stage-coach left Jonathan Wardwell's Orange Tree in Boston and ran to Rhode Island — that is, the island proper. At any rate, it was advertised in Boston newspapers as starting at that date. In 1721 there was a road-wagon over the same route. In 1737 two imported stage-coaches were advertised for this road, and doubtless many travellers used these coaches, which connected with the boats for New York.

The early coaching conveyances were variously named. In 1767 it was a "stage-chaise" that ran between Salem and Boston, while a "stage-coach" and "stage-wagon" were on other short routes out of Boston. In 1772 a "stage-chariot" was on the road between Boston and Marblehead. "Flying Mail-Stages" came later, and in 1773 Thomas Beals ran "Mail Stage Carriages between Boston and Providence.' In England there were "Flying-Machines" and "Flying-Waggons." An old English road-bill dated

Philadelphia, Albany, and Vermont
LINES OF STAGES.

FEDERAL LINE, for PHILADELPHIA, will leave New York every day at eight o'clock in the morning, (Sundays excepted); arrives at Philadelphia early next day. Fare of each passenger four dollars

ALBANY STAGES will leave New York every day at ten o'clock in the morning; arrive at Albany the fourth day at nine o'clock in the morning. Fare of each passenger seven dollars,

VERMONT STAGES will leave New York every Monday, Wednesday and Friday mornings, at eight o'clock; run to Bedford the first day, the second to Dover, the third to Stockbridge, and the fourth to Bennington, in Vermont. Also, a LINE of STAGES will run from South-east to Danbury, Brookfield, New Milford, &c. to meet the Vermont Line to and from New-York. Fare of each passenger five cents, per mile.

N. B. For seats in either of the above Lines of Stages enquire of Wm Vandervoort, No. 3, Courtlandt street, and of B. Many, No 42, John-street, corner of Nassau-street, where passengers may be accommodated with genteel Board and Lodging.

J. Douglass. Wm. Vandervoort & Co.
October 2, 1797.

1774 ends with this sentence, "The Rumsey Machine, through Winchester, hung on Steel Springs begins flying on the 3rd of April from London to Poole in One Day." On the Paulus Hook route to Philadelphia in 1772 the proprietor announced a vehicle "in imitation of a coach" — and perhaps that is all that any of these carriages could be rightfully called.

One of the clearest pictures which has come down to us of travelling in the early years of our national existence is found in the pages relating the travels of a young Englishman named Thomas Twining, in the United States in the year 1795. He journeyed by "stage-waggon" from Philadelphia, through Chester and Wilmington, to Baltimore, then to Washington, then back to Philadelphia.

He fully describes the stage-wagon in which he made these journeys : —

"The vehicle was a long car with four benches. Three of these in the interior held nine passengers. A tenth passenger was seated by the side of the driver on the front bench. A light roof was supported by eight slender pillars, four on each side. Three large leather curtains suspended to the roof, one at each side and the third behind, were rolled up or lowered at the pleasure of the passengers. There was no place nor space for luggage, each person being expected to stow his things as he could under his seat or legs. The entrance was in front over the driver's bench. Of course the three passengers on the back seat were obliged to crawl across all the other benches to get to their places. There were no *backs* to the benches to support and relieve us during a rough and fatiguing journey over a newly and ill-made road."

Mr. Jansen, who resided in America from 1793 to 1806, wrote a book entitled *The Stranger in America*. In it he described the coach between Philadelphia and New York with some distinctness : —

"The vehicle, the American stage-coach, which is of like construction throughout the country, is calculated to hold twelve persons, who sit on benches placed across with their faces toward the horses. The front seat holds three, one of whom is the driver. As there are no doors at the sides, the passengers get in over the front wheels. The first get seats behind the rest, the most esteemed seat because you can rest your shaken frame against the back part of the wagon. Women are generally indulged with it; and it is laughable to see them crawling to this seat. If they have to be late they have to straddle over the men seated further in front."

It will be readily seen that the description of this coach is precisely like that given by Weld in his *Travels*, and like the picture of it in the latter book. An excellent representation of this stage-wagon is given in Mr. Edward Lamson Henry's picture of the Indian Queen Tavern at Blattensburg, Maryland, a copy of which is shown facing page 33. Cruder ones may be seen in the various advertisements of eighteenth-century stage lines.

The coach-body of the year 1818 had an egg-shaped body and was suspended on thick leather straps, called thorough-braces, which gave the vehicle a comparatively easy motion. After being worn these frequently broke, and one side of the

coach would settle.   The patient travellers then
alighted, took a rail from an adjoining fence,
righted up the body of the coach, and went on
slowly to the next village for repairs.

This coach had a foot-board for the driver's feet,
and a trunk-rack bolted to the axletrees. One
is here shown, and an old cut on page 273.   A few
still exist and are in use.

Stage-coach of 1818.

Ten years later the fashion of coaches had
changed, and of boats, as shown by the cut on the
opposite page.   This view is at the first lock on
Erie Canal above Albany.

All the various forms of coaches were superseded
and made obsolete by the incomparable Concord
coach, first built in Concord, New Hampshire, in
1827.

The story of the Concord coach is one of profound interest, and should be given in detail.   It
has justly been pronounced the only perfect passenger vehicle for travelling that has ever been

built.   To every state and territory in the Union,
to every country in the world where there are roads
on which such a coach could run, have these Concord coaches been sent.   In spite of steam and
electric cars they still are manufactured in large
numbers, and are still of constant use.   There is
really very little difference between the older Concord coaches, such as the one used by Buffalo Bill,

Stage-coach of 1828.

shown on page 266, and one of the stanch, well-
equipped modern ones used in mountain travel,
such as is shown facing page 268.
   The word stage-coach was originally applied to a
coach which ran from station to station over a number of stages of the road, usually with fresh horses
for each stage.   It was not used to designate a
coach which ran only a short distance.   Mr. Fairman Rogers notes as an example of the curious
changes of language the custom in New York of
calling a short-route omnibus a stage.   We all
recall the tottering Broadway stages ; we still have

the Fifth Avenue stages with us. This debased
use of the word is not an Americanism, nor is it
modern. Swift speaks of riding in the six-penny
stage ; and Cowper has a similar usage. The word
drag, originally applied to a public road-coach, now
is used for a coach for private driving. The in-
correct American use of the word tally-ho, as a
general name for a coach and four, dates from 1876,
when Colonel Delancey Kane first ran his road-coach

Old Concord Coach.

from the Brunswick Hotel in New York to Pelham.
It chanced to be named Tally-ho after English
coaches of that name, and the word was adopted from
the individual to a class. Barge, as applied to a
long omnibus, is apparently a modern Americanism.
I heard it first about ten years ago. Alighting from
the cars, travel-tired and dusty, at a New England
coast town one July afternoon, we asked the distance to a certain hotel ; and we were told it was
four miles, and we could go either by sloop or

barge, and that " the barge got there first." We gladly welcomed the possibility of closing our journey with a short, refreshing water trip, but decided that the sloop might be delayed by adverse winds, and we would trust to the barge, which we inferred was propelled by steam. On stating our preference for the barge we were waved into a long, heavy omnibus harnessed with a " spike " team of three jaded horses that soon stumbled along the dry road, choking us with the dust of their slow progress. After riding nearly half an hour we called out despondingly to the driver, " When do we reach the wharf?" " We ain't goin' to the wharf," he drawled. " Where do we take the barge then, and when?" " You're a-ridin' in the barge now," he answered, and thus we added another example to our philological studies.

Our first conveyance of goods and persons was by water, and the word transportation was one of our sea terms applied to inland traffic. Mr. Ernst has pointed out that many sea terms besides the word barge have received a land use. "The conductor shouts his marine 'All aboard,' and railroad men tell of 'shipping' points that have nothing to do with navigation. We ship by rail, and out West they used to have 'prairie schooners.' Of late we go by 'trolley,' and that word is borrowed from the sailors. Our locomotives have a 'pilot' each, and even 'freight' has a marine origin."

The first line of stages established between New York and Philadelphia made the trip in about three days. The stage was simply a Jersey wagon with-

out springs.   The quaint advertisement of the route
appeared in the *Weekly Mercury* of March 8, 1759:—

" Philadelphia Stage Waggon and New York Stage Boat
perform their stages twice a week.   John Butler with his
waggon sets out on Monday from his house at the sign of
the ' Death of the Fox ' in Strawberry Alley, and drives the
same day to Trenton Ferry, where Francis Holman meets
him, and the passengers and goods being shifted into the
waggon of Isaac Fitzrandolph, he takes them to the New
Blazing Star to Jacob Fitzrandolph's the same day, where
Rubin Fitzrandolph, with a boat well suited will receive
them and take them to New York that night : John Butler,
returning to Philadelphia on Tuesday with the passengers
and goods delivered to him by Francis Holman, will set out
again for Trenton Ferry on Thursday, and Francis Holman, &c., will carry his passengers and goods with the
same expedition as above to New York."

The driver of this flying machine, old Butler,
was an aged huntsman who kept a kennel of hounds
till foxes were shy of Philadelphia streets, when his
old sporting companions thus made a place for
him.

With such a magnificent road as the National
Road, it was natural there should be splendid coaching upon it.   At one time there were four lines of
stage-coaches on the Cumberland Road: the National
Line, Pioneer, Good Intent, and June Bug.   Curiously enough, no one can find out, no one is left to
tell, why or wherefore the latter absurd and undig-
nified name was given.   An advertisement of the
" Pioneer Fast Stage Line " is given on page 270.
Relays of horses were made every ten or twelve

Concord Coach at Toll Gate.

miles.   It was bragged that horses were changed ere the coach stopped rocking.   No heavy luggage was taken, and at its prime but nine passengers to a coach.   These were on what was called Troy coaches.   The Troy coach was preceded by a heavy coach built at Cumberland, and carrying sixteen persons, and a lighter egg-shaped vehicle made at Trenton ; and it was succeeded by the famous Concord coach.   Often fourteen coaches started off together loaded with passengers.   The mail-coach had a horn; it left Wheeling at six in the morning, and twenty-four hours later dashed into Cumberland, one hundred and thirty-two miles away.   The mail was very heavy.   Sometimes it took three to four coaches to transport it ; there often would be fourteen lock-bags and seventy-two canvas sacks.

The drivers had vast rivalry.   Here, as elsewhere all over the country, the test of their mettle was the delivery of the President's message.   There was powerful reason for this rivalry ; the letting of mail contracts hinged on the speed of this special delivery.   Dan Gordon claimed he carried the message thirty-two miles in two hours and twenty minutes, changing teams three times.   Dan Noble professed to have driven from Wheeling to Hagerstown, one hundred and eighty-five miles, in fifteen hours and a half.

The rivalry of drivers and coach-owners extended to passengers, who became violent partisans of the road on which they travelled, and a threatening exhibition of bowie knives and pistols was often made.   When the Baltimore and Ohio Railroad

was completed to Wheeling, these stage-coaches had
their deathblow.

The expense of travelling in 1812 between Philadelphia and Pittsburg, a distance of two hundred
and ninety-seven miles, was twenty dollars by stage
with way-expenses of seven dollars, and it took six

days. The expense by wagon was five dollars a
hundred weight for persons and property, and the
way-expenses were twelve dollars, for it took twenty
days.

In England, in the prime days of coaching, rates
were fourpence or fivepence a mile inside, and twopence or threepence outside. The highest fares were
of course on the mail-coaches and fast day-coaches;
the lower rates were on the heavy night-coaches.

At an early date there were good lines of conveyance between Boston and Providence, and from
Providence to other towns. The early editions of
old almanacs tell of these coaching routes. *The
New England Almanack* for 1765 gave two routes
to Hartford, the distances being given from tavern
to tavern. *The New England Town & County
Almanack* for 1769 announced a coach between
Providence and Norwich, "a day's journey only,"
and two coaches a week between Providence and
Boston, also performing this journey in a day. In
1793, Israel Hatch announced daily stages between
the two towns; he had "six good coaches and experienced drivers," and the fare was but a dollar. He
closed his notice, " He is also determined, at the
expiration of the present contract for carrying the
mail from Providence to Boston, to carry it gratis,
which will undoubtedly prevent any further under-
biddings of the Envious."

"The Envious" was probably Thomas Beal,
whose rival carriages were pronounced "genteel
and easy." His price was nine shillings "and less
if any other person will carry them for that sum."

When passenger steamboats were put on the route
between Providence and New York these lines of
coaches became truly important.   Often twenty full
coach-loads were carried each way each day.   The
editor of the *Providence Gazette* wrote with pride,
" We were rattled from Providence to Boston in
four hours and fifty minutes — if any one wants to
go faster he may send to Kentucky and charter a
streak of lightning."   But with speed came increased
fares — three dollars a trip.   This exorbitant sum
soon produced a rival cheaper line — at two dollars
and a half a ticket.   The others then lowered to
two dollars, and the two lines alternated in reduc-
tion till the conquered old line announced it would
carry the first booked applicants for nothing.   The
new stage line then advertised that they would carry
patrons free of expense, and furnish a dinner at the
end of the journey.   The old line was rich and
added a bottle of wine to a like offer.

Mr. Shaffer, a fashionable teacher of dancing and
deportment in Boston, an arbiter in social life, and
man about town, had a gay ride on Monday to
Providence, a good dinner, and the promised bottle
of wine.   On Tuesday he rode more gayly back to
Boston, had his dinner and wine, and on Wednesday
started to Providence again.   With a crowd of gay
young sparks this frolic continued till Saturday, when
the rival coach lines compromised and signed a contract to charge thereafter two dollars a trip.

In 1818 all the lines in eastern Massachusetts
and New Hampshire, and others in Maine and
Rhode Island, were formed into a syndicate, the

Eastern Stage Company; and it had an unusual career. The capital stock consisted of four hundred and twenty-five shares at a hundred dollars each. Curiously enough, the contracts and agreements signed at the time of the union do not ever mention its object; it might be a sewing-machine company, or an oil or ice trust. It had at once an enormous business, for it was born great. The profits were likewise enormous; the directors' meetings were symposiums of satisfaction, and stockholders gloated

NEW OMNIBUS

New Omnibus "Accommodation."

over their incomes. In 1829 there were seventy-seven stage-coach lines from Boston; the fare to Albany (about two hundred miles) was six dollars, and eight dollars and seventy-five cents by the "Mail Line." The fare to Worcester was two dollars; to Portland, eight dollars; to Providence, two dollars and a half. In 1832 there were one hundred and six coach lines from Boston. The *Boston Traveller* was started as a stage-coach paper in 1825, whence its name. Time-tables and stage-lists were issued by Badger and Porter from 1825 to 1836. After twelve years, the Eastern Stage Company was incorporated in New Hampshire, but even then luck was turning. There was no one shrewd enough to heed the warning which might have been heard through the land, "Look out for the engine," and soon the assets of the stage company were as dust and ashes ; everything was sold out at vast loss, and in 1838 — merely a score of years, not even "come of age" — the Eastern Stage Company ceased to exist. On its prosperous routes, during the first ten years, myriads of taverns had sprung up ; vast brick stables had been built for the hundreds of horses, scores of blacksmiths' forges had been set up, and some of these shops were very large. These buildings were closed as suddenly as they were built, and rotted unused.

This period of the brilliant existence of the Eastern Stage Company was also the date of the coaching age of England, given by Stanley Harris as from 1820 to 1840. The year 1836, which saw the publication of *Pickwick*, wherein is so fine a picture of old coaching days, was the culminating point of the mail-coach system. Just as it was perfected it was rendered useless by the railroad.

In the earliest colonial days, before the official appointment of any regular post-rider, letters were carried along the coast or to the few inland towns by chance travellers or by butchers who made frequent trips to buy and sell cattle. John Winthrop, of New London, sent letters by these butcher carriers.

In 1672 " Indian posts " carried the Albany winter

mail. With a retrospective shiver we read a notice of
1730 that "whoever inclines to perform the foot-post
to Albany this winter may make application to the
Post-Master."   Lonely must have been his solitary
journey up the solemn river, skating along under
old Cro' Nest.

The first regular mounted post from New York
to Boston started January 1, 1673.   He had two
"port-mantles" which were crammed with letters,
"small portable goods and divers bags."   It was
enjoined that he must be active, stout, indefatigable,
and honest.   He changed horses at Hartford.   He
was ordered to keep an eye out for the best roads,
best ways through forests, for ferries, fords, etc., to
watch keenly for all fugitive servants and deserters,
and to be kind to all persons travelling in his company.   During the month that he was gone the
mail was collected in a box in the office of the Colonial Secretary.   The arrivals and departure of these
posts were very irregular.   In 1704 we read, "Our
Philadelphia post (to New York) is a week behind,
and not yet com'd in."

In unusual or violent weather the slowness of
mail carriage was appalling.   Salem and Portsmouth are about forty miles apart.   In March,
1716, the "post" took nine days for one trip
between the two towns and eight days the other.
He was on snowshoes, and he reported drifts from
six to fourteen feet deep; but even so, four to five
miles a day was rather minute progress.

It is pleasant to read in the *Winthrop Letters* and
other correspondence of colonial days of "journeys

with the Post." Madam Knight rode with him, as did many another fair traveller with his successors at later dates. A fragment of a journal of a young college graduate, written in 1790, tells of "overtaking the Post, who rode with six Dames, neither young nor fair, from Hartford to Boston." He tells that the patient Squire of Dames was rather surly when joked about his harem. Mrs. Quincy tells of travelling, when she was a little girl, with the Post, who occupied his monotonous hours by stocking-knitting.

NEWS! NEWS!

AARON OLIVER, *Poſt-Rider,*

WISHES to inform the Publick, that he has extended his Route; and that he now rides thro' the Towns of *Troy, Pittſtown, Hooſick, Mapletown,* Part of *Bennington,* and *Shaftſbury, Peterſburgh, Stephentown, Greenbuſh* and *Schodack.*

All Commands in his Line will be received with Thanks, and executed with Punctuality.

He returns his ſincere Thanks to his former Cuſtomers ; and intends, by unabated Diligence, to merit a Continuance of their Favours.

O'er ruggid hills, and vallies wide,
　He never yet has fail'd to trudge it ;
As ſteady as the flowing tide,
　He hands about the NORTHERN BUDGET.
June 18, 1799.

The post-riders, whose advertisements (one of which is here shown) can be found in many old-time newspapers, were private carriers. They "Resolv'd to ride Post for the good of the Publick," etc. They were burdened by law with restrictions, which they calmly evaded, for they materially decreased the government revenue in sealed mail-matter, though they were supposed to be merchandise carriers only.

In 1773, Hugh Finlay was made postal surveyor by the British government of the mail service from Quebec, Canada, to St. Augustine, Florida. He made a very unfavorable report of postal conditions. He declared that postmasters often had no offices, that tavern taprooms and family rooms in private houses were used as gathering places for the mail. Letters were thrown carelessly on an open table or tavern bar, for all comers to pull over till the owners called; and fresh letters were irregularly forwarded. The postmaster's salary was paid according to the number of letters he handled, and of course the private conveyance of letters sadly diminished his income. Private mail-carriage was forbidden by law, but the very government post-riders were the chief offenders. Persons were allowed to carry merchandise at their own rates for their own profit, so post-riders, wagon-drivers, butchers, ship captains, or any one could carry large sealed letters, provided they were tied to any bundle or box. Sham bundles of paper or straw, weighing little, were thus used as kite-tails to the letters. The government post-rider between Newport and Boston took twenty-six hours to go eighty miles, carried all way-letters to his own profit, and bought and sold on commission. If he had been complained of, the informer was in danger of tarring and feathering. It was deemed all a part of the revolt of the provinces against " slavery and oppression." The rider between

Saybrook and New York had been in his calling
forty-six years. He carried on a money exchange to
his own profit, and pocketed all way-postage. He
superintended the return of horses for travellers;
and Finlay says he was coolly waiting, when he saw
him, for a yoke of oxen that he was going to transfer for a customer. No wonder the mails were slow
and uncertain.

In 1788 it took four days for mail to go from
New York to Boston — in winter much longer.
George Washington died on the 14th of December,
1799. As an event of universal interest throughout the nation, the news was doubtless conveyed
with all speed possible by fleetest messenger. The
knowledge of this national loss was not known in
Boston till December 24. Two years later there
was a state election in Massachusetts of most profound interest, when party feeling ran high. It took
a month, however, to get in all the election returns,
even in a single state.

The first advertisement or bill of the first coaching line between Boston and Portsmouth reads
thus : —

" *For the Encouragement of Trade from Portsmouth to Boston.*

"A LARGE STAGE CHAIR,

With two horses well equipped, will be ready by Monday
the 20th inst. to start out from *Mr. Stavers*, Inn-holder at
the sign of the *Earl of Halifax*, in this town for Boston, to
perform once a week; to lodge at Ipswich the same night;
from thence through Medford to Charlestown Ferry; to tarry
at Charlestown till Thursday morning, so as to return to this

town next day : to set out again the Monday following :
It will be contrived to carry four persons besides the driver.
In case only two persons go, they may be accommodated
to carry things of bulk and value to make a third or fourth
person.   The Price will be *Thirteen Shillings* and *Six Pence*
sterling for each person from hence to Boston, and at the
same rate of conveyance back again ; though under no
obligation to return in the same week in the same manner.

"Those who would not be disappointed must enter their
names at *Mr. Stavers'* on Saturdays, any time before nine
in the evening, and pay one half at entrance, the remainder
at the end of the journey.   Any gentleman may have business transacted at Newbury or Boston with fidelity and
despatch on reasonable terms.

"As gentlemen and ladies are often at a loss for good
accommodations for travelling from hence, and can't return
in less than three weeks or a month, it is hoped that this
undertaking will meet with suitable encouragement, as they
will be wholly freed from the care and charge of keeping
chairs and horses, or returning them before they had
Finished their business.

"Portsmouth, April, 1761."

A picture and account of the Stavers Inn are
given on page 176.

These stages ran throughout the winter, except in
bad weather, and the fare was then three dollars a trip.
This winter trip was often a hard one.   We read at
one time of the ferries being so frozen over that
travellers had to make a hundred-mile circuit round
by Cambridge.   This line of stages prospered ; and
two years later "The Portsmouth Flying Stage-
coach," which held six "insides," ran with four or
six horses.   The fare was the same.

On this Stavers line were placed the first mail-coaches under the English crown. When Finlay (the post-office surveyor just referred to) examined the mail-service in the year 1773, he found these mail-coaches running between Boston and Portsmouth. Mr. Ernst says, "The Stavers mail-coach was stunning, used six horses in bad weather,

Old Coach and Sign-board, Barre, Massachusetts.

and never was late." These coaches were built by Paddock, the Boston coach-builder and Tory. Stavers also was a Tory, and during the Revolution both fled to England, and may have carried the notion of the mail-coach across the sea. At any rate the first English mail-coach was not put on the road till 1784; it ran between Bristol and London. It was started by a theatrical manager named Palmer, who had had no practical knowledge either of post-office work or coaching. The service was very imperfect and far from speedy.

Herbert Joyce, historian of the British post-office, says, " In 1813 there was not a single town in the British kingdom at the post-office of which absolutely certain information could have been obtained as to the charge to which a letter addressed to any other town would be subject." The charge was regulated by the distance; but distances seemed movable, and the letter-sender was wholly at the mercy of the postmaster. The government of the United States early saw the injustice of doubt in these matters, and Congress ordered a careful topographical survey, in 1811–12, of the post-road from Passamaquoddy to St. Mary's, and also established our peerless corps of topographical engineers. Foreigners were much impressed with the value of this survey, and an old handkerchief, printed in 1815 by R. Gillespie, at " Anderston Printfield near Glasgow," proves that the practical effects of the survey were known in England before the English people had a similar service.

This handkerchief gives an interesting statement of postal rates and routes at the beginning of this century. Around the edge is a floral border, with the arms of the United States, the front and reverse of the dollar of 1815, a quartette of ships of war, and portraits of Washington, Adams, Jefferson, and " Maddison " intertwined.

Its title is " A Geographical View of All the Post Towns in the United States of America and Their Distance from Each Other According to the Estab-

lishment of the Postmaster General in the Year
1815." By an ingenious arrangement of the towns
on the main coast line and those on the cross post-
roads, the distance from one of these points to any
other could easily be ascertained. The "main line
of post towns" extended "from Passamaquoddy in
the District of Maine to Sunbury in the State of
Georgia."

The object in publishing such a table as this was
to make a durable record by which it was possible
for the people to compute easily and with a handy
helper what the cost of postage on letters would be.
The following "rates of postage" are given on the
old handkerchief: —

"Single Letter conveyed by land for any distance not
exceeding 10 miles, 6 cents.

Over	10,	not exceeding	60 miles,	8 cents.		
"	60	"	"	100	"	10	"
"	100	"	"	150	"	12	"
"	150	"	"	200	"	15	"
"	200	"	"	250	"	17	"
"	250	"	"	350	"	20	"
"	350	"	"	450	"	22	"
For	450			"	25	" "

Double letters are charged double; and triple
letters, three times these rates, and a packet weighing one ounce avoirdupois at the rate of four single
letters.

Let us compare conditions in these matters in
America with those in Scotland. While England
had, in the first half of the eighteenth century,

coaches in enough number that country folk knew what they looked like, Scotland was barren not only of coaches but of carriages. In 1720 there were no chariots or chaises north of the Tay. Not till 1749 was there a coach between Edinburgh and Glasgow; this journey of forty-six miles could, by the end of the century, be done in twelve hours. In 1754 there was once a month a coach from Edinburgh to London; it took twelve to sixteen days to accomplish this journey, and was so perilous that travellers made their wills before setting out. There were few carts and no such splendid wagons as our Conestogas. Cadgers carried creels of goods on horseback; and sledges, or creels borne on the backs of women, were the means of transportation in northern Scotland until the end of the eighteenth century. These sledges had tumbling wheels of solid wood a foot and a half in diameter, revolving with the wooden axletree, and held little more than a wheelbarrow.

Scotch inns were as bad as the roads; "mean hovels with dirty rooms, dirty food, dirty attendants." Servants without shoes or stockings, greasy tables with no cloths, butter thick with cows' hairs, no knives and forks, a single drinking-cup for all at the table, filthy smells and sights, were universal; and this when English inns were the pleasantest places on earth.

Mail-carriage was even worse than personal transportation; hence letter-writing was not popular. In 1746 the London mail-bag once carried but a single letter from Edinburgh. So little attention was paid to the post that as late as 1728 the letters were sometimes not taken from the mail bag, and were brought back to their original starting place. Scotland was in a miserable state of isolation and gloom until the Turnpike Road Act was passed; the building of good roads made a complete revolution of all economic conditions there, as it has everywhere.

The first railway in America was the Quincy Railroad, or the "Experiment" Railroad, built to

Quincy Railway Pitcher.

carry stones to Bunker Hill Monument. A tavern-pitcher, commemorative of this Quincy road, is shown here. Two views of the Baltimore and Ohio Railroad, printed on plates and platters in rich dark blue, are familiar to china collectors. One shows a stationary engine at the top of a hill with a number of little freight cars at a very singular angle going down a steep grade. The other displays a primitive locomotive with coachlike passenger cars.

All the first rail-cars were run by horse-power.

Peter Parley's *First Book on History* says, in the chapter on Maryland : —

"The people are building what is called a railroad. This consists of iron bars laid down along the ground and made fast, so that carriages with small wheels may run upon them with facility. In this way one horse will be able to draw as much as ten horses on a common road. A part of the railroad is already done, and if you choose to take a ride upon it you can do so. You enter a car something like a stage, and then you will be drawn along by two horses at a speed of twelve miles per hour."

The horse-car system, in its perfection, did not prevail until many years after the establishment of steam cars. It is curious to note how suddenly, in our own day, the horse cars were banished by cars run by electricity; as speedily as were stage-coaches cast aside by steam. A short time ago a little child of eight years came running to me in much excitement over an unusual sight she had seen in a visit to a small town — "a trolley car dragged by horses."

Many strange plans were advanced for the new railways. I have seen a wood-cut of a railway-coach rigged with masts and sails gayly running on a track. I don't know whether the inventor of this wind-car ever rigged his car-boat and tried to run it. Another much-derided suggestion was that the motive power should be a long rope or chain, and the notion was scorned, but we have lived to see many successful lines of cars run by cable

Kites and balloons also were seriously suggested as motive powers. It was believed that in a short time any person would be permitted to run his own private car or carriage over the tracks, by paying toll, as a coach did on a turnpike.

The body of the stage-coach furnished the model for the first passenger cars on the railway. A copy is here given of an old print of a train on the Veazie

Railroad, which began to run from Bangor, Maine, in 1836. The road had two locomotives of Stevenson's make from England. They had no cabs when they arrived here, but rude ones were attached. They burned wood. The cars were also English; a box resembling a stage-coach was placed on a rude platform. Each coach carried eight people. The passengers entered the side. The train ran about twelve miles in forty minutes. The rails, like those of

Veazie Railway.

other railroads at the time, were of strap-iron spiked down. These spikes soon rattled loose, so each engine carried a man with a sledge hammer, who watched the track, and when he spied a spike sticking up he would reach down and drive it home. These "snake heads," as the rolled-up ends of the strap-iron were called, sometimes were forced up through the cars and did great damage. "Snake heads" were as common in railway travel as snags in the river in early steamboating.

The Boston and Lowell, Boston and Providence, and Boston and Worcester railroads were all opened in 1835. The locomotive used on the Boston and Worcester road was called the Meteor. The cars were coach-shaped and ran on single trucks. The freight cars were short vans or wagon-bodies covered with canvas like a Conestoga wagon. A picturesque view of an old railway train is given opposite page 288 in the picture painted by Mr. Edward Lamson Henry, called "The Arrival of the Train." It shows a train at a way station between Harrisburg and Lancaster, in the year 1839, and a comparison between the coaches on the track and the coach and horses waiting near by will show that the same model served for both.

Accidents were many on these early roads ; some were fatal, some were ridiculous. The clumsy locomotive often broke down, and horses and oxen had to be impressed to drag the cars to the nearest station and repair shop. An old print showing "Uncle Ame Morris's" oxen serving as a locomotive on a railroad near Danbury, Connecticut, is given on page 289. Coaching accidents had seldom been fatal, and ancient citizens were appalled at the deaths on the rail. Never was the cry of "the good old times" so loudly heard as in the early days of the railroad. Especially were the injuries by escaping steam and by communicated fire deemed horrible and unbearable. An old-school blood thus summarized all these sentiments: "You got upset in a coach — and there you were! You get upset in a rail-car — and, damme, where are you?"

The roadbed of the track was laid thus, as shown in the words of a State Report made to the Massachusetts Legislature on January 16, 1829: —

"A continuous stone wall, laid so deep in the ground as not to be moved by the effects of the frost; and surmounted by a rail of split granite about a foot in thickness and depth, with a bar of iron on top of it of sufficient thickness for the carriage wheels to run."

My father, who rode on one of these rock-bedded railways, told me that the jarring was inexpressibly tiring and even distressing. They were in use but a short time. But the cars had no springs, and the jarring continued to some degree. It produced headaches and an incessant itching of the skin. The primitive brake-power was a hand or foot brake, and a car stopped with a jolting which was almost as severe as the shock felt to-day in a collision. A more primitive brake-power was in vogue on the Newcastle and Frenchtown Railroad, where the engineer would open his safety valve at each station and several strong negroes would seize the end of the train and hold it back while the station agent thrust sticks of wood through the wheel-spokes. Crooked roads were favored, so the engineer and conductor could "look back and see if the train was all right." These were easily managed with the short coach-like railway carriages.

It would be impossible to repeat all the objections against the establishment of the railroads, besides the loss of life. These objections far outnumbered those made against coaches centuries pre-

The Arrival of the Train.

vious.   The farmers would be ruined.   Horses would have to be killed because wholly useless. There would therefore be no market for oats or hay.   Hens would not lay eggs on account of the noise.   It would cause insanity.   There would be constant fires from the sparks from the engine.   It

Uncle Ame Morris' Oxen serving as a Locomotive.

was declared that no car could ever advance against the wind.   The *Boston Courier* of June 27, 1827, said in an editorial : —

"The project of a railroad from Boston to Albany is impracticable, as every one knows who knows the simplest rule of arithmetic, and the expense would be little less than the market value of the whole territory of Massachusetts; and which, if practicable, every person of common sense knows would be as useless as a railroad from Boston to the moon."

Captain Basil Hall rode by stage-coach in 1829 over the present route of the Boston and Albany Railroad. He described the hills, ravines, and rivers, and said, "Those Yankees talk of constructing a railroad over this route; as a practical engineer, I pronounce it simply impossible."

All the sentimental objections of all the sentimental objectors may be summed up in the words of the best beloved of all coachmen, Tony Weller : —

"I consider that the rail is unconstitutional, and a inwader o' privileges. As to the comfort — as an old coachman I may say it — veres the comfort o' sitting in a harm-chair, a lookin' at brick walls, and heaps o' mud, never comin' to a public 'ouse, never seein' a glass o' ale, never goin' thro' a pike, never meetin' a change o' no kind (hosses or otherwise) but always comin' to a place ven you comes to vun at all, the werry picter o' the last! As to the honor and dignity o' travellin', vere can that be vithout a coachman, and vats the rail to sich coachmen as is sometimes forced to go by it, but a outrage and a insult! And as to the ingen, a nasty, wheezin', creakin', gaspin', puffin', bustin' monster always out o' breath, with a shiny green and gold back like a onpleasant beetle; as to the ingen as is alvays a pourin' out red-hot coals at night and black smoke in the day, the sensiblest thing it does, in my opinion, is ven there's somethin' in the vay, and it sets up that 'ere frightful scream vich seems to say, ' now 'eres two hundred and forty passengers in the werry greatest extremity o' danger, and 'eres their two hundred and forty screams in vun!' "

CHAPTER XIII

TWO STAGE VETERANS OF MASSACHUSETTS

THERE still stands in Shrewsbury, Massachusetts, at the junction of the Westborough road with the old " King's Highway," a weatherbeaten but dignified house, the Pease Tavern; it is shown on page 292. This house was for many years a popular resort for the teamsters and travellers who passed back and forth on what was then an important road. Behind the house was originally a large shed with roof and open sides for the protection from rain or snow of the great numbers of loaded wagons. In another covered shed at the side of the house were chairs and tables for the teamsters and shelves for any baggage they took from their wagons. This shed for the accommodation of the teamsters would indicate to me that they were not so unreservedly welcome at this tavern as at many others on the route. Miss Ward, in her entertaining book, *Old Times in Shrewsbury*, says that under this shed, in the side boards of the house, slight holes were cut one above the other to a window in the second story. These holes were large enough to hold on by, and to admit the toe of a man's boot; by dexterous use of hands and feet the teamsters were expected to climb up the outside wall to the window, and thus reach their sleeping apartments without passing through the hall and interior of the house. This was, it was asserted, for the convenience both of the family and

Pease Tavern.

the travellers. In the Wayside Inn at Sudbury a small special staircase winding in the corner of the taproom led to the four "drivers' bedrooms" above. One of the upper rooms in the Pease Tavern was a dancing hall. Across this hall from wall to wall was a swing partition which could be hooked up to the ceiling when a dance was given, but at other times divided the hall into two large bed-rooms. This was a common appurtenance of the old-time tavern.

Major John Farrar, an officer in the Revolution, first kept this Shrewsbury inn, and greatly rejoiced when Washington visited it in his triumphal journey through the country. His successor as land-lord, Levi Pease, was a man of note in the history of travel and transportation systems in Massachusetts. He was a Shrewsbury blacksmith who served through the entire Revolutionary War in a special function — which might be entitled a confidential transportation agent: he transferred important papers, carried special news, purchased horses and stores, foraged for the army, and enjoyed the full confidence of the leaders, especially of Lafayette. In 1783, when peace was established, he planned to establish a line of stages between Boston and Hartford, and thus turn his knowledge of roads and transportation to account. Wholly without funds, he found no one ready to embark in the daring project and work with him, save one young stage-driver, Reuben Sykes or Sikes, who braved parental opposition, as well as universal discouragement, and started with a stage-wagon from Hartford to Boston at the same hour that Captain Pease set out from Boston to Hartford. Each made the allotted trip in four days. The fare was ten dollars a trip. Empty stages were soon succeeded by prosperous trips, and in two years the penniless stage agent owned the Boston Inn opposite the Common, in Boston, on the spot where St.

Old Arcade, Shrewsbury, Massachusetts.

Paul's Church now stands. The line was soon extended to New York.

Josiah Quincy gives a far from alluring picture of Pease's coaches in the earliest days: —

"I set out from Boston in the line of stages lately established by an enterprising Yankee, Pease by name, which at that day was considered a method of transportation of wonderful expedition. The journey to New York took up a week. The carriages were old and shackling, and much of the harness made of ropes. One pair of horses carried the stage eighteen miles. We generally reached our resting place for the night, if no accident intervened, at ten o'clock, and after a frugal supper went to bed with a notice that we should be called at three the next morning, which generally proved to be half-past two. Then, whether it snowed or rained, the traveller must rise and make ready by the help of a horn-lantern and a farthing candle, and proceed on his way over bad roads, sometimes

with a driver showing no doubtful symptoms of drunkenness, which good-hearted passengers never fail to improve
at every stopping place by urging upon him another glass
of toddy. Thus we travelled, eighteen miles a stage,
sometimes obliged to get out and help the coachman lift
the coach out of a quagmire or rut, and arrived at New
York after a week's hard travelling, wondering at the ease
as well as expedition of our journey."

It should be added to this tale that young Quincy
was in love, and on his way to see his sweetheart,
which may have added to his impatience.

This condition of affairs was not permitted to
remain long. Captain Pease bought better horses
and more comfortable wagons, and he persuaded
townships to repair the roads; and he thus advertised in the *Massachusetts Spy*, or the *Worcester
Gazette*, under date of January 5, 1786: —

" Stages from Portsmouth in New Hampshire, to
Savannah in Georgia.

" There is now a line of Stages established from New
Hampshire to Georgia, which go and return regularly, and
carry the several Mails, by order and permission of Congress.

" The stages from Boston to Hartford in Connecticut, set
out, during the winter season, from the house of Levi
Pease, at the Sign of the New York Stage, opposite the
Mall, in Boston, every *Monday* and *Thursday* morning, precisely at five o'clock, go as far as *Worcester* on the evenings
of those days, and on the days following proceed to *Palmer*,
and on the third day reach *Hartford*; the first Stage reaches
the city of *New York* on Saturday evening, and the other on
the Wednesday evening following.

"The stages from *New York* for *Boston*, set out on the same days, and reach *Hartford* at the same time as the Boston Stages.

"The stages from *Boston* exchange passengers with the stages from *Hartford* at *Spencer*, and the Hartford Stages exchange with those from *New York* at *Hartford*. Passengers are again exchanged at *Stratford Ferry*, and not again until their arrival at *New York*.

"By the present regulation of the stages, it is certainly the most convenient and expeditious way of travelling that can possibly be had in America, and in order to make it the cheapest, the proprietors of the stages have lowered their price from four pence to three pence a mile, with liberty to passengers to carry fourteen pounds baggage.

"In the summer season the stages are to run with the mail three times in a week instead of twice in the winter, by which means those who take passage at Boston in the stage which sets off on Monday morning, may arrive at New York on the Thursday evening following, and all the mails during that season are to be but four days going from Boston to New York, and so from New York to Boston.

"Those who intend taking passage in the stages must leave their names and baggage the evening preceding the morning that the stages set off, at the several places where the stages put up, and pay one-half of their passage to the place where the first exchange of passengers is made, if bound so far, and if not, one-half of their passage so far as they are bound.

"N. B. Way passengers will be accommodated when the stages are not full, at the same rate, viz. three pence only per mile.

"Said PEASE keeps good lodging, &c. for gentlemen travellers, and stabling for horses.

"BOSTON, Jan. 2nd, 1786."

Pease obtained the first Government contract within the new United States for carrying the mails ; and the first mail in this new service passed through Worcester on the 7th of January, 1786 — such changes had three short years brought.

All was not ease for him even then ; he still drove the stage, and endured heat and cold ; and when New England snowstorms could not be overcome by the mail-coach, like many another of his drivers, he shouldered the mail-bag and carried the mail on snowshoes to Boston town.   He died in 1824, after having received from the Government the first charter granted in Massachusetts for a turnpike. It was laid out in 1808 from Boston through South Shrewsbury to Worcester, nearly parallel to the old road.   It transformed travel in that vicinity and, indeed, served to alter all town relations and conditions.   This grant and his many incessant efforts to establish turnpikes conferred on Levi Pease the title of the " Father of the Turnpike."

Many other charters were soon granted, and the state was covered with a network of turnpikes which were in general thronged with vehicles and live-stock, and were therefore vastly profitable.   From the prospectus of the Sixth Massachusetts Turn-pike Company, incorporated in 1799 to build a road from Amherst to a point near Shrewsbury, we learn that the turnpike from Northampton to Pitts-field paid twelve per cent dividend.

On these great, bustling, living thoroughfares a sad change has fallen.   In Bedford, Raystown, Somerset, Greensbury, in scores of towns, weeds and grass grow in the ruts of the turnpike. The taverns are silent; some are turned into comfortless farm-houses, others are closed and unoccupied, sad and deserted widows of the old "pikes," far gone in melancholy decline.

Many of the methods familiar to us in railroad service to-day were invented by Pease, and were crudely in practice by him. He introduced the general ticket office in 1795, and no railroad office to-day sells tickets to all the points served by Pease. His stage office was in State Street, Boston. He evolved what we now term the "limited" and "accommodation" service of railroads; in fact, the term "limited" originated with mail-coaches limiting passengers to a specific number. Pease's fast mail line took but four passengers in each coach, and ran to New York three times a week with the mails. The slower line charging lower prices ran the other days of the week and took all applicants, putting on extra coaches if required. This service began in 1793. Tolls were commuted on Massachusetts turnpikes before 1800, so that condition of railroad travel is a century old.

Not far from this Pease Tavern is a sulphur spring which has some medicinal repute, and which attracted visitors. To reach it at one time you passed close to the house of the Indian, Old Brazil, and his wife Nancy, and this was always a ticklish experience. Miss Ward tells their blood-curdling story. His real name was the gentle title Basil, but he had been a pirate on the high seas, and Brazil was more appropriate. He and his wife thriftily ran their little farm and industriously wove charming baskets and peddled them around the neighboring towns. These last leaves on the tree were, for all the perceptions of Shrewsbury folk, peaceful creatures as they were honest; but when Brazil had been treated to a good mug of hard cider at tavern or farm-house (and no one would fail thus to treat him) he told of

Harrington Tavern, Shrewsbury, Massachusetts.

his past life with such fierce voice and horrid gesture as made him equally a delight and a terror to the children and to many older folk as well.

He had been a bloodthirsty villain; scores, perhaps hundreds, of helpless souls on captured craft had perished at his gory hands. He detailed to the gaping loungers at the tavern with a realism worthy a modern novelist how he split the heads of his victims open with his broadaxe — exactly in the middle — " one half would fall on one shoulder, tother half on tother shoulder ! ugh ! ugh ! " and with another pull of cider, husband and wife trotted contentedly home. About 1850 they died as they had lived, close — and loving — companions. As a fitting testimonial to the pirate's end, the village boys put a charge of gunpowder in the brick oven of the peaceful little kitchen and blew the pirate's house in fragments.

At a time when he could not afford to pay high Boston rents, Pease made Shrewsbury his headquarters. This may account for the large number of old taverns in the town, several of which are portrayed in these pages, — the Old Arcade on page 294, Harrington's Tavern on page 299, Balch Tavern on page 301.

The Exchange Hotel, still standing and still in use as a public house, was the stage office for Pease's stage line in Worcester. This interesting old landmark, built in 1784, was owned by Colonel Reuben Sykes, the partner of Pease ; and other coach lines than theirs centred at the Exchange, and made it gay with arrival and departure. As the United States Arms, Sykes's Coffee-house, Sykes's Stage-house, Thomas Exchange Coffee-house, and Thomas Temperance Exchange in the days of the Washingtonian movement, this hotel has had an interesting existence. President Washington in 1789 " stopped at the United States Arms where he took breakfast, and then proceeded on his journey. To gratify the inhabitants he politely passed through town on horseback. He was dressed in a brown suit, and pleasure glowed in every countenance as he came along." Lafayette was also a guest; and through its situation opposite the Worcester court-houses on Court Hill the tavern has seen within its walls a vast succession of men noted in law and in lawsuits.

Balch Tavern, Shrewsbury Massachusetts.

From 1830 to 1846 a brilliant comet flashed its way through the stage-driving world of New England; it was Hon. Ginery Twichell, who was successively and successfully post-rider, stage-driver, stage proprietor, most noted express rider of his times, railroad superintendent, president of the Boston and Worcester Railroad, and member of Congress. Some thirty years ago or more a small child sat in the " operating room " of a photographer's gallery in Worcester. Her feet and hands were laboriously placed in a

tentatively graceful attitude and the back of her
head firmly fastened in that iron " branks-without-
a-gag " fixture which then prevailed in photogra-
phers' rooms and may still, for all that I know.   A
sudden dashing inroad from an adjoining room of
the photographer's assistant with the loud and excited
exclamation, " Ginery's coming, Ginery's coming," led
to the immediate and unceremonious unveiling of the
artist from the heavy black cloth that had enveloped
his head while he was peeping wisely through the
instrument at his juvenile sitter, and to his violent
exit ; he was followed with equal haste and lack of
explanation by my own attendant.   Thus basely
deserted I sat for some minutes wondering what a
Ginery could be, for there was to me a sort of men-
agerie-circus-like ring in the word, and I deemed it
some strange wild beast like the Pygarg once exhibited at the old Salem Tavern.   At last, though fully
convinced that my moving would break the camera,
I boldly disengaged myself from the claws of the
branks, ran to a front window, and hung peering
out at the Ginery over the heads of the other occupants of the gallery, who regarded with eager delight
no wild or strange beast, but a great stage-coach with
six horses which stood reeking, foaming, pawing, in
front of the Baystate House across the street.   A
dignified and self-contained old man, ruddy of face,
and dressed in a heavy greatcoat and tall silk hat,
sat erect on the coachman's seat, reins well in hand
— and suddenly Ginery and his six horses were off
with rattle of wheels and blowing of horn and
cheers of the crowd ; but not before there was im-

printed forever in unfading colors on my young brain a clear picture of the dashing coaching life of olden days. It was an anniversary of some memorable event, and the member of Congress celebrated it by once more driving over his old-time coaching route to meet the cheers and admiration of all beholders.

The predecessor of Baystate House, the old Central Hotel, was the headquarters of Twichell's stage line during the sixteen years of his connection with it. It was built in 1722, and rooms in it served various purposes besides those of good cheer — one being used as a county jail.

I do not doubt that the coach which I saw was the one thus referred to in the *Boston Traveller* of June 1, 1867, as Mr. Twichell occasionally drove it until the year of his death : —

"The venerable coach built by Moses T. Breck of Worcester, and used 30 years ago in the heart of the Commonwealth by Hon. Ginery Twichell for special occasions before railroads were fairly in vogue, passed through our Boston streets on Friday. The vehicle was of a most substantial pattern; no repairs have been needed through all these years except an occasional coat of varnish and new upholstering. In 1840, by request of the citizens of the town of Barre, seats were added on the top of the vehicle, so that a party of 32 persons could be accommodated (12 inside and 20 outside). The largest load ever carried by the ponderous carriage was a party of (62) sixty-two young ladies of Worcester who, uniformly dressed, were driven on a blackberry excursion to the suburbs by Mr. Twichell himself, eight matched horses being required on the occasion. During the exciting Presidential Campaign of 1840,

the staunch vehicle was used for conveying the sovereigns
to and from political gatherings in the town surrounding
old Quinsigamond."

There is still living in Boston, at an advanced
age, but of vigorous mental powers, Mr. Henry S.
Miner, the last stage-driver of Ginery Twichell's
stage-route, perhaps the last person living who was
connected with it.   He has scores of tales of stage-
coach days which he has capacity to frame in interesting language.   I am indebted to him for many
letters full of information and interest.   He says:

"Ginery Twichell was a shrewd, quiet, persevering
man of but few words, and those to the point; his voice
was clear and low, never raised to horses or men. Affable,
sociable, he was a man that would make friends and hold
them.   He was smooth-shaven and red-faced, but strictly
temperate.   He had one habit of rubbing his hands rapidly
when in earnest conversation.   He had but a common
school education and might be called a self-made man.
Before through railroads were completed, Mr. Twichell
collected the November election votes on horseback, from
Greenfield to Worcester, 54 miles, covering the distance
in four and one-half hours.   He had relays of horses and
men every 6 to 10 miles.   As the work always came in
the night, he was many times thrown by his horse stumbling,
but always came out all right.   At one time he slept in his
clothes with buckskin underwear, at the American House
in Worcester, in wait for despatches from English steamers.
He had men and horses on the road to Norwich for one
week waiting also.   When the dispatches arrived he
mounted his horse and started for Norwich; he met the
boat, and the despatches were in New York hours ahead of

Advertisement of Twichell's Stage Line.

any other line. I am the only one of his drivers living,
and one hostler is living."

A friend who remembers riding with Twichell
eulogizes him in the warmest terms for his accom-
modating spirit and happy faculty of making all his
passengers as comfortable as possible. He had an
inexhaustible fund of racy anecdotes which he would
tell so well that it was a perfect treat to ride upon the
box with him. He was a general favorite, especially
with the country folks, and the boys and girls on
the road, and with these he always had a joke to
crack whenever it came his way to do so, to the
infinite amusement of the travellers whom he had in
charge. He carried many small and valuable par-
cels, and executed commissions for the people like
an expressman. After a period of self-denial in
early life, throughout which he had saved his liberal
earnings carefully, he was enabled to purchase from
Mr. Stockwell the stage and two horses which he
drove between Athol and Barre. About 1837 he
started with Mr. Burt and Mr. Billings a stage line
from Brattleboro to Worcester.

In 1843 he was engaged in driving a stage of
his own between Barre and Worcester. Not long
afterwards he was sole owner of a line from Greenfield, Massachusetts, to Brattleboro, Vermont. The
Postmaster-general about this time advertised for
mail contracts, and Ginery Twichell went to Washington. It was supposed by the owners of the other
lines, who knew he had gone thither, that he would
not undertake to execute more than one contract,

Ginery Twichell's Ride.

but his own private views, it appears, were somewhat broader, for he contracted with the Government to carry the mails upon a number of routes,
greatly to the astonishment of others in the business;
and what was better still, he accomplished what he
had undertaken very satisfactorily to the Postmaster-
general, and came to be regarded as a sort of Napo-
leon among mail contractors. He became the owner
of a large number of fine stages and horses.   He
ran a line from Worcester to Northfield, sixty miles,
three times a week; from Worcester to Winchester,
fifty-five miles, daily; from Worcester to Keene,
fifty-four miles, three times a week; to Templeton
twenty-five miles, daily; from Templeton to Greenfield, forty-eight miles, daily; from Barre to Worcester, forty-four miles, daily. In all this was two
hundred and eighty-six miles of stage-route, and it
took a hundred and fifty-six horses to do the work.

The picture shown on page 306 is from a litho-
graph published in 1850, entitled, —

" The Unrivaled Express Rider, Ginery Twichell,
who rode from Worcester to Hartford, a distance of
Sixty miles in Three hours and Twenty minutes
through a deep snow, January 23, 1846."

It commemorates an exploit of his which was
much talked of at the time it took place.

CHAPTER XIV

A STAGING CENTRE

THE story of the tavern and stage life of the town of Haverhill, New Hampshire, may be told as an example of that aspect and era of social history, as developed in a country town. It shows the power the stage-coach was in bringing civilization and prosperity to remote parts of the states, what an illumination, what an education.

Haverhill is on the Connecticut River somewhat more than halfway up the western boundary line of the state of New Hampshire, at the head of the Cohos valley. It is a beautiful fertile tract of land which had been cleared and cultivated by the Indians before the coming of the white man. It is lovely and picturesque with its broad intervales, splendid mountains, and peaceful river winding in the sweeps and reaches of the Oxbow; so lovely that Longfellow declared Haverhill the most beautiful spot he ever had seen. The town has but little colonial history. It had no white settlers till 1761; but the first who did take up land and build there were, as was the case with nearly all New Hampshire towns, men of unusual force of character and energy of purpose; by Revolutionary times the town was well established, and its situation and resources made it the authorized place of rendezvous for the troops destined for Canada. At the end of the war, when the danger of Indian invasion lessened, the town grew rapidly, but there were still only bridle-paths blazed through the woods by which to connect with the world, and until this century its only roads were the river road, the Coventry Road over Morse Hill, and the old Road from Plymouth, New Hampshire.

But the day of the turnpike and vast changes was dawning. In 1805, in this town, still poor and struggling, were men who contributed their share to the building of the old Cohos Turnpike from Plymouth through Warren to Haverhill. The old post-rider, faithful John Balch, who had carried on foot and on horseback the scant letters throughout the dangerous days of the Revolution, was succeeded by Colonel Silas May in a Dutch wagon, carrying packages and the mail. As he drove into town blowing his horn he inaugurated a change for Haverhill that was indeed a new life. By 1814 a permanent stage line was established between Concord and Haverhill through Plymouth; and the first coach came down the long hill on its first trip, with loud and constant blasts of the horn, with a linchpin gone, but wheel safely in place clean up to the tavern door, thanks to Silas May's skilful driving. A leading spirit in obtaining the turnpike charter and one of the proprietors of the first stage line was Colonel William Tarleton (or Tarlton), then a dashing young fellow of great elegance of manners; he kept the Tarleton Tavern on Tarleton Lake on the Pike till

his death. Every stage and team that went down
or up the Pike stopped there to water the horses,
with water in which was thrown salt; and every
passenger had at least a hot drink. His hostelry
was famous for two generations, and all the while
there swung in the
breezes that swept over
Tarleton Lake the old
sign-board which is
shown here. It is an
oaken board on which
is painted on one side
an Indian and the name
William Tarlton and
date, 1774; on the
other a symbol of
Plenty. It is owned
by his grandson, Amos
Tarleton, of Haverhill,
to whose cordial inter-
est and intelligent help
I owe much of this
story of Haverhill's
coaching days.

Sign-board of Tarleton Inn.

The turnpike line
from Concord to
Haverhill was scarcely under way when a rival line
was started which came through Hanover, and connected with the stage line to New York. Others
followed with surprising quickness; the chief were
lines to Boston, New York, and Stanstead, Canada;
lesser lines of coaches ran to the White Mountains,

to Montpelier, Vermont, to Chelsea, Vermont, and elsewhere. The reason for this sudden growth of Haverhill was found in its position with regard to the neighboring country; the topography of upper New England made it a proper and natural travel centre.

As many coaches came into Haverhill every night and started out early the next morning, as many passengers changed coaches there, it can be readily seen that the need of taverns was great, and a number at once were opened. Often a hundred and fifty travellers were set down daily in Haverhill. The Bliss Tavern was one of the first to be built and is still standing, a dignified and comfortable mansion, as may be seen from its picture on page 314. Its landlord, Joseph Bliss, was a man of influence in the town, and held several important offices; his house was the headquarters where the judges of the court and the lawyers stopped when court was held; for Haverhill was a shire town, a county seat, from 1773. At some of the courts of the General Sessions of the Peace as many as twenty-two justices were present; and court terms were longer then than now, so justices, lawyers, clients, sheriffs, deputies, jurors, and witnesses came and remained in town till their law business was settled. Sometimes the taverns, were crowded for weeks. The court and bar had a special dining room and table at Bliss's Tavern, to which no layman, however high in social standing, was admitted. On Sundays all went to the old meeting-house at Piermont, where there was a " Judges' Pew."

Sometimes executions took place in town — a grand day for the taverns. When one Burnham was hanged there in 1805, ten thousand people witnessed the sight. Old and young, mothers with babes, lads and lasses, even confirmed invalids thronged to this great occasion.

Sign-board of Tarlton Inn.

Besides the court and its following, and the pampered travellers in stage-coaches, Haverhill taverns had by 1825 other classes of customers. Backward and forward from upper New Hampshire and Vermont to Boston, Portsmouth, and Salem, rolled the great covered wagons with teams of six or eight horses bearing the products of the soil and forest to the towns and the products of the whole earth in return. These wagons, which were the Conestoga wagons of Pennsylvania, made little appearance in New England till this century; they were brought there by the War of 1812; but they had there their day of glory and usefulness as elsewhere throughout our whole northern continent.

The two-wheeled cart of the earliest colonists, clumsily built and wasteful of power, was used long in New England for overland transportation; though the chief transfer of merchandise was in the winter by "sledding." There seems to have always been plentiful snow and good sledding every year in every part of New England in olden times, though it is far from being so to-day. The farmer, at that season of the year, had little else to do, and the ancient paths were soon made smooth by many sleighs and sleds.

Mr. Henry S. Miner gives me a very interesting account of these freight wagons in New England as he remembers them in ante-railroad days. Though the traffic was small in amount compared with that of the present day, it was carried on in a way which gave a sense of great life and action on the road. As even little towns furnished freight for several teams, the aggregate was large, and as they neared Boston the number of teams on the highway seemed enormous. These passed through towns on the turnpike every day, Sundays included. No vocation called for sturdier or better men. The drivers were almost invariably large, hearty, healthy Yankees, of good sense and regular habits, though they were seldom total abstainers. They could not be drunkards, for their life was too vigorous; long whip in hand, they walked beside their teams. The whip was a sign of office, seldom applied to a horse. They had to be keen traders, good merchants, to sell advantageously the goods they carried to town and to choose wisely for return trips. Country merchants seldom went to the cities, but depended wholly on these teamsters for supplies.

The wagons were of monstrous size, broad and high. Each horse had a ton of freight. No one was a regular teamster who drove less than four horses. But there were other carriers. A three-horse team called a "spike," a two-horse team

Bliss's Tavern.

called a "podanger," and a single horse with cart called a "gimlet," were none of them in favor with tavern-keepers or other teamsters. Still, if the smaller teams got stuck in the mud or snow, the regulars would good-humoredly help them out. Whatever accident happened to a teamster or his wagon or horses, his fellow-craftsmen assisted him, while stage-drivers, drovers, or any other travelling citizens were never looked upon for help.

An old man who drove one of these teams in his youth says : —

"When these large teams were hooked to the wagons, the starting word was 'whoo-up'; and the horses would at once place themselves in position. Then, 'Order, whope, *git*.' To turn to the left, 'Whoa, whoa,' softly; to the right, 'Geer there.' For a full stop, 'Whoa who-oof,' in louder voice, and all would come to a standstill. It was a fine sight to see six or eight good horses spread out, marching along in each other's steps, and see how quick they were to mind the driver's voice. Good drivers always spoke to their teams in a low voice, never shouted. The teamsters walked beside their teams, twenty miles a day the average. The reins were done up on each horse's hames, allowing them to spread apart with ease, a check-rein from the bit over the hames to keep them where they belonged. You could never teach a horse anything that wasn't checked up. The wagons weighed from eighteen hundred to twenty-two hundred pounds. Some wagons had an adjustable seat called a lazy-board."

With winter snows the wagons were generally housed; hundreds, yes, thousands of sleighs, pods, and pungs took their place. The farmer no longer sent to town by wagon and teamster; he carried his farm produce to town himself, just as his grandfather had in the days of the cart and sled before the Revolution. Winter brought red-letter days to the New England farmer; summer and autumn were his time of increase, but winter was his time of trade and of glorious recreation.

Friendly word was circulated from farm to farm, spread chiefly at the Sabbath nooning, that at stated

date, at break of day the long ride to market
would begin.   Often twenty or thirty neighbors
would start together on the road to town.   The two-
horse pung or single-horse pod, shod with steel shoes
one inch thick, was closely packed with farm wealth
— anything that a New England farm could produce that could be sold in a New England town.

Old Sleigh with Double Dashboard.

Frozen hogs, poultry, and venison ; firkins of butter,
casks of cheeses, — four to a cask, — bags of beans,
peas, sheep-pelts, deer hides, skins of mink, fox, and
fisher-cat that the boys had trapped, perhaps a
splendid bearskin, nuts that the boys had gathered,
shoe pegs that they had cut, yarn their sisters had
spun, stockings and mittens they had knitted, homespun cloth and linen, a forest of splint brooms

strapped on behind, birch brooms that the boys had whittled. So closely packed was the sleigh that the driver could not sit; he stood on a little semicircular step on the back of the sleigh, protected from the cutting mountain winds by the high sleigh back. At times he ran alongside to keep his blood briskly warm.

To Troy and Portland went some winter commerce, but Boston, Portsmouth, and Salem took far the greatest amount. On the old Cohos Turnpike trains of these farm sleighs were often a half mile long. The tavern-keepers might well have grown rich, had all these winter travellers paid for board and lodging, but nearly all, even the wealthiest farmers, carried their own provender and food. Part of their oats and hay for their horses sometimes was deposited with honest tavern-keepers on the way down to be used on the way home; and there was also plenty of food to last through the journey: doughnuts, cooked sausages, roast pork, " rye and injun " bread, cheese, and a bountiful mass of bean porridge. This latter, made in a tub and frozen in a great mass, was hung by loops of twine by the side of the sleigh, and great chunks were chopped off from time to time. This itinerant picnic was called in some vicinities tuck-a-nuck, an Indian word; also mitchin. It was not carried from home because tavern-fare was expensive, — a " cold bite " was but twelve and a half cents, and a regular meal but twenty-five cents; but the tavern-keeper did not expect to serve meals to this class or to such a great number of travellers. His profits were made on liquor he sold and sleeping room he gave. The latter was often simple enough. Great fires were built in barroom and parlor; each driver spread out a blanket or fur robe, and with feet to the fire, the semicircle slept the sleep of the healthy and tired and cider-filled. Ten cents this lodging cost; but the sale of rum and cider, toddy and flip, brought

Old Passenger Pung.

in dimes and dollars to the tavern-keeper. Many a rough story was told or old joke laughed at before the circle was quiet; quarrels, too, took place among so many strong and independent men.

It can readily be seen how important the tavern must have been in such a town as Haverhill, what a news centre, what an attraction, what an education. Newspapers were infrequent, but none were needed when newcomers from all points of the compass brought all there was to tell from everywhere. Mine host was the medium through which information was spread; he came into close contact with leaders in law, politics, and business, and dull he must have been if he did not profit in mental growth. But he could not be dull, he had to be companionable and intelligent; hence we find the tavernkeeper the leading man in town, prominent in affairs, and great in counsel, and it was to the stagecoach he owed much of his intelligence and influence.

CHAPTER XV

THE STAGE-DRIVER

IN a home-library in an old New England town there were for half a century two sets of books which seemed strangely alien to the other staid occupants of the bookshelves, which companions were chiefly rows of encyclopædias, Scott's novels, the *Spectator* and *Tatler*, a large number of books of travel, and scores of biographies, autobiographies and memoirs of pious "gospellers," English and American, chiefly missionaries. These two special sets of books were large volumes, but were not placed primly and orderly with others of their own size ; they were laid on their sides thrust high up among the smaller books on the upper shelves as if to escape notice under the frames of the glazed doors. They were strictly tabooed to all the younger members of the family, and were, indeed, well out of our reach ; but Satan can find library steps for idle and very inquisitive little souls to climb, and we had read them eagerly before we were in our teens. One set was that inestimable and valuable work *London Labour and London Poor*, which was held to be highly improper reading for the young, but which I found very entertaining, as being of

folk as remote from my life as if they were gnomes
and elves. The other volumes were Pierce Egan's
Book of Sports; and one, a prince of wicked books,
entitled *Life in London: or the Day and Night
Scenes of Jerry Hawthorne, Esq., and his elegant friend
Corinthian Tom accompanied by Bob Logic, the Oxonian,
in their Rambles and Sprees through the Metropolis.*
This also was by Pierce Egan.

Relay House.

That this latter most reprehensible book (from
the standard of the Puritan household in which it
was found) should have been preserved at all must
have been, I think, from the fact that the illustrations were by Cruikshank, and delightful pictures
they were. Though this book was so ill-regarded in
New England, its career in England was a most brilliant one. It was the most popular work in British

literature in the years 1820 to 1850 ; in fact, to many Englishmen it was *the* book, *the* literature, of the period.   One claim it has to the consideration of the reading public to-day : it is perhaps the best picture existing of Society, or, as it was termed in the words of the day, of " Life, Fashion, and Frolic," in the times of George IV.   Thackeray tells, in his article on George Cruikshank, of the lingering fondness he had for this old book, but even when he wrote could find no copy either in the British Museum or in London circulating libraries.   It was dramatized by several hands, and had long runs on the stage both in England and the United States ; and I do not doubt wealthy young men in the large American cities tried to emulate the sports of the London Tom and Jerry.   In the peculiar affectations of the bucks and bloods of that day, from the king down, shown in the love of all low sports, in association, even familiarity, with low sportsmen, and in the domination of the horse in sporting life, we see the reason for the high perfection and participation of the rich in coaching in England — a perfection which was aped in some respects in America.   Coaching is less talked about than other sports by Jerry and the elegant Corinthian Tom (whose surname is never once given), probably because their dissipations and sprees were those of the city, not of turnpike roads and green lanes.   But the life of the day, perhaps the idlest, most aimless era of fashion in English history, the life most thoroughly devoid of any spirituality or intellectuality, yet never exactly un-intelligent and never dull, lives forever in Pierce

Egan's pages; and lives for me with the intensity of reality from the eager imprinting on the fresh memory of a little child of unfamiliar scenes and incomprehensible words, knowledge even of whose existence was sternly forbidden.

I obtained from these books a notion of an English coachman, as an idealized being, a combination of Phœbus Apollo, a Roman charioteer, and the Prince Regent. I fancied our American coach-drivers as glorious likewise, though with a lesser refulgence; and I distinctly recall my disappointment at the reality of the first coachman of my first coach-ride from Charlestown, New Hampshire. A man, even on a day of Indian Summer, all in hide and fur: moth-eaten fur gloves, worn fur cap with vast ear-flaps and visor, and half-bare buffalo-hide coat, and out of all these ancient skins but one visible feature, a great, shining, bulbous nose. But even the paling days of stage-coaches were then long past; and the ancient coachman had long been shorn of his glory. In the days of his prime he was a power in the land, though he was not like the English coachman.

From Mr. Miner and others who remember the great days of stage-coach travel, I learn that our American drivers were a dignified and interesting class of men. Imposing in bearskin caps, in vast greatcoats, and with their teams covered with ivory rings, with fine horses and clean coaches, they and their surroundings were pleasant to the eyes. They acquired characteristic modes of speaking, of thinking. They were terse and sententious in expression,

had what is termed horse sense. They had prudence
and ability and sturdy intelligence. They carried
from country to town, from house to house, news
of the health of loved ones, or of sickness when
weary nurses were too tired to write. . A kindly
driver would stop his horses or walk them past a
lane corner where an anxious mother or sister waited,
dreading; and passengers in the coach would hear
him call out to her, " John's better, fever's all gone."

They were character-readers, of man and horse
alike. They had great influence in the community
they called home, and their word was law. They
were autocrats in their own special domain, and respected everywhere. No wonder they loved the life.
Harrison Bryant, the veteran Yankee whip, inherited
a fine farm in Athol. He at once gave up his hard
life as a driver, bade good-by to the cold and exposure, the long hours of work, the many hardships,
and settled down to an existence of sheltered prosperity. On the third day of his life on the farm he
stood at the edge of a field as a stage passed on the
road. The driver gave " the Happy Farmer " a
salute and snapped his whip. The horses started
ahead on the gallop, a passenger on top waved
good-by to him; the coach bounded on and disappeared. Farmer Bryant walked sombrely across
the field to his new home, packed his old carpet-bag,
went to the stage-office in the next town, and two
days later he swept down the same road on the same
coach, snapping his whip, waving his hand, leaving
the miles behind him. He was thus one week off
the coach-box, and at the end of his long life had a

The Relay.

well-established record of over one hundred and
thirty-five thousand miles of stage driving, more
than five times round the world.

A letter written by an " old-timer " says : —

" I remember many of the old stage-drivers. What a
line was the old ' accommodation ' put on by Gen. Holman and others ! What a prince of drivers was Driver
Day ! Handsome, dressy, and a perfect lady's man ! How
many ladies were attracted to a seat on the box beside him!
Then such a team, and with what grace they were guided !
How many young men envied his grace as a driver ! So,
also, what gentlemen were the tavern-keepers of that day !
They studied to please the public by their manners, though
behind the scenes some of them could spice their conversation with big words."

A very vivid description of the dress of the old
stage-drivers of Haverhill and other New Hampshire
towns was given me by Mr. Amos Tarleton, an
old inhabitant of the town. He says : —

" The winter dress of these old drivers was nearly all
alike. Their clothing was of heavy homespun, calfskin
boots, thick trousers tucked inside the boots, and fur-lined
overshoes over the boots. Over all these were worn Cana-
dian hand-knit stockings, very heavy and thick, colored
bright red, which came up nearly to the thighs, and still
over that a light leather shoe. Their coats were generally
fur or buffalo skin with fur caps with ear protectors, either
fur or wool tippets. Also a red silk sash that went round
the body and tied on the left side with a double bow with
tassels."

Can you not see one of those hairy old bears
peering out of his furs, vain in scarlet sash and

tassels, and with his vast feet planted on the dashboard? What were on his fore paws? double-pegged
mittens, leather gauntlets, fur gloves, wristlets, and
muffettees?

Mr. Twining declared that the skill of American
drivers equalled that of English coachmen, though
they had little of the smart appearance of the latter,
"neither having the hat worn on one side, nor
greatcoat, nor boots, but wearing coarse blue jackets, worsted stockings, and thick shoes."

A traveller calling himself a Citizen of the World,
writing in 1829, noted with pleasure that the drivers on American coaches neither asked for nor took
a fee, but simply wished the passengers a polite
good morning. Other Englishmen greeted this
fact with approval. Mr. Miner tells us "tipping"
was unknown — which was so customary, indeed so
imperative, in England. Sometimes travellers who
went frequently over the same route would make a
gift to the driver.

The custom of "shouldering," which was for the
coachman to take the fare of a way-passenger — one
who did not register or start at the booking-office
— and pocket it without making any return to the
coach agent or proprietor, was universal in England.
Some coach companies suffered much by it, and it
was a tidy bit of profit to the unscrupulous coachman. Shouldering was common also in the new
world, and called by the same name. There were
no "spotters" on coaching lines as on street railways.

As in every trade, profession, or calling, stage-
coaching had a vocabulary — call it coaching slang

View of Middletown, Connecticut.

if you will. Among English coachmen "skidding" was checking with a shoe or drag or "skid-pan" the wheels of the coach when going down hill, thus preventing them from revolving, and slackening the progress of the coach. "Fanning" the horses was, in coachman's tongue, whipping them; "towelling" was flogging them; and "chopping" the cruel practice of hitting the horse on the thigh with the whip. "Pointing" was hitting the wheeler with the point of the whip. A "draw" was a blow at the leader. If the thong of the whip lapped round any part of the harness, it was called "having a bite." "Throat-lashing" was another term.

Another and expressive use of the word bite was to indicate a narrow strip of gravel or broken stone on the near side of a winding road on a steep hill. The additional friction on the wheel on one side made a natural drag or brake, while the wheels of the ascending coach did not touch it.

The drivers on local lines grew to be on terms of most friendly intimacy with dwellers along the route. They bore messages, brought news, carried letters and packages, transacted exchange, and did all kinds of shopping at the citywards end of the route. An old coach-driver in Ayer, Massachusetts, told me with much pride that he always bought bonnets in Boston for all the women along his route who could not go to town; and that often in the spring the bandboxes were piled high on the top of his coach; that he never bought two alike, and that there wasn't another driver on the road that the women would trust to perform this important duty save himself.

The great bell-crowned hat which the driver wore in summer on lines leaving Boston often was crammed with papers and valuables, and one of the rules of the Eastern Stage Company at one time was, "No driver shall carry anything except in his pocket." It is said many of the drivers grew bald from the constant weight on their heads.

The constant imbibing of ale, brandy, and rum-and-milk by English coachmen at coaching inns was echoed in America by drivers at every tavern at which the stage-coach stopped. The driver was urged to drink by coach passengers who had far better have implored him not to drink. Many an old driver showed by the benignant purple glow of his nose that the importunities of the travellers had been duly silenced by more than ample hard cider, gin, and New England rum.

A great day on the coaches was when schoolboys and college boys went home on their vaca-
tions. The tops of the coaches were filled with
their square boxes, which packed like cord-wood.
On these boxes and within the coach swarmed the
boys, pea-shooters in hand. A favorite target was
the pike-keeper at the toll-gate, and those who left
the coach first fared worst. Our boys have but a
feeble imitation of these good times when they riot
into a railway car together for a few hours of hurried travel to their city homes.

The stage-drivers were universally kind and
careful of all children placed under their charge;
even young children, boys and girls, were intrusted
to their care.

One old gentleman tells me that in the days of
his youth he rode by stage-coach to and from school,
and so strong was his longing for a seafaring life,
with such a flavor of salt water and tar did he
englamour every unusual event, that it was inevitable
with the imaginativeness of a child he should compare this trip by stage to a sea voyage; the roads
and fields he mentally termed the ocean, the driver
was the captain, the inside of the coach the cabin,
the top the deck, and so on. He was honored by
having a seat with the driver; and as the day waned,
and the ship came to anchor, and all disembarked
for supper at a stage tavern, he was further honored
by eating supper with the driver and being treated
to a glass of toddy. After the coach was again
under way the driver had some tardy compunctions
that the toddy had been rather strong drink for a

growing boy, and said plainly that he feared the young traveller felt the liquor and might tumble from his high seat. He was not reassured when the boy answered dreamily, "Never mind, I can swim." After glancing sharply at him, the driver stopped his horses, and ignominiously forced the boy to descend and make the rest of the journey inside the coach.

Nothing is more marked than the changes in travelling-bags and trunks from those of stage-coach days. When our ancestors crossed the ocean they transported their belongings in wooden chests — common sea-chests and chests of carved wood. I have seen no mention of *trunks* in any old colonial inventories, though trunks existed and are named by Shakespere. These old trunks were metal coffers, and usually small. When Judge Sewall went to England in 1690, he bought trunks for his little daughters — trunks of leather or hide with their initials studded in metal nails. This shape of trunk lasted till the days of the railroad. Nearly all old families have one or more of these old trunks in their garrets. They were stout enough of frame, and heavy enough of frame to have lasted in larger numbers, and for centuries, but their heavy deerskin or pigskin covering often grew sorely offensive through harboring moths; and as they held but little, and were very heavy, they were of no use for a modern wardrobe. Their long narrow forms, however, were seen laden on every stage-coach, in company with carpet bags and leather sacks, and the schoolboy who owned one was a proud fellow.

An ancient travelling bag is shown on page 333. It is of a heavy woollen homespun stuff ribbed like corduroy, mounted with green leather bindings, straps, handles, etc. It is shaped like a mail-bag, and the straps laced through large eyelet holes.

Deer's Hide and Pigskin Trunks.

This bag is believed by its owners to have held the possessions of John Carver on the *Mayflower*.

Not only were stage-drivers respected by all persons in every community, but they had a high idea of their own dignity and of the importance of their calling. Little Jack Mendum, who drove the Salem mail-coach, did not deem it an exaggeration of his position when he roared out angrily in answer to a hungry passenger who kept urging him to drive faster, "When I drive this coach I am the whole United States of America."

One coachman who drove from Boston to Hartford was deeply tanned by summer suns and winter winds, and his mates spoke to each other of him as Black Ben. An English traveller, bustling out of the coach office with importance, shouted out: "I and my people want to go with Black Ben; are you the coachman they call Black Ben?" "Blackguards call me Black Ben," was the answer, "but gentlemen call me Mr. Jarvis."

The list of the coach-drivers employed by the Eastern Stage Company still exists, and has been printed by Mr. Rantoul. From it we learn that coach-driving went by families — it was an hereditary calling. Many families had two sons in this work, there were four Potter brothers, three Ackermans, and three Annables, all coachmen. Their names were often curious, Moses Caney, John Foss, Perley Annable, Eppes Potter, Ben Savory, Fortune Tozzer.

Mr. Miner writes thus of stage-terms and stage-horses : —

"Every horse had a name. It was 'Git up, Jo; gwan, boys or gals; you are shirky, Bill; you want touching up, Ben; if you don't do better, Ben, I'll swap you for a mule.' All kinds of expressions. Some drivers would fret a team to death, while others would get over the road and you would never hear hardly a loud word to the team. It was

just as drivers themselves were constituted.   All kinds of
horses were used in a stage team, runaways, kickers, biters,
and all kinds of tricksters.   If the owners could not manage them they went on stage teams, and did good work,
and never died.   They were seldom sick, as they were
well-fed and groomed, and had quick time and short trips.
We had some fine teams of matched horses, especially on
the Connecticut River roads, which would have sold for
seven hundred to a thousand
dollars a pair.   The horses
were usually what were
termed native horses, large,
full of muscle and gimp, of
English descent."

It was the testimony
of John Lambert, an
English gentleman who
travelled here in the early
years of this century, that
the horses used on
coaches in all settled
parts of the United States
were as good as English
coach-horses.

Old Carpet Bag.

It serves to show with force the pride and vanity
of coach owners and drivers to be told that on the
Boston and Salem line the coachmen sometimes
attached false sweeping tails to the horses, to dress
them up as it were and put on a good appearance
—this is ante- if not anti-docking days.

Elaborate rules for coach-driving are given in old-
time and modern manuals of coaching.   Mr. Fair-

man Rogers's descriptions are the plainest. Mr.
Miner tells very simply of the old modes of driving
in his day : —

"On four-horse teams were four reins. The near
wheel-horse rein came under the little finger of left hand,
the leader over the next finger. The off wheel-horse rein
over third finger, right hand, leader over first finger. Six
horses would require two more reins, and one more finger
on each hand. Some drivers would wear mittens, and have
one rein over and one under the fingers. These among
good reinsmen were called Dummies or old Farmers. The
whip was carried in the right hand, horizontally pointing
to the left, toward the ground, not as pictured at the present day. A good driver who was interested in his team
always sat up straight, and kept his reins and whip in a
stylish manner. He talked to his horses as he would to a
person. Every horse knew him; they knew him by his
voice whether they were late for cars or early, and just
where to make up time if late. A driver of this kind always
had a good team, able to respond under all conditions."

Even the whip of good drivers was of regulation
size. The rule of perfection was that it should be
five feet one and one-half inches from butt to holder
and twelve feet five inches long from holder to end
of point of lash — so it was an imposing machine.

On summer routes in the mountains of New
Hampshire the stage-driver lingered long. Over
the backbone of Vermont he guides in our own
day a few rusty coaches.

Among the popular stage-drivers of the New
Hampshire mountains before the advent of frequent
railroads, were Charles Sanborn, of Pittsfield, who

drove between Centre Harbor and West Ossipee; and H. P. Marden, who drove between Plymouth and the Profile House, White Mountains, during the summer months; and James F. Langdon, of Plymouth, — the three being among the last to give up the reins and the whip, when called to that far-away country "from whence no traveller returns." In 1861, Mr. Sanborn drove between Centre Harbor and North Conway, a distance of thirty-five miles. He drove over that route eleven years, at first requiring but forty horses, while in 1872 no less than one hundred and twenty were in constant use, besides a large number of coaches, wagons, and sleighs. On one of his round trips, Mr. Sanborn took three hundred and fifty dollars in passenger fares alone, while the express business was proportionately large. Of course all this seems small to those who know little of the days before railroads ran by every man's dooryard, but those who have "staged it" in the old times will understand what a busy time the driver on such a route must have had. Mr. Sanborn was over six feet in height and of Herculean frame, his broad shoulders and sturdy gait betokening a strength which gave his passengers the greatest confidence in his ability to carry them safely through any accident. He seldom lost his temper, even under the most trying circumstances, and was a jolly man withal. Major Lewis Downing of Concord tells me that on his route Sanborn had the good-will of every one, and in Pittsfield, where was his home, he was highly esteemed for his sterling character and strict integrity.

In England the coachmen and coaches had an Annual Parade, a coaching-day, upon the Royal Birthday, when coach-horses, coachmen, and guards all were in gala attire. In America similar annual meetings were held in many vicinities. In Concord, New Hampshire, which was a great coaching centre, an annual coaching parade was given in the afternoon and a "Stagemen's Ball" in the evening. "Knights of the whip" from New Hampshire and neighboring states attended this festival. The ball was held in the celebrated Grecian Hall — celebrated for its spring floor — which was built over the open carriage-houses and woodsheds attached to the Eagle Coffee-house, called now the Eagle Hotel. This dancing hall, built in 1827, took its name from the style of its architecture. At one end was a great painting of the battle of New Orleans, with Jackson on horseback. It was the rallying-point for all great occasions, — caucuses, conventions, concerts, even a six weeks' theatrical season.

Political economists solve the problem of a sudden loss of one trade by saying that others can easily be found. But it is difficult for a man learned in one handicraft to become proficient in others; and it is most difficult for the old or even middle-aged to learn a new trade.

No more melancholy example of an entire class of workmen deprived of work and subsistence through no fault of their own can be found than in these old coachmen, especially in England. Their work left them with astonishing rapidity, and they refused to realize the fact that their occupation was going out of existence, and that railroads would supersede coaches. In England the employment of the drivers of coaches on the railroads was almost unknown ; they ended their days as humble workers in stables or as omnibus drivers, or, worse still, upon carts working on the road ; sorry lives com-pared to the cheery work on a coach. A few took to farming, and made pretty poor work of it.

Sign of David Reed's Tavern.

In America, espe-cially in New England if they were young and strong and quick-witted enough to read coming events and ad-just themselves early in the day to altered conditions, they ob-tained positions on the railroads, as brakemen, conductors, ticket-sellers, express-agents, depot-masters, never as engineers — driving horses does not fit a man to drive an engine. Often these brakemen and conductors advanced in position as the railroads grew. It was not unusual a decade ago in the obituary notices of men who had acquired wealth through the railways, to read that these men had in early life been stage-drivers ; but they were usually men who had amassed some capital before the era of the railroad, or very young stage-drivers when steam carriage came.

Benjamin Pierce Cheney, one of the wealthiest men of Boston, an owner of vast railroad properties, founder of the rich Cheney Express Company, chief owner of the American Express Company, one of the Wells-Fargo Company, one of the builders of the Northern Pacific and other great Western railroads, began his business life a strong boy of seventeen driving the coach from Exeter, New Hampshire, to Nashua. For six years he drove fifty miles every day; then he became stage agent, and agent for the Lowell and Nashua Railroad, then railroad owner. Chester W. Chapin (afterwards president of the Boston and Albany Railroad) ran a stage line between Springfield and Hartford. The early members of the firm which formed Harnden's Express were nearly all connected with stage-coach lines.

Certainly much consideration was shown the old employees of the stage roads.

It was said by an old coachman of the Eastern Stage Company that all its men were given positions on the railroads if so desired; "All who wished had something to do," and facilities were given them also to benefit by the new railroads. For instance, after the steam cars were running between Salem and Boston the stage-drivers from Portsmouth and other towns were given free passes on the railroad. They could thus go to Boston and transact their old "errand-business," from which they had so much profit. The fast-growing express companies of

Harnden and Adams also employed many of the
old workers on the stage-coach lines. Some resisted
the new mode of travel. Major Shaw of Salem
threatened to ruin the railroad with a new opposition
stage line, but Americans in general have been ever
quicker to accept changes and innovations than the
English. They were more "uptaking," as the Scotch
say, — that is, quicker to perceive, accept, and adopt;
we breathe in that trait with the air of the new world;
so American coach employees accepted the railroad
and profited by it.

CHAPTER XVI

THE ROMANCE OF THE ROAD

THE traveller in the old stage-coach was not tantalized by the fleeting half-glimpse of places which we gain in railroad travel to-day. He had ample time to view any unusual or beautiful spot as he passed, he had leisure to make inquiry did he so desire, he had also many minutes, nay hours, to hear any traveller's tale that could be told him by a fellow-journeyer or by the driver. This last-named companion, going over the stage road day after day, talking constantly, querying frequently, grew deeply versed in its lore, its history. He knew the gossip, too, of each house he passed, he knew the traditions and tales of each locality; hence in his company every mile of the road had some point of deep interest.

Roger Mowry's Tavern was the first one established in the town of Providence. It escaped destruction in King Philip's War, when nearly all the town was burned, and stood till the present day. When a coach started out from that old tavern, it passed the burying ground and a dense growth of barberry bushes which grew along the roadside. There seems to have been, in many

places, a suspicion of uncanny reputation connected
with barberry bushes.   In one spot a dense group
of bushes was said to harbor a vast snake; in
another it shaded an Indian's grave; a third concealed a ghost.   The barberry was not a native of
America; it is an immigrant, and has the further ill
name of blasting any wheat near which it is planted.
The grewsome growth of barberry bushes near
Mowry's Tavern was the scene of the first serious
crime of the settlement of Providence Plantations.
The town carpenter, a thrifty and much respected
young man named Clauson, much beloved by Roger
Williams, was found dying one winter morning in
1660 near " a clump of barberry bushes " at the parting of the paths "near Roger Mowry's Tavern." His
head was cloven open with an axe, and the dying
man accused a neighbor named Herndon of being
the instigator of the crime; and with a spirit never
learned from his old master, the gentle Williams, he
left a terrible curse upon the children and children's
children of John Herndon, that they should ever
" be marked with split chins and be haunted by barberry bushes."   An Indian named Wanmanitt was
arrested for having done this terrible deed, and was
locked up in the Mowry Tavern.   He was probably
executed for it, though the town records only con-
tain a preliminary story of his trial.   With bills for
interpreters and for a boat and guard and powder
and shot and liquor, all to go with the prisoner to
Newport jail, the Indian murderer vanishes down
the bay out of history.   John Herndon lived on
peacefully for many years, branded, doubtless, in the

minds of many; but there is no record that the futile
imprecation of the dying man ever was fulfilled.

As the stage-coach runs along through old Narragansett, it comes to another scene of crime, of horrible crime and horrible punishment — that of hanging
in chains. This demoralizing sight was almost unknown in America. You can scarcely read a tale, a
history of old English life, without hearing of men
"hanging in chains." That most popular of children's books, *The Fairchild Family*, has a typical
English scene, wherein the solemn English father, in
order to make his children love each other the more,
takes them through a lonely wood to see the body
of a man hanging in chains on a gibbet, a horrible
and revolting sight. Travellers on the Portsmouth
Road in England, after the year 1786, passed at
Hind Head a gibbet with three men swinging in
chains, three barbarous murderers of an unknown
sailor — not a pleasant outlook for tired riders on
the coach. By the old South Ferry in Narragansett, a man was murdered by a fellow-traveller. At
the inn where they had rested the last night one of
them spent on this earth, a woman had dressed his
hair, and she noted a curious white lock which grew
like our artist Whistler's in a thick head of black
hair. On this single identification was built a chain
of evidence which ended in that unusual and terrible
sight in the new world, the body of a criminal hanging in chains. It swung there till the poor bones
dropped to the earth, and finally the great chains
rusted apart. Then schoolboys took the heavy
links which had bound a sight they had not seen,

and with equal bravado and apprehension cracked open their winter store of hickory nuts and butternuts with the last emblem of an obsolete law.

Not far from this scene is a crossroads which could be viewed from the stage-coach, but I trust no traveller saw there the execution of a law as obsolete and as barbaric as hanging in chains.

For on this crossroads took place several of those eccentric, ridiculous performances known as "shift-marriages." Any widow, about to be married again, could be free from all debts of her dead husband's contracting by being married at the crossroads, "clad only in her shift." Sometimes she was enjoined to cross the King's Highway four times thus scantily clad.

George Hazard, Justice, made entry in the town book of South Kingston, Rhode Island, that Abigail Calverwell on the 22d of February, 1719, was taken in marriage "after she had gone four times across the highway in only her shift and hair low and no other clothing." Think of this poor creature, on this winter's night, going through such an ordeal. Another Narragansett widow, Jemima Hill, was married at midnight "where four roads meet," clad only in her shift. Another entry in a town record-book specifies that the bride had "no other clothing but shifting or smock." Let me hasten to add that these marriages were not peculiar to Rhode Island; they took place in many of the colonies, certainly in Pennsylvania and in all the New England states.

As the old Narragansett coach sped on through Connecticut, it passed lonely spots which were noted

for other sad tales and traditions, but were ever of
keen interest to all passers-by. For at the crossroads " where four roads meet," were buried sui-
cides, with a stake thrust through the heart. This
was a cruel old English and Dutch law. We learn
from Judge Sewall all of the public obloquy and
hatred of a suicide in Massachusetts. One poor
fellow found dead was buried in disgrace under a
pile of stones at a Connecticut crossroads, but the
brand of self-destruction was taken from him at a
later date, when much evidence was secured that he
was murdered.

If our Narragansett coach went over the Ridge
Hill, the driver surely pointed out the spot where
a lover once hid his coach and horses till there rode
up from a bridle-path near by the beauty of Narragansett, " Unhappy Hannah Robinson," who
jumped from her horse into the coach and drove
off headlong to Providence to be married. An
elopement should end happily, but the adjective ever
attached to her name tells the tale of disappointment, and it was not many years ere she was borne
back, deserted and dying, lying on a horse-litter, to
the spacious old home of her childhood, which is
still standing. And one day down this road there
came hotly lashing his horses a gay young fellow
driving tandem a pair of Narragansett pacers, and
he scarcely halted at the tavern as he asked for the
home and whereabouts of the parson. But the
tavern loungers peeped under the chariot-hood and
saw a beautiful blushing girl, and they stared at a
vast, yawning, empty portmanteau, strapped by a

Midsummer along the Pike.

single handle to the chariot's back. And soon two angry young men, the bride's brothers, rode up after the elopers, who had been tracked by the articles of the bride's hastily gathered outfit which had been strewn from the open portmanteau along the road in the lovers' hasty flight. Who that rides on a railway car ever hears anything about elopements or such romances! Parson Flagg, of Chester, Vermont, made his home a sort of Yankee Gretna Green; the old stage-drivers could tell plenty of stories of elopers on saddle and pillion who rode to his door.

The traveller by the coach learned constant lessons from that great teacher, Nature. Even if he were city bred he grew to know, as he saw them, the various duties of country life, the round of work on the farm, the succession of crops, the names of grains, and he knew each grain and grass when he saw it, which few of city life do now. He saw the timid flight of wild creatures, rabbits, woodchucks, squirrels, sometimes a wily fox. My father once, riding on a stage-coach in Vermont, chased down a mountain road a young deer that ran, bewildered, before its terrible pursuer. At night the traveller heard strange sounds, owls and a smothered snarl as the coach entered the woods — a catamount perhaps. He heard the singing birds of spring and noted the game-birds of autumn; and in winter they could watch the broad and beautiful flight of the crows, free in snowy woods and fields from the rivalry of all fellow feathered creatures. He saw the procession of wild flowers, though he, perhaps, did not consciously heed them, and he knew the trees by name. The stage-driver showed his passengers "the biggest ellum in the county," and "the best grove of sugar-maples in the state." He pointed out a lovely vista of white birches as "the purtiest grove

A Vista of White Birches.

o' birch on the road," and there was a dense grove of mulberry trees, the sole survivors of silk-worm culture in which were buried so many hours and years of hard labor, so much hard-earned capital, so many feverish hopes. And towering a giant among lesser brothers, a glorious pine tree still showing the mark of the broad arrow of the King, chosen to be a mast for his great ships, but living long after he was dead and his ships were sunken and rotten, living to be a king itself in a republican land.

The foot-farer, trudging along the outskirts of the village, is often shut out by close stone or board barriers from any sight of the flowering country gardens, the luxuriance of whose blossoming is promised by the heads of the tall hollyhocks that bend over and nod pleasantly to him; but the traveller on the coach could see into these old gardens, could feast his eyes on all the glorious tangle of larkspur and phlox, of tiger lilies and candytuft, of snowballs and lilacs, of marigolds and asters, each season outdoing the other in brilliant bloom.

And what odors were wafted out from those gardens! What sweetness came from the lilacs and deutzias and syringas; from clove-pinks and spice bush and honeysuckles; how weird was the anise-like scent of the fraxinella or dittany; and how often all were stifled by the box, breathing, says Holmes, the fragrance of eternity! The great botanist Linnæus grouped the odors of plants and flowers into classes, of which three were pleasing perfumes. To these he gave the titles the aromatic, the fragrant, the ambrosial — our stage-coach traveller had them all three.

From the fields came the scent of flowering buckwheat and mellifluous clover, and later of newmown hay, sometimes varied by the tonic breath of the salt hay on the sea marshes. The orchards wafted the perfumes from apple blossoms, and from the pure blooms of cherry and plum and pear; in the woods the beautiful wild cherries equalled their domestic sisters.

How sweet, how healthful, were the cool depths of the pine woods, how clean the hemlock, spruce,

The Hollyhocks' Promise.

fir, pine, and juniper, and how sweet and balsamic their united perfume. And from the woods and roadsides such varied sweetness! The faint hint of perfume from the hidden arbutus in early spring, and the violet; the azalea truly ambrosial with its

The Cool Depths of the Pine Woods.

pure honey-smell; the intense cloying clethra with the strange odor of its bruised foliage; the meadow-sweet; the strong perfume of the barberry; and freshest, purest, best of all, the bayberry throwing off balm from every leaf and berry. Even in the late autumn the scent of the dying brakes and ferns were as beloved by the country-lover as the fresh smell of the upturned earth in the spring after the farmer's plough, or the scent of burning brush.

Fruit odors came too to the happy traveller, the faint scent of strawberries, the wild strawberry the most spicy of all, and later of the dying strawberry leaves; even the strong and pungent onions are far from offensive in the open air; while the rich fruity smell of great heaps of ripe apples in the orchards is carried farther by the acid vapors from the cider mills, which tempt the driver to stop and let all taste new apple-juice.

In the days of the stage-coach we had on our summer journeys all these delights, the scents of the wood, the field, the garden; we had the genial sunlight, the fresh air of mountain, plain, and sea; and all the wild and beautiful sights which made the proper time for travel — the summer — truly joyful. Now we may enjoy a place when we get there, but we have a poor substitute for the coach for the actual travelling — a dirty railway car heated almost to tinder by the sun, with close foul air (and the better the car the fouler and closer the air) filled, if we try to have fresh air, with black smoke and cinders; clattering and noisy ever, with occasional louder-shrieking whistles and bells, and some-

times a horrible tunnel — it has but one redeem-
ing quality, its speed, for thereby the journey is
shortened.

Cheerful friends on the old roads were the milestones and guideposts. Milestones had an assured
position in social life, a dignified standing. It would
be told of a road as a great honor and distinction,

Taylor's Tavern, 1777.   Danbury, Connecticut.

and told fitly in capitalized sentences thus, "This
Elegant road is fully Set with well-cut Milestones."
A few of the old provincial milestones remain, and
put us closely in touch with the past. In Governor
Hutchinson's day milestones were set on all the
post-roads throughout Massachusetts. Several of
these are still standing; one is in Worcester, in the
heart of the city, marked " 42 Mls. to Boston, 50

Mls. to Springfield, 1771." Another is in Sutton. It is five feet high and nearly three feet wide. It is marked "48 mls. to Boston. B. W." The letters B. W. stand for Bartholomew Woodbury, a genial tavern-keeper of Sutton. It shows a custom which obtained at that date. It was deemed most advantageous to a tavern to have a milestone in front of it. Possibly the tale of the stone shown in its lettering urged wayworn travellers to halt and rest within the welcoming door. Bartholomew Wood-

bury's Tavern was a few rods from the spot marked for the stone, but the government permitted him to set this stone by his doorside, at his own expense, beside the great horse-block. Tavern-keeper and tavern are gone, and the old road sees few travellers. Occasionally some passer-by, inquisitive like myself of

M. M. Taylor's Milestone.

the presence of the old stone, will halt as did the traveller of old, and pull away the curtain of vines, and read the lettering of this gravestone of the old Woodbury Tavern.

Another landlord who appreciated that the milestone served as a magnet to draw customers to the tavern taproom was Landlord Taylor, who kept the old tavern known as "Taylor's," in Danbury, Connecticut. The house with the milestone is shown on page 350 and the milestone alone on page 351.

Judge Peleg Arnold was one of the most active patriots in northern Rhode Island during the Revolution; for many years he carried on a tavern at Union Village, a suburb of Woonsocket, and his house was noted for its excellence and hospitality. Not far from his tavern to the northward the "Great Road" from Smithfield into Mendon wound through woods and meadows and over the northern hills of Rhode Island. In 1666 this great road was a small footpath through the woods, and was indicated by marked trees leading from cabin to cabin; but in 1733 it had taken upon itself the dignity of a cart-path and then became the subject of discussions on town-meeting days. Peleg Arnold had been one of the men to re-lay the old road, and it was near the northern boundary of his farm that he set up the old milestone shown here. For more than a hundred and twenty-five years this stone has served

Peleg Arnold's Milestone.

to brighten the hearts of travellers, for they have learned to know that this silent and inanimate guide can be relied upon as to distances with much more certainty than can the words of residents in the neighborhood.

When Benjamin Franklin was Postmaster-general, he set an indelible postmark in many ways on the history of our country; and many mementos of him still exist. Among them are the old milestones set under his supervision. He transacted this apparently prosaic business with that picturesque originality which he brought to all his doings and which renders to every detail of his life an interest which cannot be exceeded and scarcely equalled by the events recorded of any other figure in history.

He drove over the roads which were to be marked by milestones, seated in a comfortable chaise, of his own planning, and followed by a gang of men, and heavy carts laden with the milestones. Attached to the chaise was a machine of his invention which registered by the revolution of the wheels the number of miles the chaise passed over. At each mile he halted, and a stone was dropped which was afterward set. The King's Highway, the old Pequot Trail, was thus marked and set. A few of these milestones between Boston and Philadelphia are still standing, one in New London, another at Stratford, and are glanced at carelessly by the hundreds of thousands who glide swiftly past on wheels bearing more accurate cyclometers than that of Franklin.

Guide-boards always stood at the crossings of all travelled roads ; indeed, they stood where the roads were scarce more than lines among the grass and low shrubs. Since our day of many railroads, and above all, since the interlacing network of trolley lines has spread over all our Eastern lands where once the stage-coach ran, many guide-boards have disappeared and have not been replaced. You find them often at the angles of the road lying flat in grass and bushes ; or standing split, one-sided, askew, pointing the road to the skies, or nowhere. When in trim and good repair in the days of their utility and helpfulness, they were friendly things, and the pointing hand gave them a half-human semblance of cheerful aid. Where the road led through woods or rarely frequented ways, they were friends indeed, for all ways looked alike, and one might readily go far astray. The mile of the guide-board was an elastic one, and sometimes a weary one.

Guide-boards, even poor ones, are still most welcome. No one in the country ever has any correct estimate of distances ; a distance " a little better than three miles " before you usually increases by an extraordinary law instead of decreases after you have driven nearly a mile to " about four mile." The next road-jogger says " nigh on to a mile " ; and then you may be sure a few hundred feet farther on to jump back to a slow and wise rejoinder of the original distance, " hard on to four mile."

Another wayside friend of the traveller in coaching days was the watering trough. It was frequently a log of wood hollowed out, Indian fashion, like a dug-out, filled with the lavish bounty of untrammelled Nature by a cool pure rill from a hillside spring. One of these watering troughs is shown on this page. In the days of the glory of the stage-coach and turnpike, fine stone troughs chiselled like an Egyptian sarcophagus took the place of the

The Watering Trough.

log dug-out. They had their supply from a handled pump, which was a more prosaic vehicle than the pipe made of hollowed tree-trunks which brought the spring-water; but it had also a certain interest as the water spouted out in response to the vigorous pumping, and it has been immortalized by Hawthorne. Our artesian wells, and sunken pipes, and vast reservoir systems are infinitely better than the old-time modes of water supply, but we miss the

pleasure that came from the sight of the water,
whether it was borne to us on the picturesque well-
sweep by wheel and bucket, or old chain pump; it
was good to look at as well as to taste, and it refreshed man even to see cattle and horses drinking
from the primitive trough.

There is always something picturesque and pleasant in an old bridge, and of historic associations as
well.   The great logs such as form a wooden bridge
over a narrow stream are the most natural water-
spans, those of the primitive savages.   By fallen
tree-trunks placed or utilized by the Indians, the
colonists first crossed the inland streams, adding
parallel trunks as years passed on and helping
hands multiplied; and finally placing heavy, flat
cross-timbers and boards when hand-saws and saw-
mills shaped the forests' wealth for domestic use.

The old arched stone bridges are ever a delight
to the eye and the thoughtful mind.   Look at the
picture of the old Topsfield Bridge shown on the
opposite page.   It was built in 1760 over the Ipswich
River.   It shows the semicircle — simplest of all
arched forms — which is happily within the compass
and ever the selection of rustic builders.   The
shallow voussoirs speak of security and economy
rather than of monumental effect; the irregular
shape and size of the stones tell a similar tale, that
there was ample and fitting material near by, in
every field.   The arched stone bridge is a primitive
structure; the sort of construction that may be
found in the so-called " Cyclopean " walls of earliest
Greece; and this very simplicity is a distinct beauty,

that, added to its fitness and durability, makes the bridge a thing of satisfaction.

How charming are the reflections in the stilly waters, the arch making the perfect circle, ever an

Topsfield Bridge.

attractive and symbolic form. How cool and beautiful is the shadowy water under these stone arches; but it cannot be reached by the rider in stage-coach or on horseback, as can the brook spanned by a wooden bridge. This has often a

watering place which spreads out on one side
of the road, a shoal pool of clear, crystal, dancing
water. The bottom is cut with the ruts of travellers'
wheels, but the water is pure and glistening; the
pool is edged heavily with mint and thoroughwort
and a tangle of greenery pierced with a few glorious
scarlet spires of cardinal flowers, and some duller
blooms. How boys love to wade in these pools,
and dogs to swim in them, and horses to drink from
them. The wooden bridge seems in midsummer a
useless structure, fit only to serve as a trellis for
clematis and sweet brier and many running vines,
and to be screened with azalea, clethra, and elder,
and scores of sweet-flowered shrubs that add their
scent to the strong odor of mint that fills the air, as
the sensitive leaves are bruised by careless contact.

There was a closeness of association in stage-
coach travel which made fellow-passengers companionable. One would feel a decided intimacy with
a fellow-sufferer who had risen several mornings in
succession with you, at daybreak, and ridden all
night, cheek by jowl. Even fellow-travellers on
short trips entered into conversation, and the characteristic inquisitiveness was shown. Ralph Waldo
Emerson took great delight in this experience of his
in stage-coach travel. A sharp-featured, keen-eyed,
elderly Yankee woman rode in a Vermont coach
opposite a woman deeply veiled and garbed in
mourning attire, and the older woman thus entered
into conversation: " Have you lost friends ? "
" Yes," was the answer, " I have." " Was they
near friends ? " " Yes, they was." " How near

The Shadowy Water under the Arches.

was they?" "A husband and a brother." "Where
did they die?" "Down in Mobile." "What did
they die of?" "Yellow fever." "How long was
they sick?" "Not very long." "Was they seafaring men?" "Yes, they was." "Did you save
their chists?" "Yes, I did." "Was they hope-
fully pious?" "I hope so." "Well, *if you have
got their chists* (with emphasis) and they was hope-
fully pious, you've got much to be thankful for."
Perhaps this conversation should be recorded in
the succeeding chapter, but in truth the pleasures and pains of stage-coach travel ran so closely
side by side that they can scarce be separated.
Many pleasant intimacies and acquaintances were
begun on the stage-coach; flirtations, even court-
ships, were carried on. One gentleman remembers that when he was a big schoolboy he rode on
the coach from Pittsfield, New Hampshire, to
Dover, and he cast sheep's-eyes at a pretty young
woman who was a fellow-passenger. He had just
gathered courage to address her with some bold,
manly remark when the coach stopped and a
middle-aged man of importance entered. Soon all
other passengers got out and the three were left
in the coach; and the Boy heard the Man recall himself to the Girl as having been her teacher
when she was a child. He soon proceeded to
make love to her, and made her a proposal of
marriage, which she did not refuse, but asked a
week's time to consider. "And during all this
courting," said my informant, with indignant remi-
niscence after fifty years, "they paid no more atten-

tion to my presence than if I had been Pickwick's Fat Boy."

The pleasures of coaching days have been written by many an English author in forcible and beautiful language. Thomas De Quincey sang in most glowing speech the glories of the English mail-coach. He says:—

"Modern modes of travelling cannot compare with the old mail-coach system in grandeur and power. They boast of more velocity, not, however, as a consciousness, but as a fact of our lifeless knowledge, resting upon *alien* evidence; as, for instance, because somebody *says* that we have gone fifty miles in the hour, though we are far from feeling it as a personal experience; or upon the evidence of a result, as that we actually find ourselves in York four hours after leaving London. Apart from such an assertion, or such a result, I myself am little aware of the pace. But seated on the old mail-coach we needed no evidence out of ourselves to indicate the velocity. . . . The vital experiences of the glad animal sensibilities made doubts impossible on the question of our speed. We heard our speed, we saw it, we felt it a-thrilling; and this speed was not the product of blind insensate energies that had no sympathy to give, but was incarnated in the fiery eyeballs of the noblest among brutes, in his dilated nostril, his spasmodic muscles and thunder-beating hoofs."

Nothing more magnificent and inspiring could be written than his *Going Down with Victory* — the carrying the news of the victory at Waterloo on the mail-coach to English hamlets and towns; it is a gem of English literature.

CHAPTER XVII

THE PAINS OF STAGE-COACH TRAVEL

IN describing the pleasures and pains, the delights and dangers, the virtues and vicissitudes of the travel of early days by stage-coach in America, I have chosen to employ largely the words and descriptions of contemporary travellers rather than any wording of my own, not only because any such description of mine would be simply a transcription of their facts, but because there is a sense of closeness of touch, a pleasant intimacy, and indeed a profound sympathy thereby established with those old travellers and modes of travel which cannot be obtained by modern wording; nor indeed can their descriptions and travellers' tales be improved. Careless or ignorant writers often portray early stage-coach travel in America in the same terms as would be used of similar travel in England, and as having the same accessories; it was in truth very different in nearly all of its conditions, as different as were the vehicles used in America.

I do not believe that travellers in coaching days found much pleasure in long journeys by stage-coach. They doubtless enjoyed short trips, or possibly a day on a coach, as we do now, but

serious travel was serious indeed. In winter it
must have appeared a slow form of lingering death.

Grant Thorburn, the New York seedsman, tells
of the first journey he ever made by land. It was in
the winter of 1831; he was then fifty-eight years old.

"We left Hoboken with about fifteen passengers closely
packed in a stage with wheels, and a very neat coach, and
so foolish was I and ignorant (never having travelled on
land) I thought this same fine close carriage would go
through thick and thin with me all the way to Albany:
in two short hours my eyes were opened. We stopped in
Hackensack at a tavern grocery grogshop and post-office
all under one roof, for we carried Uncle Sam's letter bags,
which was another grievance, as we had to stop every few
miles to change the mails. The keeper of the office began
to bluster and swear he had neither carriages covered or
uncovered to forward so many passengers. He said the
Jockey Club in New York took all the money and gave
him all the trouble. In short, says he, unless you remain
here till four o'clock P.M. you must go on with such
conveyance as I can furnish. We applied to our Hoboken
driver. He said his orders were to drop us at Hackensack and bring back the coaches; and sure enough he
turned about and back he went. I stepped into the barroom — a large place. In the centre stood a large old-
fashioned tin-plate stove, surrounded by fifteen or twenty
large lazy fellows. After waiting an hour we were sent forward, viz. two in an open chair, four in an open wagon, and
the remainder, eight I think, in a common Jersey farming
wagon, all the machines being without covers. It now
commenced raining, and by the time we got to the next
stage, we looked like moving pillars of salt, our hats and
coats being covered to the thickness of an eighth of an inch
with ice transparents. At the town of Goshen we changed

Dalton Winter Stage.

the mail, thawed our garments, and ate our dinner.   As we got north the sleighing got better, so we were accommodated with a covered box and runners, but alas! it was like the man's lantern without a candle.   The cover was of white wood boards placed a quarter of an inch apart without paint, leather, or canvas to protect them from the weather.

"We travelled all night.   The rain and snow descending through the roof, our hats were frozen to our capes, and our cloaks to one another.   In the morning we looked like some mountain of ice moving down the Gulf Stream. I thought the machine used at the Dry Dock would have been an excellent appendage to have lifted us bodily into the breakfast room : and this is what the horse-flesh fraternity in New York advertise as their *safe*, *cheap*, *comfortable*, and expeditious winter establishment for Albany."

This latter account is certainly a hard blow to the lover of the " good old times."   Of tough fibre and of vast powers of endurance, both mental and physical, must have been our grandfathers who dared to travel overland in winter time.   Coaches were often " snowed up " and had to be deserted by the passengers, who were rescued in old pods and pungs, such as are shown on pages 316 and 318, and the journey had to be continued in some of the awkward coach-bodies or " boobies " set on runners like those on pages 362 and 364.   Coaches were also overturned or blown off bridges by heavy winds.

Somewhat varied was Captain Hall's experience on the trip from Fredericksburg to Richmond during the following January.   The stage-coach was appointed to start at 2 A.M., but at the blank looks of the captain, the stage agent said, " Well, if it is so disagreeable to the ladies, suppose we make it five?" The fare was five dollars. It took seventeen hours to travel the sixty-six miles, and the coach stopped at ten taverns on the way. At each his fellow-passengers all got out and took a mint

Chepachet Winter Stage.

julep; perhaps he did likewise, which might account for the fact that he pronounced the trip a pleasant one, though it rained; "your feet get wet; your clothes become plastered with mud from the wheel; the trunks drink in half a gallon of water apiece; the gentlemen's boots and coats steamed in the confined air; the horses are draggled and chafed by the traces; the driver got his neckcloth saturated"—

and yet, he adds, "the journey was performed pleasantly."

There were days in July, in midsummer, when in spite of the beauties of Nature, the journey by stage-coach on the unwatered roads was not a thing of pleasure. Whether on "inside" or "outside," the traveller could not escape the dust, nor could he escape the fervor of the July sun. And when the eye turned for relief to green pastures and roadsides, there was reflected back to him the heated gold of the sunlight, for the fields flamed with yellow and orange color. Sometimes accidents occurred. One may be described, using the contemporary account of it to show what danger was incurred and through what motive powers. In January, 1823, there was a sharp competition between the two stage lines running between Albany and New York, and apparently the stage-drivers on the rival lines could no more be kept from racing than the old-time steamboat captain. The accident was thus told in a newspaper of the day : —

" *To the Public :* The stage from New York to Albany was overset on the Highlands, on Friday last, with six passengers on board ; one of whom, a gentleman from Vermont, had his collar-bone broken, and the others were more or less injured, and all placed in the utmost jeopardy of their lives and limbs by the outrageous conduct of the driver. In descending a hill half a mile in length, an opposition stage being ahead, the driver put his horses in full speed to pass the forward stage, and in this situation the stage overset with a heavy crash which nearly destroyed it, and placed the wounded passengers in a dreadful dilemma, especially as the driver could not assist them, as it required all his efforts to restrain the frighted horses from dashing down the hill which must have destroyed them all.   It was, therefore, with the greatest difficulty, and by repeated efforts, the wounded passengers extricated themselves from the wreck of the stage.   Such repeated wanton and wilful acts of drivers to gratify their caprice, ambition, or passions, generally under the stimulus of ardent spirits, calls aloud on the community to expose and punish these shameful aggressions."

It should be added, in truth, that accidents on stage-coaches were seldom with fatal results.   Stage-coach travel was more disagreeable than deadly.   A stage-coach driver who had driven three hundred days a year for thirty-five years, could boast that there had never been a serious accident while he was driving, and scarcely any injury had been received by any passenger.

Before the days of the turnpike the miserable bridges, especially of the Southern colonies, added to the terrors of travel, though I have not learned of frequent accidents upon them.   The poet Moore wrote in the year 1800 of Virginia bridges : —

> " Made of a few uneasy planks
>   In open ranks,
>   Over rivers of mud."

Near Fayetteville, North Carolina, in 1812, a traveller by coach thus found the bridge : —

"Three large logs were stretched across the creek, called sleepers, and these supported a number of misshapen pieces called rafters, thrown on at random, without being

fixed either by nails or pins.   They had been disturbed by
a freshet, and the driver alighted to adjust them.   On
entering the bridge, the fore wheels gathered the rafters
in a heap which stopped the progress of the coach.   This
was just as the driver was whipping up the fore horses.
They sprang forward, and disengaging themselves with a
jerk, by pulling out the staple of the main singletree, they
set off at full speed with the singletree rattling at their
heels."

One horse was killed, the patient passengers
alighted and pulled the coach free themselves.   At
the next creek the horses plunged in the water and
swam across, while the passengers held up the mail-
bags to keep them dry.   Weld tells of similar
bridges and experiences in 1795 in Virginia.

Many of the bridges were rickety floating bridges.
Mr. Twining experienced the sense of insecurity,
the dread of sinking, which I have also felt in crossing a floating bridge in a heavy vehicle.

Mr. Twining tells also of the constant necessity
of trimming and balancing of the stage-wagon by
all the passengers leaning to one side to prevent it
from overturning in the deep ruts which abounded.
Mr. Weld wrote that the driver " frequently called
out, ' Now, gentlemen, to the right,' upon which all
the passengers stretched their bodies halfway out of
the carriage to balance on that side.   ' Now, gentlemen, to the left,' and so on."

One traveller tells of a facetious travelling companion, —

" ' A son of Neptune and of Mars also,' and could
adapt the technical language of these professions to the

different movements of the stage. When the coach heeled to one side he would call out, ' To the right and left and cover your flanks — Whiz ! ' — and when we passed a stream or ford he would sing out, ' By the deep nine,' accompanied with all the movements of heaving the lead. The day was clear, pleasant, and healthy ; and in this strain of merriment and good humor we prosecuted our journey much to our satisfaction."

Folk were easily amused in coaching days. One of the old stage-drivers tells the following incident of stage travel. He was driving from Dover, New Hampshire, to Haverhill, Massachusetts. During the spring months the roads were often in a bad condition, and six horses and sometimes ten were needed to draw the coach. In Epping, New Hampshire, was a particularly hard place, locally known as the "Soap mine." Through this mine of mud the driver hoped to guide his coach and six. But the coach was heavily loaded, and in spite of the efforts of the skilful driver the team was soon fast in the mud, the wheels settling to the hubs. All attempts of the horses to start the coach were in vain. The driver finally climbed down from his seat, opened the coach door and told the passengers the condition of things, and politely asked them to get out and thereby lighten the load. This they all positively refused to do ; they had paid their fares and did not think it their duty to get out into the mud. The driver said, "Very well," quietly closed the door, and seated himself by the roadside. In a few minutes the passengers asked, "What are you doing there ? "

J. H. & I. COOKE,

Coach Makers,

RESPECTFULLY inform the public that they continue to carry on the Coach-making business, in all its branches. They have on hand, finishing, a great variety of the most fashionable GIGS and CHAISES, of every description, which they offer to the public on the most liberal terms, for cash or approved credit. Those who wish to purchase are requested to call and examine their work and materials.

An active LAD, about the age of fifteen, will find good encouragement at the above business.

May 15. 64

STEAM-BOAT HOTEL,
WATER STREET, New-Haven.
MRS. A. BABCOCK.

HAS removed her establishment from the New-England Coffee-House, in Church-St. New-Haven, to that large and commodious house in Water-Street, near Tomlinson's Bridge, formerly owned and occupied by Mr. Platt. This house, being located, near the place where the Steam-Boat FULTON arrives, affords to Gentlemen and Ladies, who may be travelling to and from New-York, conveniences equal to other public houses in this city. Every attention will be paid to her guests to render their stay agreeable. The best of liquors kept constantly on hand.

She returns her thanks to those who encouraged her former establishment, and will spare no pains to merit a patronage of her present one.

Gentlemen and Ladies who may visit the sea shore for their health, can be accommodated in no better situation than hers, as it directly fronts the Sound, in view of all vessels passing and repassing, and during the summer season is delightfully situated to receive refreshing breezes from the sea.

June 12. tf 85

WAGGONS
ON AN IMPROVED PLAN.

THE objection to waggons as a pleasure carriage, has been for the want of an easy motion, the difficulty in getting in and the rattling—Those who are in want of Carriages of the above description, will find those difficulties which attend waggons, obviated, by calling at the shop of the subscriber—The principle on which Waggons can be built, is much lighter than those of other carriages; they can be built in a handsome style, for one or two horses, at much less expence; besides the consideration that it does not cost so much to keep them in repair—Other Carriages made as usual, and all Repairing done on the shortest notice.

N. B. All orders thankfully received and punctually attended to, by the public's humble servant,

JAMES BREWSTER.

Elm-st. North of the Colleges,
Dec. 12, 1814. tf 59

WAGGONS FOR SALE.

THE subscriber has on hand, and now finishing, at the new building directly opposite the public Well, in Broadway, a great variety of one and two-horse WAGGONS, which are warranted to be finished as substantial and neat as any others which can be purchased elsewhere, and are offered for sale at a reasonable price.

ALSO, FOR SALE,

A variety of HARNESES.

Several second hand Chaises and Waggons

JAMES HEADLEY, Jun.

N. B. Cash paid for White Oak Spokes, Ash and Oak Plank.

New-Haven, June 12. 85

STEAM-BOAT FULTON.

For the better accommodation of the public, the proprietors of the Steam-Boat FULTON, have determined to run her six times a week between New-York and New-Haven. This new arrangement commenced on Monday, the 12th inst. The days of starting are as follows, viz:—From New-York every Monday, Wednesday and Friday morning: from New-Haven every Tuesday, Thursday and Saturday morning.

June 30. 88

WAGGON TO LET.

A GENTEEL one horse Waggon to let, by D. S. GLADDING.

Chapel-Street, June 19. 86

WANTED,

Advertisements from Connecticut Journal, July 3, 1815.

The driver calmly replied : " The horses cannot draw the load. There is only one thing I can do. I shall wait until the mud dries up."

It is needless to say that they did not wait for the mud to dry.

The state of the roads and the regard of some persons for stage-coach travelling is shown in a letter written early in this century by a mother to a girl of eighteen, visiting at Cambridge, and impatient to return home. As the roads were bad her father delayed his going for her. Her mother says : —

"Your papa would not trust your life in the stage. It is a very unsafe and improper conveyance for young ladies. Many have been the accidents, many the cripples made by accidents in those vehicles. As soon as your papa can go, you may be sure he will go or send for you."

There was one curious and most depressing, even appalling, condition of stage-coach travel. It seemed to matter little how long was your journey, nor where you were going, nor whence you started, your coach always started before daybreak. You had to rise in the dark, dress in the dark most feebly illumined, eat a hurriedly prepared breakfast in the dark, and start out in the blackness of night or the depressing chill of early morning. We read that the greatest number of deaths take place in the early morning, at daybreak, and it is not surprising, since it is the time, of all the hours of the day, when earth offers the least to the human soul to tempt it to remain here. It is no unusual thing to read in travellers' accounts of journeys by stage-coach, of riding ten miles on the coach, and then — breakfasting. We cannot wonder, therefore, at the records of incessant dram-drinking during coach travel which we always find in any minute accounts.

An English eye-witness, Captain Basil Hall, thus described the beginning of a trip from Providence to Hartford in October, 1829 : —

" The nominal hour of starting was five in the morning; but as everything in America comes sooner than one expects, a great tall man walked into the room at ten minutes before four o'clock to say it wanted half an hour of five : and presently we heard the rumbling of the stage coming to the door upwards of thirty minutes before the time specified. Fortunately there were only five passengers, so we had plenty of room; and as the morning was fine we might have enjoyed the journey much, had we not been compelled to start so miserably early. At the village of Windham we dined in a cheerful sunny parlour on a neatly dressed repast excellent in every way, and with very pleasant chatty company."

So forehanded were American coach-agents and coach-drivers that such premature starts were not infrequent. Many a time an indignant passenger, on time, but left behind, was sent off after the coach in a chaise with a swift horse at full gallop.

Josiah Quincy tells thus of a trip on the Lancaster road during the winter of 1826 : —

" At three o'clock this morning the light of a candle under the door and a rousing knock told me that it was time to depart, and shortly after I left Philadelphia by the

"A Wet Start at Daybreak."

Lancaster stage, otherwise a vast illimitable wagon, capable of holding some sixteen passengers with decent comfort to themselves, and actually encumbered with some dozen more. After riding till eight o'clock we reached the breakfast house, where we partook of a good meal."

Longfellow wrote of his first acquaintance, in the year 1840, with the Wayside Inn, otherwise Howe's Tavern, at Sudbury, Massachusetts: "The stage left Boston about three o'clock in the morning, reaching the Sudbury Tavern for breakfast, a considerable portion of the route being travelled in total darkness, and without your having the least idea who your companion might be."

Charles Sumner, writing in 1834 of a trip to Washington, says: "We started from Boston at half-past three Monday morning with twelve passengers and their full complement of baggage on board, and with six horses. The way was very dark, so that, though I rode with the driver, it was some time before I discovered we had six horses."

The unfortunate soul who wished or was forced to travel from Boston to New York in 1802 was permitted a very decent start at ten in the morning. He arrived in Worcester at eight at night. Thereafter at Worcester, Hartford, and Stamford he had to start at three in the morning and ride till eight at night. We can imagine his condition when arriving in New York. The Lancaster and Leominster stages left Boston at sunrise. John Melish, the English traveller, in 1795, was called to start at two in the morning, when he set out from Boston to New York. Badger and Porter's Stage Register

for 1829 gives the time of starting of the stage to
Fitchburg as 2 A.M.; the Albany stage was the same
hour.   The stage for Keene set out at 4 A.M., and
the one for Bennington at 2 A.M.   The stage for
Norwich, Connecticut, in 1833 started at 3 A.M.
In 1842, the Albany coach left at 4 A.M.   When
we remember the meagre "light of other days," the
pale rays of a candle, usually a tallow one, the
smoky flicker of a whale-oil lamp, the dingy shadow
of an ancient lantern, we can fancy the gloom of
that early morning departure; and when it was
made in snow, or fog, or rain, there seemed but
scant romance in travel by stage-coach.   A fine
picture by Mr. Edward Lamson Henry, "A Wet
Start at Daybreak," is reproduced opposite page 370.
It is interesting and picturesque — to look at; but
it was not interesting to experience.

The Wayside Inn.

CHAPTER XVIII

KNIGHTS OF THE ROAD

IT is impossible to read of the conditions of life on the public highway in England and not wonder at the safety and security with which all travel was carried on in the American colonies. In Great Britain shop-robbing, foot-padding, street assaults, and highway robberies were daily incidents. Stage-coach passengers were specially plundered. From end to end of England was heard the cry of "Stand and deliver." Day after day, for weeks together, the Hampstead, Islington, Dover, and Hackney coaches were stopped in broad daylight, and the passengers threatened and robbed. The mail from Bristol to London was robbed every week for five weeks. Scores of prisoners were taken, and scores more strung up on the gallows; many were shipped off to the Plantations because on hanging day at Tyburn, there was not room enough on the gallows for the convicted men. All classes turned outlaws. Well-to-do farmers and yeomen organized as highwaymen in the Western counties under the name of "the Blacks." Justices and landed gentry leagued with "the Owlers" to rob, to smuggle, and defraud the customs. Even Adam Smith confessed to a weakness for smuggling.

Travellers journeyed with a prayer-book in one hand and a pistol in the other. Nothing of this was known in America. Citizens of the colonies travelled unhampered by either religion or fear. Men and women walked through our little city streets by night and day in safety. The footpads and highwaymen who were transported to this country either found new modes of crimes or ceased their evil deeds.

Not only on convict ships came highwaymen to America. As redemptioners many rogues came hither, sure thus of passage across-seas and trusting to luck or craft to escape the succeeding years of bound labor. Among the honest men seized in English ports, kidnapped, and shipped to America were found some thieves and highwaymen, but all — whether "free-willers," convicts, or "kids" — seemed to drop highway robbery in the new world. We were nigh to having one famous thief. Great Moll Cutpurse, had her resources been of lesser sort, had been landed in Virginia, for she was trapanned and put aboard ship, but escaped ere ship set sail. Perhaps 'twould have been of small avail, for in Virginia, with its dearth of wives, even such a sturdy jade as Moll, "a very tomrig and rumpscuttle," sure had found a husband and consequent domestic sobriety.

There was one very good reason why there was little highway robbery in America. Early in our history men began to use drafts and bills of exchange, where the old world clung to cash. English travellers persisted in carrying gold and banknotes, while we carried cheques and letters of credit.

To this day the latter form of money-transfer is more common with Americans than with the English. Express messengers in the far West carrying gold did not have to wait long for a Jesse James.

But our typical American scamp has ever been the tramp, formerly the vagabond, not the highwayman; though the horse thief kept him close companion.

By this absence of the highwaymen, our story of the road has lost much of its picturesqueness and color. I have envied the English road-annalists their possession of these gay and

Sign-board of Perkins Inn, Hopkinton, New Hampshire.

dashing creatures. Their reckless buoyancy, their elegance, their gallantry, their humor, make me long to adopt them and set them on our staid New England roads or on Pennsylvania turnpikes. Dick Turpin, Claude Duval, Beau Brocade — how I should love to have them hold up Benjamin Franklin or John Adams!

There was no lack of rogues in the colonies, but their roguery did not take the outlet of highway robbery. One Henry Tufts, a famous vagabond, has left an amusing and detailed history of his life and deeds. He stole scores of horses by sneaking methods, but never by open seizure on the road. He began his wrong-doing after the universal custom of all bad boys (but why be invidious ? — of all good boys, too), by robbing orchards. He soon raised himself to be a leader in deviltry by the following manœuvre. A group of bad boys were to have a stolen feast of bread and cucumbers ; for the latter esteemed viand they raided a cucumber patch. As they seated themselves to gorge upon their ill-gotten fare, Henry Tufts raised a cry that the robbed cucumber farmer was upon them. All fled, but Tufts quickly returned and ate all the feast himself. He survived the cucumbers, but pretended to his confederates that he had been captured and had promised to work out the value of the spoils in a week's hard labor. This work sentence he persuaded them to share ; he then farmed out the lot of young workmen at a profit, while they thought themselves nobly sharing his punishment. He lived to great old age, and, though at the last he " carried his dish pretty uprightly," it was by taking a hand at forgery and counterfeiting that he lived when burglary became arduous ; his nature, though irretrievably bad, was never bold enough to venture his life by robbing on the highway.

A very interesting thread of Tuft's story is his connection with the War of the Revolution ; and it awakens deep compassion for Washington and his fellow-generals when we think how many such scamps and adventurers must have swarmed into the Federal army, to the disorder of the regiments

and to their discredit and to the harassment alike
of patriot officers and patriot soldiers. There were
frequent aggressions at the hands of rogues in the
Middle states, and they became known by the
name of Skinners. Cooper's novel, *The Spy*, gives
an account of these sneaking bands of sham patriots.
Among those who allied themselves on the side of
the King was a family of notorious scoundrels, five
brothers named Doane.

The story of the Doanes is both tragic and
romantic. They were sons of respectable Quaker
parents of Bucks County, Pennsylvania, and during
the Revolutionary War became celebrated for their
evil deeds. They were all men of remarkable physical development, tall, strong, athletic, and all fine
horsemen. Before the war they were of good reputation, and it is said proposed to remain neutral;
but the Doanes were not permitted to take a middle
course, and soon enrolled themselves as Tories,
which at once engendered a bitter feeling between
them and their Whig neighbors. They began
their career of infamy by robbing and plundering in
the neighborhood, gradually extending their field
of operations into neighboring counties. Sabine's
Loyalists gives the names of three other Doanes —
kinsmen who were allied with the five brothers in
their evil deeds. Their place in historical books
and history comes to them through their services
to the British officers during the war. In a dingy
chap-book entitled *Annals of the Revolution, or a
History of the Doanes*, full credit is assigned to
Moses Doane for giving information to General

Howe, and planning with him the stratagem which led to the victories of the British on Long Island. The Edge Hill skirmish, laid out by Doane and agreed to by Howe and Lord Cornwallis, was to be an important move of the British. The move was lost by the prompt and brave action of Mrs. Lydia Darrach, who overheard the plot and carried news of it to Washington. In the terrible massacre at Wyoming the Doanes took prominent part. The close of the war seemed but to increase their career of crime. Each brother had a sled drawn by four horses. There was heavy snow and a long season of sleighing in 1782, and they fairly raided the entire state, robbing again and again on the highway. At last an act was passed by the General Assembly of Pennsylvania " to encourage the speedy apprehending and bringing to justice of divers Robbers, Burglars, and Felons," naming the Doanes, and offering a large reward for their capture and a gift of £150 to any person injured in helping to arrest them, or £300 to the family of such a helper should he be killed while aiding the cause of justice.

Joseph Doane was finally secured in prison. He broke jail, however, and escaped to New Jersey, where, like many another thief and rogue of his day, he found occupation as a school-teacher. He then fled to Canada, and died peacefully at an advanced age. Two brothers, Abraham and Mahlon, were hanged in Philadelphia. Moses, the leader of the outlaws, had the most tragic end. He was the most cruel and powerful of them all; of famous athletic powers, it was said he could run and jump

Russel Tavern, Arlington, Massachusetts.

over a Conestoga wagon. In the latter part of the summer of 1783, the Doanes went to the house of one Halsey who lived on Gallows Run, and asked for something to eat, and Halsey sent his son to a neighboring mill to get flour for them. The boy told that the Doanes were at his father's house, and the miller sent the word to a vendue in the neighborhood. A party of fourteen armed and mounted men promptly started to capture them. The house was surrounded. On approaching the men saw through the clinks of the logs the Doanes eating at table, with their guns standing near. William Hart opened the door and commanded them to surrender, but they seized their arms and fired. Hart seized Moses Doane, threw him down, and secured him. Then Robert Gibson rushed into the cabin and shot Doane in the breast, killing him instantly. Colonel Hart sent the body of the dead

outlaw to his unhappy father, who was also tried
for sheltering the robbers, and burnt in the hand
and imprisoned.

The most noted scourge of the eighteenth century
was Tom Bell. He was for years the torment of
the Middle colonies, alike in country and in town.
He was the despair of magistrates, the plague of
sheriffs, the dread of householders, and the special
pest of horse-owners. Meagre advertisements in
the contemporary newspapers occasionally show his
whereabouts and doings. This is from the *New
York Weekly Post Boy* of November 5, 1744 : —

"The noted Tom Bell was last week seen by several
who knew him walking about this city with a large Patch
on his face and wrapt up in a Great Coat, and is supposed
to be still lurking."

Two years later, in April 14, 1746, we read : —

"Tuesday last the famous and Notorious Villain Tom
Bell was apprehended in this city and committed to Jail on
Suspicion of selling a Horse he had hired some time ago
of an Inhabitant of Long Island. His accuser 'tis said has
sworn expressly to his Person, notwithstanding which he
asserts his Innocence with a most undaunted Front and
matchless Impudence. We hear his trial is to come off
this week."

His most famous piece of deviltry was his im-
personation of a pious parson in New Jersey. He
preached with as much vigor as he stole, and his
accidental resemblance to the minister increased his
welcome and his scope for thieving. So convinced
was the entire community that it was the real parson

who robbed their houses and stole their horses, that on his return to his parish he was thrust into prison, and a clerical friend who protested against this indignity was set in a pillory in Trenton for false swearing. Still, Tom Bell was not a highwayman of the true English stamp; he more closely resembled a sneak thief.

In the year 1741 the little child of Cornelius Cook, the blacksmith of Westborough, Massachusetts, and of his wife Eunice, lay very close to death. As was the custom of the day, the good old parson, Dr. Parkman, and his deacons prayed earnestly over the boy, that the Lord's will be done; but his mother in her distress pleaded thus: "Only spare his life, and I care not what he becomes." Tom Cook recovered, and as years passed on it became evident by his mischievous and evil deeds that he had entered into a compact with the devil, perhaps by his mother's agonized words, perhaps by

Sign-board of Gifford's Tavern.

his own pledge. The last year of this compact was at an end, and the devil appeared to claim his own as Tom was dressing for another day's mischief. Tom had all his wits about him, for he lived upon them. "Wait, wait, can't you,"

he answered the imperative call of his visitor, " till
I get my galluses on ? "   The devil acquiesced to this
last request, when Tom promptly threw the suspenders
in the fire, and therefore could never put them on
nor be required to answer the devil's demands.

Tom Cook became well known throughout Massachusetts, and indeed throughout New England,
as a most extraordinary thief.
His name appears in the
records of scores of New
England towns; he was called
" the honest thief"; and his
own name for himself was
" the leveller." He stole
from the rich and well-to-do
with the greatest boldness
and dexterity, equalled by
the kindness and delicacy
of feeling shown in the be-
stowal of his booty upon
the poor and needy.   He
stole the dinner from the
wealthy farmer's kitchen and
dropped it into the kettle or
on the spit in a poor man's
house.   He stole meal and

Sign-board of Wells' Tavern.

grain from passing wagons and gave it away before
the drivers' eyes.   A poor neighbor was ill, and her
bed was poor.   He went to a thrifty farm-house,
selected the best feather bed in the house, tied it in
a sheet, carried it downstairs and to the front door,
and asked if he could leave his bundle there for a

few days. The woman recognized him and forbade him to bring it within doors, and he went off with an easy conscience.

In Dr. Parkman's diary, now in the library of the American Antiquarian Society at Worcester, under the date of August 27, 1779, is this entry: " The notorious Thom. Cook came in (he says) on Purpose to see me. I gave him w^t admonition, Instruction, and Caution I could — I beseech God to give it force! He leaves me with fair Words — thankful and promising." There came a time when his crime of arson or burglary led to his trial, conviction, and sentence to death. He heard the awful words of the judge, " I therefore sentence you to be hanged by the neck till you are dead, dead, dead," and he called out cheerfully, " I shall not be there on that day, day, day." And when that day came, surely enough, his cell was empty.

Tom Cook was most attractive in personal appearance; agile, well formed, well featured, with eyes of deepest blue, most piercing yet most kindly in expression. He was adored by children, and his pockets were ever filled with toys which he had stolen for their amusement. By older persons he was feared and disliked. He extorted from many wealthy farmers an annual toll, which exempted them from his depredations. One day a fire was seen rising from the chimney of a disused schoolhouse in Brookline, and Tom was caught within roasting a stolen goose, which he had taken from the wagon of a farmer on his way to market. The squire took him to the tavern, which was filled with farmers and carters, many of whom had been his victims. He was given his choice of trial and jail, or to run a gantlet of the men assembled. He chose the latter, and the long whips of the teamsters paid out many an old score of years' standing.

A very amusing story of highway robbery is told of John Buckman of Buckman's Tavern, of Lexington, Massachusetts (which is shown on page 23). An old toper bought a bottle of rum, and the bystanders jokingly asked him what he would do if he were attacked on the road. He answered solemnly that he would rather give up his life than his rum. John Buckman slipped out of the room, took a brass candlestick that had a slide that could be snapped with a noise like the trigger of a pistol. He waylaid the rum-lover not far from the tavern, and terrified him so that he quickly gave up his beloved bottle. This was a famous joke when John told it in the tavern taproom, but John did not laugh the next day when he was arrested for highway robbery and fined fifty dollars.

In the year 1818 there took place the nearest approach to a highway robbery on the English methods that had ever happened in America. It was the robbery of the mail-coach which ran between Baltimore and Philadelphia. The story is thus told by one of the victims : —

"HAVRE DE GRACE,
"Thursday morning, 4 o'clock.

"JOHN H. BARNEY, Esq.,

"Sir : I take the earliest opportunity to send you by an express an account of what happened to the mail last evening. About 2 miles from this place the driver of your mail wagon and myself were attacked by three highwaymen, each armed with a double barrelled pistol and a dirk. They had, previous to our arrival, built a rail fence across the road, and immediately on our driving up they leaped from behind the same, where they lay concealed, and presented their pistols, threatening to blow our brains out if we made any resistance. We were then carried some distance from the road into the woods; there they tied the driver and myself to a tree and commenced searching the mail. Every letter was opened and all the bank notes taken out; they showed me a large bundle of bills, and I much fear the loss will be found very great. They were from 11 until 3 o'clock busily employed in opening the letters. After they had done this they tied us to the back of the wagon, mounted three of the horses and galloped off towards Baltimore. They were all white men — had their faces blackened, and neither of them appeared more than 20. I have just arrived at this place and have stated the facts to the deputy postmaster, who will use every exertion to recover the letters that remain in the woods. They did not take anything belonging to me, & appeared not to wish anything but bank notes. They were all dressed in sailor's trowsers and round jackets, & were about the middle size; two wearing hats & the other having a silk handkerchief tied around his head.

" I am your obt. servt.
" THOS. W. LUDLOW.

" P. S. They called each other by their several names — Johnson, Gibson, and Smith, but I expect they were fictitious."

At that date and season of the year the " Eastern mail," on account of the heavy roads, was carried in a light carriage called a dearborn, with four horses.

This Lieutenant Ludlow of the United States Navy
obtained permission to accompany the driver in this
mail-carriage.   They left Baltimore at three o'clock
and were held up at eleven.   One robber desired to
shoot Lieutenant Ludlow and the driver, but the
others objected, and, on leaving, offered the driver
ten dollars.   They took no money from Ludlow,
and though they looked at his handsome gold
repeater to learn the time, they carefully returned it
to his pocket.   The very next day two men named
Hare, known to be journeymen tailors of Baltimore, entered a clothing shop in that city, and made
such a lavish display of money that they were
promptly arrested, and over twenty thousand dollars in money and drafts was found upon them.
They were puny fellows, Levi Hare being but twenty
years old, and contemporary accounts say " one person of average strength could easily manage them
both."

The total amount of bills and drafts recovered
amounted to ninety thousand dollars, and made the
robbery the largest ever attempted.   A few days
later a third brother Hare was arrested, and thirteen
hundred dollars was found in his house.   The third
robber proved to be John Alexander.

A Baltimore newspaper dated May 18, gives an
account of the sentence of the three men after their
interesting trial : —

"On Thursday last John Alexander, Joseph T. Hare,
and Lewis Hare were brought before Court to receive
sentence.   Judge Duval presided — first addressed Lewis

Hare and sentenced him to ten years' imprisonment —
J. T. Hare and Alexander sentenced to death. As Jos. T.
Hare was proceeding from the Court House to prison
accompanied by the constable, they had to cross Jones'
Falls, over which the trunk of a tree was laid for foot
passengers to walk on; when they arrived in the middle
of the creek Hare made an attempt to release his hands
from his irons, and to knock the constable into the creek;
it proved fruitless, but in the scuffle Hare tore off the
lappelle of the constable's coat. After he reached prison
he made an attack on the turnkey and nearly bit off his
finger."

I have seen an amusing old chap-book entitled
*The Life of the Celebrated Mail Robber and Dar-
ing Highwayman Joseph Thompson Hare*, and it
has a comical illustration of " The Scuffle between
Hare and the Constable," in which the constable,
much dressed up in tight trousers, tailed coat,
and high silk hat, struggles feebly with the outlaw
as they balance like acrobats on the narrow tree-
trunk.

The whole account of this mail robbery has a
decidedly tame flavoring. The pale tailors, so
easily overcoming a presumably brave naval officer
and a government mail-carrier; the leisurely ransacking of the mail-bags; the speedy and easy arrest
of the tailors and recovery of their booty, and the
astonishing simplicity of transporting the scantily
guarded felon across a creek on a fallen tree as
though on a pleasant country ramble, all combine
to render it far from being a tale of terror or
wild excitement.

The account of the death of the highwayman is thus told in the *Federal Republican and Baltimore Telegraph* of September 11, 1818.

"THE EXECUTION.

"Agreeably to public notice, the awful sentence of death was yesterday inflicted on J. Thompson Hare and John Alexander, in the presence of a vast concourse assembled to witness the ignominious ceremony. Their lives have expiated the crime for which they suffered. Justice has no demands on them in the grave.

"The gallows was sufficiently elevated above the walls of the prison to afford a distinct view of the unfortunate men to spectators at the distance of several hundred yards.

"Hare has made a confession which is now hawking about town for sale. In it he observes that, 'for the last fourteen years of my life I have been a robber, and have robbed on a large scale, and been more successful than any robber either in Europe or in this country that I ever heard of.'"

This lying dying boast of Hare fitly closes his evident failure as a highwayman.

An account of a negro highwayman is given in the *Federal Republican and Baltimore Telegraph* of September 11, 1818.

In the early years of this century there existed in eastern Massachusetts an organized band of thieves. It is said they were but one link in a chain of evil night-workers which, with a home or shelter in every community, reached from Cape Hatteras to Canada. This band was well organized, well trained, and well housed; it had skilful means of concealing stolen goods in innocent-faced cottages, in barns of honest thrift, and in wells and haystacks in simple dooryards. One mild-manered and humble house had a deep cellar which could be entered by an ingeniously hidden broadside door in a woodshed; into this cave a stolen horse and wagon or a pursued load of cribbed goods

Relay House, Mattapan Tavern.

might be driven, be shut in, and leave no outward sign. Other houses had secret cellars, a deep and wide one beneath a shallow, innocuous storage place for domestic potato and apple bins, and honest cider barrels. In a house sheltering one of these subterranean mysteries, a hard-working young woman was laboriously and discreetly washing clothes when surprised by the sheriff and his aids, who wisely invaded but fruitlessly searched the house. Nothing save the simplest household belongings was found in that abode of domesticity; but in later years, after the gang was scattered, a trap-door and ladder were found leading to the sub-cellar, and with chagrin and mortification the sheriff remembered that the woman's washing tubs stood unharmed upon the trap-door during the fruitless search.

An amusing battering ram was used by another woman of this gang on the sheriff who came to her house to arrest one of those thieves. The outlaw fled upstairs at the approach of the officer, but his retreat was noted, and the man of law attempted to follow and seize him. The wife of the thief — his congenial mate — opposed the passage of the sheriff, and when he attempted to push her one side and to crowd past her, she suddenly seized the crosspiece over the staircase, swung back by her hands and arms, planted both feet against the officer's chest, and knocked him down with such a sudden blow and consequent loss of wind, that the thief was far away ere the sheriff could move or breathe.

The leader of this band of thieves was an ingenious and delightful scamp — one George White. He was hard to catch, and harder to keep than to catch. Handcuffs were to him but pleasing toys. His wrists were large, his hands small; and when the right moment came, the steel bracelets were quickly empty. Locks and bolts were as easily thrust aside and left far, far behind him as were the handcuffs. At last he was branded on his forehead H. T., which stands for horse thief; a mean trick of a stupid constable who had scant self-confidence or inventiveness. Curling lovelocks quickly grow, however, and are ill in no one's sight; indeed, they were in high fashion in similar circles in England at that time, when various letters of the alphabet might be seen on the cheeks and brow of many a gay traveller on the highway when the wind blew among the long locks.

Wilde Tavern, 1770.   Milton, Massachusetts.

Term after term in jail and prison were decreed to George White when luck turned against him. Yet still was he pardoned, as he deserved to be, for his decorous deportment when behind bars; and he had a habit of being taken out on a writ of *habeas corpus* or to be transferred; but he never seemed to reach his journey's end, and soon he would appear on the road, stealing and roistering. The last word which came from him to New England was a letter from the Ohio Penitentiary, saying he was dying, and asking some of his kin to visit him. They did not go, he had fooled them too often. Perhaps they feared they might put new life into him. But the one time they were sure he lied he told the truth — and his varied career thus ended.

Flying once along a Massachusetts highway on a stolen horse, George White was hotly pursued. At the first sharp turn in the road he dismounted in a flash, cut the horse a lash with his whip, altered the look of his garment with a turn of his hand, tore off his hat brim and thus had a jaunty cap, and started boldly back on foot. Meeting the sheriff and his men all in a heat, he fairly got under their horses' feet, and as they pulled up they bawled out to know whether he had seen a man riding fast on horseback. "Why, yes," he answered ingenuously, "I met a man riding as though the devil were after him." They found the horse in half an hour, but they never found George White.

He once stole a tavern-keeper's horse, trimmed the mane, thinned out the tail, and dyed the horse's white feet. He led the renovated animal in to the bereft landlord, saying innocently that he had heard his horse was stolen, and thought he might want to buy another. He actually sold this horse back to his owner, but in a short time the horse's too evident familiarity with his wonted stable and yard and the fast-fading dye revealed the rascal's work. To another tavern-keeper he owed a bill for board and lodging, which, with the incongruity of ideals and morals which is often characteristic of great minds, he really wished to pay. The landlord had

a fine black horse which he had displayed to his
boarder with pride. This horse was kept temporarily in a distant pasture. White stole the horse
one night, rode off a few miles, and sold it and was
paid for it. He stole it again that night from the
purchaser, sold it, and was paid. He stole it a third
time and returned it to the pasture from whence it
never had been missed. He then paid his board-
bill as an honest man should.

Ashburnham Thief Detecting Society.

These gangs of horse thieves became such pests,
such scourges in the Northern states, that harassed
citizens in many towns gathered into bands and
associations for mutual protection and systematic
detection of the miscreants. A handbill of the
" Ashburnham Thief Detecting Society " had an
engraved heading which is reproduced on this page,
which showed a mounted thief riding across country
with honest citizens in hot pursuit. The Thief
Detecting Society of Hingham had, in 1847, eighty-
seven members. It used a similar print for a
heading for handbills, also one of a boy stealing
apples — as a severe lesson to youth.

In the year 1805 an abrupt and short but fierce attempt was made at highway robbery and burglary in Albany. The story as told in a chap-book is so simple, so antique, so soberly comic, that it might be three centuries old instead of scarce one. The illustrations, though of the date 1836, are of the standard of art of the seventeenth century.

It seems a piece of modern Philistinism to spoil the story — as I must — by condensation. The title of the book is *The Robber, or Pye and The Highwayman*, and the irony of giving Pye place before the highwayman or any place at all will be apparent by the story. In this tale two sturdy Albany dames shine as models of courage and fearlessness by the side of the terror-stricken burghers of the entire town, whose reputation to a man was only saved from the branding of utter and universal cowardice by the appearance and manly carriage and triumph at the end of the night's fray of old Winne the pennypost.

There put up that year in December at an Albany tavern a young man who gave his name as Johnson; he was aristocratic in bearing and dress, dark of complexion, sombre of aspect, but courteous and pleasant, "with a daring but cultivated eye." When questioned of himself and his business, however, Johnson was silent and taciturn. His magnificent horse and pair of splendid pistols were noted by the solid Dutch burghers and sharp Yankee traders who smoked and drank beer within the tavern walls; and one wintry afternoon the stranger was seen carefully cleaning the pair of pistols.

On that bitter night, a man — none other than our black-browed highwayman — rode clattering up to the toll-gate two miles below the town, and called out to open the gate; when the wife of the toll-keeper appeared to do that duty he jumped from his horse, rushed in toward the house, demanding in a terrible voice all the money in the toll till and chest.   The woman was terrified at this demand, yet not so scared but she could at his first approach throw the fat bag with all the accumulation of toll money under the porch, and do it unseen by the highwayman; and she at once asserted tearfully, with the alacritous mendacity born of sharp terror (the account says with great earnestness and woman-ish simplicity), that her husband had gone to the agent in town with all the month's collections, leav-ing her but a few shillings for change, which she displayed in the gate-drawer for proof.   Disgusted but credulous, the villain rode off with loud oaths, baffled in the simplest fashion by Dame Trusty No. 1.

He then went to the tavern of John Pye, the wealthy landlord, on the West Troy road.   He found the house locked peacefully for the night, but forced a window and entered.   In the barroom and kitchen, the fire was carefully covered to keep till morning.   Lighting his dark lantern with the coals, he then poured water on both fires and extinguished them, and I have puzzled long in my mind wonder-ing why he dallied, risking detection by doing this. He then went to the room where Pye and his wife were peacefully reposing, and rudely awakened them.

Mrs. Pye, promptly assuming the rôle she carried throughout, jumped from her bed and asked him what he wished. He answered, the chap-book says, "silently," "I deal with your husband, Madam, not with you " — and a more fatuous mistake never

Sign-board of Williams Tavern.

issued from lips of highwayman. To Pye he then said, "Your money or your life." Pye, heavy with sleep — and natural stupidity — seemed to fancy some trick was being played on him in mischief, and to the highwayman's demand for money answered, half alarmed, half peevish, "It's damned little money you'll get out of me, my lad, as the thing is but indifferently plenty with me." But he was roused at last by the fierceness of threats and gestures, and whimpered that his money was below; and the two proceeded downstairs to the taproom by the light of the robber's lantern. The moment they left the room, Mrs. Pye ran softly to a bedroom where slept two sojourners at the inn, wakened them with hurried words of the robber's visit and her beloved Pye's danger, and made appeals for help;

and as an emphatic wakener pulled them out of bed upon the floor. Then she ran swiftly back to bed.

In the meantime the terrified Pye recalled that his wife had the keys of the taproom till which held his money, and he and the highwayman returned to her bedroom and demanded them from her. "I'll give the keys to thee nor no man else," she stoutly answered. "Thee must, I tell thee," whined Pye, "or worse may happen." "Pye, I'll not give up my keys," still she cried, and seized a loaded gun by the bedside; for fierce answer the highwayman fired his pistol at Pye. With lamentable outcries Pye called out he was a dead man, and his arm fell to his side. His wife thrust the gun in his hands, shouting, "Fire, Pye, fire! he's feeling for another pistol." "I cannot," he quavered out, "I cannot hold the gun." She pushed it into his hands, held up his arm, aimed for him, and between them they pulled the trigger. In a second all was utter darkness and stillness: they had hit the highwayman. He pitched forward, fell on his lantern, put it out, and lay as one dead. Here was a situation for a good, thrifty, staid Albany vrouw, a dying husband on one side, a dead highwayman on the other, all in utter darkness. She ran for coals to the barroom and kitchen fires. Both were wet and black. She had no tinder box, coals must be brought from a neighbor's. She suddenly bethought of an unusual fire that had been lighted in the parlor the previous evening for customers, where still might be a live coal. This was her good fortune, and with lighted candle she proceeded to the scene of attack. Pye lay in a swoon on the bed, but by this time the highwayman had vanished; and safe and untouched under the bed were five hundred dollars in gold and five hundred more in bills, which, it is plain, Pye himself had wholly forgotten in his fright.

In the meantime where were the two "knights of the bedchamber," as the chap-book calls them? Far more silently than the robber they feared had they slid downstairs, and away from the tavern into hiding, until the highwayman rode past them.

They then tracked him by trails of blood, and soon saw him dismounted and rolling in the snow as if to quench the flow of blood. Though they knew he was terribly wounded and they were two to one, they stole past him at a safe distance in silence to the protection of the town, where they raised the cry of "A robber! Watch! Murder! Help! A band of highwaymen! Pye is dead!" Oh, how bravely they bawled and shouted! and soon a hue and cry was started from end to end of Albany town.

With an extraordinary lack of shrewdness which seemed to characterize the whole of this episode of violence, and which proved Johnson no trained "swift-nick," as Charles II. called highwaymen, instead of making off to some of the smaller towns or into the country, he rode back to Albany; and soon the night-capped heads thrust from the little Dutch windows, and terrified men leaning out over the Dutch doors, and the few amazed groups in the streets saw a fleet horseman, hatless, with bloody handkerchief bound around his head, come galloping and thundering through Albany, down one street, then back again to the river. When he reached the quay, the horse fearlessly sprang without a moment's trembling a terrible leap, eight feet perpendicular, twenty feet lateral, out on the ice. All screamed out that horse and rider would go through the ice and perish. But the ice was strong, and soon horse and rider were out of sight; but mounted men were now following the distant sound of hoofs, and when the outlaw reached what he thought was the opposite shore, but what was really a marshy island, one bold pursuer rode up after him. The robber turned, fired at him at random, and the Albany brave fled in dismay back to his discreet neighbors.

But honor and courage was now appearing across the ice in the figure of Captain Winne, the pennypost, who was heard to mutter excitedly in his semi-Dutch dialect: "Mine Cott! vat leeps das horse has mate! vull dwenty feet! Dunder and bliksem! he's der tuyfel for rooning!" Winne was an old Indian fighter, and soon he boldly grappled the highwayman, who drew a dagger on him. Winne knocked it from his hand. The highwayman grappled with him, wrenched away his club, and hit the pennypost a blow on his mouth which loosened all his front teeth (which, the chap-book says, "Winne afterwards took out at his leisure"). Winne then dallied no longer; he pulled down the handkerchief from the robber's forehead, twisted it around his neck, and choked him. In the morning twilight the great band of cautious Albanians gravely advanced, bound the highwayman securely, and carried him in triumph back to jail. He was placed in heavy irons, when he said, " Iron me as you will, you can hold me but a short time." All thought he meant to attempt an escape, but he spoke with fuller meaning; he felt himself mortally wounded.

Sign-board of Williams Tavern.

They put an iron belt around his waist and fastened it by a heavy chain to a staple in the floor. They placed great rings around his ankles, chained them to the floor, and then chained ankle-bands and belt together. They would have put an iron collar and chain on him also, but he said, " Gentlemen! have some mercy!" and a horrible wound at the base of the brain made them desist.

Poor Mrs. Pye visited him, with much distress of spirit, and sympathized with him and grieved over him as he lay face downward on the stone floor. And it arouses a sense of amused indignation to know that he asked earnestly for Pye and expressed deep regret at having injured him — he wasn't badly hurt, anyway. Our heroine, Dame

Pye, certainly deserved a better and braver husband, and it is pleasant to know that she outlived Pye and found, if not a more courageous mate, certainly a very fine young one — her bar-keeper, forty years younger than herself.

The highwayman escaped the tree, for he died in jail. There is reason to believe he was a Southerner of good birth. The horse was so widely described and exploited that his story reached a Virginia gentleman, his real owner, from whom he had been stolen. The sagacious animal had been trained to follow a peculiar whistle, and to jump at anything. The gentleman proved his ownership and took the splendid animal-hero home.

In the year 1821 a highwayman was executed in Massachusetts, Mike Martin, or Captain Lightfoot, who really was a very satisfactory outlaw, a real hightoby-crack, though he was only an imported one, not a native production. His life, as given by himself, is most entertaining. He had to his father a Kilkenny Irishman, who apprenticed the boy early in life to his uncle, a brewer. The brewer promptly beat him, he ran home, and got a bigger beating. In truth, he was a most beatable brat. When sixteen years old he joined the Ribbonmen, a political organization that committed many petty crimes and misdemeanors, besides regulating landlords. When his father found out the kind of company kept by the young rascal, he beat him again. Mike promptly took as a salve five guineas from his father's trunk, opening it with a master-key which had been kindly made for him by a Ribbonman, and which he was enjoined to keep constantly with him as a conveniency. He says, "I had always stolen in a small way." With his five guineas he ran away to Dublin, and pretended reformation and remorse so successfully to a cousin that the latter employed him in a distillery. In return he stole petty amounts continually from his cousin's money chest, by help of his master-key. Soon he was a settled outcast, and at this juncture met at an inn a fine, handsome clergyman, about forty years of age, over six feet tall, dark-eyed, of great muscle and strength ; his name was John Doherty. In spite of his black clerical dress he seemed somewhat mysterious in character, and after pumping Martin he disclosed in turn that he was the famous highwayman, Captain Thunderbolt.

He at once claimed Martin as one of the real sort, and they were talking over a union of forces and schemes when a party of dragoons came to the inn in pursuit of Thunderbolt. He escaped through a window, but in a week's time came back dressed as a Quaker and joined his companion, who at the age of twenty-one thus blossomed out as a real knight of the road, as Captain Lightfoot, with a pair of fine pistols and a splendid horse, "Down the Banks," to keep company with Thunderbolt's "Beefsteak." Thus equipped, these two gentlemen rode as gentlemen should, to the hunt. There, alone, to prove what he could do, Mike Martin robbed four huntsmen, and to his pride was mistaken by them for Thunderbolt himself. But the huntsmen soon had their turn ; sheriffs and soldiers drove the two knights to the woods ; and after weeks of uncomfortable hiding Mike Martin was properly penitent and longed for an honest man's seat in a tavern taproom. There is no retreat, however, in this career; the pair of robbers next entered a house, called all the people together, and robbed the entire trembling lot. Through Scotland and Ireland they rode till the highways got too hot for them, advertisements were everywhere, a hue and cry was out, and Thunderbolt fled to America.

Mike Martin, terrified at the multiplying advertisements and rewards, disguised himself, and sailed for New York. Quarrels and mutiny on shipboard brought him ashore at Salem, where he worked for a time for Mr. Derby. He soon received a sum of money from his father's estate and set up as a brewer. But Salem Yankees were too sharp for the honest highwayman, and he lost it all and had to take again to the road. From Portsmouth to Canada, — from pedlers, from gentlemen, — on horseback, in chaises, — he ran his rig ; finally, in spite of advertisements in newspapers and printed reports and handbills at every country inn, he worked his way back to New Hampshire ; and on a moonlight night he found himself horseless in the bushes. Two men rode up, and one held back as Mike Martin stepped forth. "Who's that?" said the foremost man. "I'm the bold Doherty from Scotland," said he, taking Thunderbolt's name and not in vain. "And what are you after?" said the shaking traveller. "Stop and I'll show you." Mike then presented his pistol and demanded of the gentleman his money or his life. Promptly money and papers were turned over. "Stand back by the fence," said the highwayman. "Here, Jack, look after this fellow," he swaggered to make the traveller think he had an accomplice; and he mounted the fine horse and rode off. He robbed some one in some way every few miles on the road till he was back in Salem. There he promptly acquiesced to the decorous customs of the New England town, and went to a lecture; on his way home from his intellectual refreshment, he asked the time of a well-dressed man. "Can't you hear the clock strike?" was the surly answer. "I'll hear your watch strike or strike your head," was the surprising reply. Out came watch and money with the cowardly alacrity ever displayed at his demands. From thence to the Sun Tavern in Boston, where he learned of a grand party at Governor Brooks's at Medford. He said in his confession, "I thought there might be some fat ones there and decided to be of the company." After an evening of astonishing bravado and recklessness, displaying himself at taverns and on the road, he held up Major Bray and his wife on the Medford turnpike, near the Ten Mile Farm which once belonged to Governor Winthrop. The gentlefolk were in "a genteel horse and chaise." Madam Bray began to try to conceal her watch-chain, but Captain Lightfoot politely told her he never robbed ladies. Major Bray turned over his watch and pocketbook, but begged to keep his papers. Martin said later, "The circumstances as given by Major Bray at the trial were correct, only he forgot to state that he was much frightened and trembled like a leaf." After stopping other chaises, he took the surprisingly foolhardy step of going to the tavern at Medford, where he found already much excitement about the robbery of Major Bray, and

Poore Tavern and Sign-board.

met many suspicious glances. He rode off, and soon a crowd was after him crying, " Stop Thief."

In his mad flight his stirrup broke, he fell from his horse and dislocated his shoulder; thence through fields and marshes on foot till he dropped senseless from pain and fatigue. When he recovered, he tied his suspenders to a tree at one end and the other end to his wrist and

pulled the shoulder into place.   Then by day and
night through farms and woods to Holliston.   In the
taproom of the tavern he called for brandy, but he
saw such a good description of himself with a
reward for his capture, while he was drinking off his
glass, it took away his appetite for the dinner he
had ordered.

He was then tired of foot travel, and stole a
horse and rode to Springfield.   Here he put up at
a tavern, where he slept so sound that he was only
awakened by landlord, sheriff, and a score of helpers
who had traced the horse to Springfield.   Major
Bray's robbery was unknown there, but he was
tried for it, however, when it was found out, on
October 21, and convicted and sentenced to death.
He cheerfully announced that he should escape if
he could, but he was put in heavy irons.   When in
jail at Lechmere Point he struck the turnkey, Mr.
Coolidge, on the head with his severed chain.   He
pushed past the stunned keeper, thrust open the
door, and ran for his life.   He was captured in a
cornfield and Coolidge was the man who grabbed
him.   It was found that he had filed through the
chain with a case-knife, filled the cut with a paste
of tallow and coal-dust, and though the link had
been frequently examined the cut had never been
noted.   He declared he would have escaped, only
the heavy chain and weight which he had worn had
made him lose the full use of his legs, and he had
to run with one end of the chain and a seventeen-
pound weight in his hand.

He was executed in December and behaved with

Monroe Tavern, Lexington, Massachusetts.

great propriety and sobriety. He showed neither cant, levity, nor bravado. He prayed silently just before his death, professed penitence, and went to the gallows with composure. He arranged his dress and hair carefully before a glass, showed a kind disposition to all, and finally gave the signal himself for the drop. A tall and handsome scamp, with piercing blue eyes and fine complexion, his marked intelligence and sweetness of expression made him most attractive. His frame was perfect in symmetry, and he was wonderful in his strength and endurance — truly an ideal highwayman ; it must have been a pleasure to meet him.

Thus it is very evident that neither highway robbery nor highwaymen thrived in America. They mended their ways very promptly — and apparently they wanted to. A very striking example of this is in the American career of Captain Thunderbolt, the friend and teacher of Mike Martin. When he set foot on American soil, he tamely abandoned all his old picturesque wicked ways. He settled first in Dummerston, Vermont, where he taught school and passed his leisure hours in seclusion and study. He then set up as a physician, in Newfane, Vermont, calling himself Dr. Wilson, and he moved from thence to Brattleboro, where his house stood on the present site of the railroad station. He married the daughter of a prominent Brattleboro farmer, but was too stern and reserved to prove a good American husband. He lived to be about sixty-five years old, and had a good and lucrative professional practice.

I know two authentic cases of highway robbery of stage-coaches in New England; one was from the driver, of a large sum of money which had been entrusted to him.   It was his wife who stole it.   She was not prosecuted, for she returned the money, and it was believed she would not have taken it from any one else.   The other theft was that of a bonnet.   Just as a stage was to start off from a tavern door, a woman jumped on the step, seized the bonnet of a woman passenger, tore it from her head, and made off with it before the outraged traveller's shrieks could reach the driver and stop the coach ; and — as the chronicler solemnly recounted to me — the robber was never heard of more.   These two highwaywomen have the honors of the road.

It may be deemed somewhat grandiloquent to term to-day this theft of a bonnet "highway robbery"; but I can assure you a fine bonnet was a most respected belonging in olden times, and if of real Dunstable or fine Leghorn straw and trimmed with real ostrich plumes it might be also a costly belonging, and to steal it was no light matter — indeed it was a hanging matter.   For in Boston, when John Hancock was governor, a woman was hanged for snatching a bonnet from another's head and running off with it.

CHAPTER XIX

ENGLAND was ever the birthplace and abiding-place of ghosts. Thoroughly respectable most of these old residents were, their manifestations being stereotyped with all the conventionalities of the spirit world. When the colonists came to the new world the friendly and familiar spectres did not desert their old companions, but emigrated also, and "sett down satysfyed" in enlarged log cabins, and houses built of American pine, just as the planters did; and in these humbler domiciles both classes of inhabitants were soon as much at home as they had been in oaken manor houses and stone castles in the "ould countrie."

In New England the tavern was often the chosen place of abode and of visitation of spirits; like other travellers on life's weary round, these travellers on the round of the dead found their warmest welcome at an inn. Naturally new conditions developed new phenomena; the spirits of unhappy peasants, of cruel barons, of hated heirs at law, of lovelorn ladies, found novel companions, among whom the manitous and wraiths of the red men cut the strangest figure. The ghosts of pirates, too, were prime favorites in America, especially in seaboard towns, but were never such frequent visitors, nor on the whole such picturesque visitors, as were the spirits of Indians : —

"The ghosts that come to haunt us
From the kingdom of Ponemah,
From the land of the Hereafter."

I have known a good many tavern ghosts of Indians — though their deeds as recounted are often far from being original or aboriginal. Reuben Jencks owned a tavern that had a very good Indian ghost. This ghost was not one of the inconsiderate kind that comes when you are awake, and half scares you to death; this noble red man stole in silently by night, so silently that the sleeper never awakened, and hence was never frightened, for nothing seems overstrange, uncanny, or impossible in a dream. Even when the Indian brandished his tomahawk and seized the visited one by the hair of the head, it never seemed to be anything more than might be expected, nor did he ever appear overfierce in his threats and gestures. Nevertheless in course of time his appearances gave a name to the apartment he visited; it came to be known as the Indian Chamber. And travelling

Sign-board of Dewey Tavern.

chapmen, pedlers, or traders who had been over the route frequently, and had heard the tale at every trip, sometimes objected to sleeping in the room — not that they were afraid — but it was somewhat of a nuisance.

It was not known that any Indian ever had received aught of injury at the hands of any at the Black Horse Tavern, save the derivative injury from too frequent and liberal draughts of hard cider, which was freely dealt out to every sorry brave who wandered there. There were some simpletons who said that the Indian's visits were to resent the injury done to another old inn, a rival down the road, named The Pine Tree, but which bore the figure of an Indian on its sign-board, and was oftener known as The Indian Tavern. This was nonsense. The Pine Tree had no visitors because it did not deserve them, had a vile table and a worse stable, while the Black Horse Tavern gave the best of the earth to its guests.

Reuben Jencks had not been born in this tavern. He inherited it from an uncle, and he was already married and had a family of small children when the tavern came to him. Another baby was born soon after, and as the Indian Chamber was the largest in the house, Mrs. Jencks quietly disposed of the objections of timid and superstitious chapmen and pedlers by taking the room for her own sleeping apartment.

It would seem to be a brave warrior, albeit a savage and a ghost, who would enter a room as densely populated as that of Mr. and Mrs. Jencks.

There was for the repose of landlord and landlady a vast four-post bedstead with curtains, valance, and tester of white dimity ; and under this high bed was thrust by day a low trundle bed.   At night it was drawn out, and upon it slept the three little daughters of the Jencks family.

Cutter's Tavern Sign-board.

Upon an old high-backed settle set on rockers slept Reuben Jencks, Jr., the deposed king of the family.   Adjustable bars slipped in the front of this settle made it a safe crib. This stood on one side of the fireplace, and the new baby reposed, when he slept at all, in a deeply hooded mahogany cradle.   There was a great fire ever and cheerfully burning in the fireplace — and yet to this chamber of infantile innocence and comfort came the saturnine form of the Indian ghost.

He was, in one sense, a thoroughly satisfactory apparition, being suitably clad in full trappings of war, buckskin and turkey feathers, bear's teeth and paint ; he was none of those miserable half-breed travesties of Indians who sometimes still sneaked round to the tavern kitchen, clad in vile clothes of civilization, so greasy and worn and dirty that a blanket would have been as stately in comparison as a Roman toga ; Indians devoid of bravery, dignity, and even of cunning, whose laziness, high cheek-bones, and hair coarse as a horse's tail, and their unvarying love of rum, were the only proofs of Indian blood ; whose skin, even, had turned from copper tawny to dingy yellow.

To Mrs. Jencks, reposing in state among her abundant goose feathers on the high bedstead, came one night the spectre in her dreams, pulled off her nightcap, seized her by her long hair, dragged her downstairs and out of doors, pointed fiercely to the roots of the great cedar at the gate, muttering all the while in broken English of avenging an insult to his race. As Mrs. Jencks awoke wholly uninjured, she merely laughed at her vision, saying that all the talk she had heard had made her dream it. But when she had dreamt it three times, three nights running, and the ghost kept speaking of an act of insult to him, that it must be avenged, removed, etc., and kept ever pointing to the base of the cedar tree, Ben Jencks insisted on digging for what he felt sure was hidden treasure. He and his menials dug deep and dug wide, and nearly killed the splendid old cedar, but found nothing. The next time the ghost appeared he dragged the astral body of Mrs. Jencks down to the other cedar tree on the right-hand side of the gateway. Ben Jencks dug again with the same result. Neither he nor the ghost was daunted, and a fine apple tree in the garden next the orchard was the

next victim.   It was a Sapson apple tree, the variety which all the children loved, and it ceased
bearing for several years.   As it
wilted and pined after the rough
spading at its roots, Mrs. Jencks
doggedly vowed never to repeat
any of the ghost's lies again.

We must not be too contemptu-
ous of this unprincipled Indian
spirit.   He simply belonged to a
class of ghosts of whom Andrew
Lang says complainingly that they
have a passion for pointing out
places and saying treasure or skele-
tons are buried therein; whereas
it always proves that nothing of
the sort is ever found.   There are
liars among the living as well as of
the dead, and Mrs. Jencks's Indian
never said it was a treasure — he
only hinted darkly at the buried
thing being associated with some
degradation or insult to the Indian
race.   The treasure was all in Ben
Jencks's brain — and the brains of
his friends.   Mrs. Jencks's silence
to her husband did not prevent

Clock with Painting of
Pahquoique House.

her however from having several
treasure-hunts alone by herself, after the Indian's
renewed visits and pointing finger, for he changed
nothing in his programme save the spot he indicated.   She spent an entire day pulling and poking

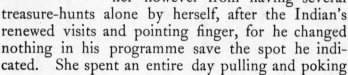

among the attic rafters. She rolled out several empty cider barrels from a distant cellar corner, and even dug a hole there secretly. Her husband at last discovered her mysteriously poking a hole down a disused well, and promptly had the well cleaned out; but of course nothing was found save the usual well contents, and thus the years rolled on.

One morning Lucy Jencks whimpered that the Indian had pulled her out of bed in the night and pointed out to her where to hunt. Lucy was nearly eleven years old; a clever, sharp, active little Yankee, who helped to shell peas and string beans and scour pewter, and who could knit famously and spin pretty well. This brought her naturally in the company of her elders, and she proved the influence of the ghost talk she had heard by repeating the Indian's words that "the derision of his ancient race, the degradation of his ancient customs, must be avenged." Derision and degradation are too big words for a little girl to use untutored, or for an Indian ghost either; and in truth they were not the precise words he had spoken at first. But Parson Pillsbury had been present at the digging under the Sapson apple tree, a piously sceptical but secretly interested spectator, and he had thus explained the somewhat broken "Injun-talk" which Mrs. Jencks reported. It proves the tractability and intelligence of this ghost of a heathen that he ever after used the words of the Puritan minister.

The ghost pointed out to Lucy Jencks a very inaccessible spot to be searched. It was the farther end of a loft over a shed, and had to be entered by

a short ladder from a leanto. This loft was packed
solidly with the accumulated débris of three-quarters
of a century, portions of farm tools, poor old furniture, boxes, barrels, every old stuff and piece that
was too mean even for the main attic, in which were
poor enough relics. It had never been searched or
sorted out since Ben Jencks came to the tavern,
and I doubt whether Mrs. Jencks would have listened to a ransacking then but for one circumstance,
the Jencks family were going to leave the Black
House Tavern — and they really ought to know exactly what was in it ere they sold it with its contents.
They had not been driven from the family home by
this Indian spirit of dreams, but by a more powerful
spirit — that of emigration. Neighbors and friends
in Rutland and Worcester were going to Ohio —
that strange new territory, and they would go too.
A single dead Indian, and such a liar, too, seemed
of but little account when they thought of the infinite bands of very live Indians in their chosen home.

Mrs. Jencks and Lucy climbed the ladder to the
loft, opened the single shutter, and let in a narrow
dancing ray of dusty sunlight on the crowded deso-
lation within. Lucy pointed between bars and barrels and bags, with slender white finger, at a large and
remote box which a slender, strong, copper-colored
hand had pointed out to her in her dreams. Her
mother sternly sent her below to do her stent at
quilt-piecing, and she tearfully and unwillingly de-
scended. It was nearly an hour ere the strong arms
of Mrs. Jencks had dislodged and repacked the
unutterable chaos to the extent of reaching the box.

Clouds of dust dimmed the air. She untied and removed a rotten rope that bound the box, which even in the dim litter looked like the upper half of a coffin. Within lay something swathed in linen bands and strips of old flannel — newspapers were

Wright Tavern, Concord, Massachusetts.

then too precious for wrappings. She struck it, and there came a faint rattle of metal. The thought came to her of the description of a mummy which she had read a few nights before in the almanac. She paused; then twisted in and among the boxes to the head of the ladder. She could hear the sound of Perseverance singing a hymn. Perseverance Abbott was the "help," the sister of a farmer neighbor, and she was baking "rye and Injun" bread for the teamsters who would stop there at nightfall. Mrs. Jencks called down, "Persy, come here a minute!" "I'll tell her to come," piped up the shrill voice of Lucy, who was hovering at the base of the ladder and evidently meant to be "in at the death." Perseverance appeared, floury and serene, at the foot of the ladder. "I'll come," she said, in answer to Mrs. Jencks's appeal for assistance, "because I know you're scairt, and I ain't a-goin' to see Ben Jencks a-huntin for them Indian bones again. I've been dyin', anyway, to clear this out ever since I come here, an' this'll be the beginnin'." "Persy," said Mrs. Jencks, hesitatingly, "it seems to be something dead." "Dead!" answered her handmaid, "I'll bet it's dead after layin' here forty, perhaps a hundred year!" An atmosphere of good sense and fearlessness seemed to halo her about; still both women unwrapped the heavy thing, the mummy, with care. A bare shining scalp came first to view. "It's a wig-block," shouted Perseverance in a moment, "yes, and here's curling irons and wire wig-springs."

It was "grandpa's wig-block," so Reuben Jencks said, when he saw it later; his grandfather had added to his duties of tavern-keeper, roadmaster, selectman, and deacon, that of wig-maker. And in that day, when all men of any station wore handsome flowing wigs, and all, even poor men, wore wigs of some kind, it was a calling of importance.

Moreover, an Indian with a tomahawk cut but a sorry figure when he tried to scalp a man who wore a wig; it was a deriding insult to the warlike customs of the whole Indian race.

There is a fine old brick tavern still standing in a New England seaboard town, and now doing service as a rather disreputable road house. It is a building rigidly square, set due north, south, east, and west, with four long, narrow doors opening over broad doorstones to the four ends of the earth. A

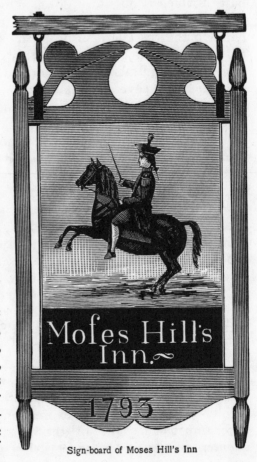

Sign-board of Moses Hill's Inn

long tail of summer and winter kitchens, a washroom, brew-house, smoke-house, wood-rooms, sheds,

barns, piggeries, pigeon-houses, hen-houses, once
stretched a hundred feet or more adown the road,
part of which is now torn down. Each joint of the
tail helped loyally in olden times to furnish good
cheer to the traveller. The great square rooms of
the main house are amply furnished; one was a
taproom, and in each second-story room still are two
double beds, save in the corner room next the
kitchen tail of the house, where stands nailed firmly
to the floor of the room a somewhat battered oaken
table. A little open staircase in the corner of this
room leads down to the working end of the house,
and was used in olden days to carry supplies to the
upper table from the lower kitchen.

It has been many a year since good cheer was
spread on that broad oaken board, though at one
time it was the favorite dining place of a choice
brotherhood of old salts, called the Mariners' Club,
who gathered there when on shore to tell tales of
wild privateering, and of sharp foreign trade, and
to plan new and profitable ventures. Many of
these Mariners' Clubs and Marine Societies existed
in seaport towns at that golden time in New England's marine commercial history.

This room was the scene about seventy-five years
ago of a somewhat unusual expression of feminine
revolt — that is, both the expression and the revolt
were unusual. One of the most constant frequenters of the tavern, the heaviest eater and deepest drinker, the greatest money-spender at these
Mariners' dinners, was one Captain Sam Blood, who
ran a large coasting brig, which made but short

trips to Atlantic seaports. Thus he was ever on hand for tavern fun. He had a large and rather helpless family which he kept somewhat in retreat on a gloomy farm two miles inland; his mother old and feeble, yet ever hard-working; a large number of untidy children, and, worst of all, a sickly wife, a tall, gaunt woman who whined, and whined, and ever whined from her patch-covered couch, over the frequent desertions of her spouse to the tavern-table, and his wilful waste of money, while she could never leave the house. One night a specially good dinner was set in the Mariners' room, roast and boiled meats, pies and puddings, a grand array of full pitchers, decanters, and bottles; the assembled group of old salts were

Sign-board of John Nash's Tavern.

about to ascend from the taproom to seat themselves comfortably at the round table for solid work, when a terrible crash and scream were heard, each seeming louder than the other, and before the startled eyes of the landlord and his guests, as they rushed up and into the room, there were all the steaming dishes, all the streaming bottles, with table-cloth and plates in a disorderly hopeless wreck on the floor. "Who could have done it?" "There he goes," shouted one captain, as he ran to the window; and, surely enough, a slender man in nautical garb was seen striking out from under the sheltering walls of the ell-kitchens and sheds, and running desperately across the snowy fields. Full chase was given and the marauder finally captured; he was swung roughly around with oaths and blows, when sudden silence fell on all. It was Sam Blood's wife in Sam Blood's togs. "I'll settle for this dinner," said Sam Blood, blackly.

On his next voyage Mrs. Blood sailed with the captain. With the usual ethical inconsistencies which prevail in small communities, Mrs. Sam Blood the despoiler attracted more attention and sympathy than Mrs. Sam Blood the poor, hard-working, sickly wife; it was the universal talk and decision of all the women in town that the captain's wife needed a change of scene; and she had to take it in that ironical form decreed to the wives of old-time ship-owners, in a voyage of uncertain length and certain discomfort on a sailing vessel, with no woman companion and the doubtful welcome of the male members of the crew. Off she went to Savannah. At that port she was no better, cried all the time (the first mate wrote home), and seemed little like the woman of spirit who had wrecked the Mariners' dinner. The captain decided to go with a cargo to South America to see how the tropics would serve the ailing woman. His old home crew shipped back to Boston, not caring for the trip far south, and a crew of creoles and negroes was taken on the supplemental trip.

When Captain Blood and his schooner at last came into port at home, he landed with sombre countenance, a mourning widower, and soon was properly clad in trappings of woe. Mrs. Sam Blood was no more. Her husband stated briefly that she had died and was buried at sea off the island of Jamaica. A discreet and decent term of mourning passed, and Mrs. Blood, as is the way of the living — and of the dead — was quite forgotten. Once more the Mariners' Club was to have a dinner, and once more the table in the Mariners' room was spread with good cheer and ample drink. Captain Blood, in somewhat mitigated bereavement, was among the thronging guests who lingered over a final stomach-warmer at the bar. The landlord ran out of the room and roared down the main stairs that dinner was ready, and even as he spoke, crash! smash! came a din from the Mariners' room, and there was all the dinner and all the broken bottles with the table-cloth and the upset table on the floor. It was a very unpleasant reminder to Sam Blood of a very mortifying event, and his friends sympathized with him in silence. This time no miscreant could be found in house or on farm, but the landlord suspected a discharged and ugly servant, who might have run down the little corner staircase, as Mrs. Blood had before him.

The ruined dinner was replaced by another a week later. The guests were gathered, the landlord was bearing a last roast pig aloft, when smash! crash! came again from the Mariners' room. Every one in the house rushed up in tremendous excitement: the table-cloth was off, table upset, bottles smashed. An ominous silence and a sense of the uncanny fell on all in the room; some glanced askance at Sam Blood. More than one sharp-eyed old salt noted that the great, hairy, tattooed hands of the widower shook amazingly, though his face was the calmest of all the bronzed, weather-beaten figure-heads staring around.

There has never been a meal served from that table since, though many a meal has been spread on it. The landlord, a stubborn man of no nonsense and no whims, grimly nailed the legs of the table to the floor, and proceeded to set the succeeding dinner on the bare boards. It mattered not, cloth or no cloth, every dinner small or great was always wrecked. Watchers were set, enjoined not to take their eyes from the table, nor themselves from the room. Something always happened, an alarm of fire, a sudden call for help, an apparent summons from the landlord — this but for a single moment, but in that moment smash! crash! went the dinner.

Captain Blood lived to a rather lonely and unpopular old age, for he was held responsible for the decay and dissolution of the Mariners' Club; and unjustly enough, for Neptune knows it was no wish of his. When occasional dinners and suppers were given by nautical men in wholly mundane rooms in

other taverns, with no spiritual accompaniments, —
that is, in the form of ghosts, — the captain was
left out. Men did not hanker for the companionship of a man who left port with a wife and came
home with a ghost. He has been dead for decades,
and is anchored in the old Hill graveyard, where
he sleeps the quiet sleep of the righteous; and the

Montague City Tavern.

name and virtues of Elvira, his beloved wife, are
amply recorded on his tombstone. But her ghost
still walks, or at any rate still wrecks. I don't like
ghosts, but I really should like to meet this lively
and persistent Yankee wraith, clad in the meek and
meagre drooping feminine attire which was the mode
in the early part of this century, or perhaps tentatively mannish in peajacket and oilskins as in her

day of riot of old.   I really wish I could see the
spry and spiteful spirit of Mrs. Sam Blood, with
her expression of rampant victory as she twitches
the table-cloth off, and wrecks the bottles, and says
in triumphal finality, "I'll settle for this dinner";
thus gaining what is ever dear to a woman, even to
the ghost of a woman — the last word.

Late on a November night in the early part of
this century the landlord and half a dozen teamsters
sat drinking deep in the taproom of the Buxton
Inn.   These rough travellers had driven into the
yard during the afternoon with their produce-laden
wagons; for a heavy snow was falling, and it was
impossible wheeling, doubtful even whether they
could leave the inn in forty-eight hours — perhaps
not for a week.   Their board would not prove very
costly, for they carried their own horse-provender,
and much of their own food.   Some paid for a bed,
others slept free of charge round the fire; but all
spent money for drink.   It was a fierce storm and a
great fall of snow for the month of the year —
though November is none too mild any year in
New England.   Though this snow was too early
by half to be seasonable, yet each teamster was
roughly merry at the others' expense that he had
not "come down" on runners.

With dull days of inaction before them there was
no need for early hours of sleep, so all talked loud
and long and drank boisterously, when suddenly a
series of heavy knocks was heard at the front door
of the inn.   Bang! bang! angrily pounded the iron
knocker, and the landlord went slowly into the little

front entry, fumbled heavily at the bolt, and at last threw open the door to a fine young spark who blustered in with a great bank of snow which fell in at his feet, and who was covered with rolls and drifts of snow, which he shook off debonairly on all around him, displaying at last a handsome suit of garments, gold-laced, and very fine to those country bumpkins, but which a "cit" would have noted were somewhat antiquated of cut and fashion.

He at once indicated and proved his claim to being a gentleman by swearing roundly at the landlord, declaring that his horses and servant were housed ere he was, that they had driven round and found shelter in the barn before he could get into the front door. He could drink like a gentleman, too, this fine young fellow, and he entered at once into the drinking and singing and story-telling and laughing with as much zest as if he had been only a poor common country clown. At last all fell to casting dice. The stakes were low, but such as they were luck all went one way. After two hours' rounds the gentleman had all the half-dollars and shillings, all the pennies even, in his breeches pocket; and he laughed and sneered in hateful triumph. Sobered by his losses, which were small but his all, one teamster surlily said he was going to sleep, and another added, "'Tis high time." And indeed it was, for at that moment old Janet, the tavern housemaid, came in to begin her morning round of work, to pinch out the candles, take up part of the ashes from the chimney-hearth, fill the kitchen pots and kettles, gather in the empty bottles and glasses; and as she

did so, albeit she was of vast age, she glanced with
warm interest at the fine figure of fashion slapping
his pockets, sneering, and drinking off his glass.
"Why, master," she said, staring, "you do be the
very cut of Sir Charles off our sign-board." "Let's
see how he looks," swaggered the young blade;
"where's a window whence we can peep at him?"
All trooped to a nigh window in the tavern parlor
to look at the portrait of Sir Charles Buxton on the

The Old Abbey, Bloomingdale Road, New York.

swing-sign, but to no avail, for there was yet but
scant light without, and they peered out only on
thick snowdrifts on the window panes. But when
they reëntered the kitchen, lo! their gay companion
was gone. Gone where? Back on the sign-board,
of course. All who heard the oft and ever repeated
wonder-tale would have scoffed at the fuddled notions
of a drunken group of stupid teamsters, but the
dollars and shillings and pennies were gone too —
the devil knows where; and who was to pay the

score for the double bowl of punch and the half-dozen mugs of flip Sir Charles Buxton had ordered while the dicing was going on, and a large share of which he had drunk off with all the zest of flesh and blood? Besides, Janet had seen him, and Janet's eye for a young man could never be doubted.

I spent one night a few summers ago in a tavern haunted by the ghost of a dead past. A sudden halt in our leisurely progress from town to town, caused by a small but unsurmountable accident to our road-wagon, found us in a little Massachusetts village of few houses. The blacksmith had gone to a neighboring village to spend the night. It was twilight, and we decided not to attempt to reach our intended place for sojourning, six miles distant. We asked of a passer-by which house was the tavern. "There isn't any," was the cheerful answer; "if you stay here over night you'll have to stay at the poorhouse." Now this was rather an unalluring alternative to any self-respecting citizen, but the night was coming on, and, after vainly searching for some resident who had ever had summer boarders, we determined to investigate the poorhouse. We found it the best house in the village. It was the almshouse, but it had been for half a century a tavern in reality, when the post-road lay through the town and travellers were more frequent than to-day. There was evidence of its tavern days in the old taproom, which had been converted into a store-room. The house with twenty acres of land had been bequeathed to the town by one of the old Bourne family that had lived in it so long. This last Bourne owner was a childless widower, a St. Louis man, who had been away from the home of his youth since early child-hood and had little love of it from old associations.

The poormaster and his wife we found to be tidy, respectable folk, even folk of a certain dignity, who

Tavern Pitcher. Apotheosis of Washington.

owned the adjoining farm. Their own house had burned down. So for ten years they had run the poorhouse. It had not proved a very difficult task. Often there were no occupants; one year there were two Portuguese cranberry pickers, stricken with rheumatism from exposure in the cranberry bogs.

After the Shower.

Now both are married to American wives and own prosperous cranberry bogs of their own. The poorhouse had its usual quota on the night of our sojourn ; we found two paupers living there.

There was not time to prepare an extra meal of extra quality for the travellers who came so suddenly for a night's shelter, but the good tea, plentiful milk, fine bread and butter, honey, hot griddle-cakes, and fried bacon bore testimony of ample fare and good housewifery. The two paupers sat at the table and ate with us — a silver-haired old man of exquisite cleanliness, and a grotesque little humpback. We noted that the old man was ever addressed by all who spoke to him as Mr. Bourne, and during his short absence from the room after supper the poormistress told us that the almshouse had been the home and this the farm of his grandfather. The supper was served in the great kitchen, and here we sat till a curfew bell rang from the little church belfry at nine o'clock.

Considerable jealousy was shown by both paupers in their eager desire to talk with us, and we learned that the dwarf was regarded as a genius ; he composed wonderful epitaphs, and had written poetry for the county newspaper. He could set type, and could thus earn his living, but was temporarily more feeble than usual, on account of a weight falling on his back; after a few months he would go to work again. He represented the brilliant and intellectual element of communal life, but was hopelessly plebeian ; while Mr. Bourne stood for blood and breeding. This the dwarf Peter scorned, being a Socialist in his creed. A curious and touching atmosphere of simplicity and confidence filled the old kitchen. The farmer and his wife were deeply solicitous for the comfort and health of their two charges; and as I sat there, tired by my long drive, a little lonely from the strangeness of the surroundings, there was nevertheless a profound sense that this poorhouse was truly a home.

Sign-board Grosvenor Inn.

It was in the middle of this night that the experience came to me of the greatest sense of passive comfort that I have known — and think of the absurdity, in a poorhouse! We heard at midnight a light patter of quick rain, and soon soft footsteps entered and our window shutters were carefully closed. "It's me," said our landlady, ungrammatically and pleasantly. "I didn't mean to wake you, but I always go to Mr.

Bourne's room when it rains to close his window for fear he'll take cold, so I looked at yours," and the old-time figure in petticoat, shawl, and ruffled nightcap withdrew as quietly as it had entered. Then came the hour of half-sleep, a true "dozy hour," as Thackeray said. In this poorhouse, with no book, no ready light, I fain must lie in silence, hence an hour such as has been told in perfection in a simple yet finished piece of descriptive English; let me give the classic prose of Sam Pepys — the words are his — but the happy hour was mine as well as his : —

"Rode easily to Welling, where we supped well, and had two beds in the room, and so lay single, and still remember it that of all the nights that I ever slept in my life I never did pass a night with more epicurism of sleep; there being now and then a noise of people stirring that wakened me, and then it was a very rainy night, and then I was a little weary, that what between waking, and then sleeping again one after another, I never had so much content in all my life."

When we awoke the following morning Mr. Bourne was awaiting our coming with some eagerness. The dwarf was absent, and the old man apologized for one or two of Peter's remarks the night before which had seemed to him uncivil. These were, however, only some of Peter's mild bitternesses about division of property, the injustice of modern laws, the inequalities of taxation, etc., which had seemed harmless enough in the mouth of a pauper.

While waiting the leisurely repairs of our vehicle

at the hands of the captured blacksmith, I yielded to
Mr. Bourne's eager invitation to come with him to
see a piece of land he owned. " It's been in the
family near two hundred years," he said proudly.
"Peter says I ought to be ashamed to tell of my folks'
grasping all them years God's gift of the soil that
ought to be just as free as the ocean and the sky;
but I'm glad I've got it. Peter's folks came from
Middleboro way, and never did own no land nor
nothin', and I've noticed it's them sort that's always
maddest at folks as does have family things."
After a few minutes of silence he added : " Peter
can't help it. It's born in him to feel that way,
just as it's born into me to feel proud of my property." We walked along the sandy road under the
beautiful autumnal sky. A dense group of stunted
cedars and one towering fir tree rose sombrely in a
little enclosed corner below the church. " This is
my property," said the old man, cheerfully, " and
they're all Bournes and Swifts in it. There lies
my great-grandfather, the old parson, under that flat
stone come from England. Here is my mother.
That slate headstone over there is for my brother
lost at sea on one of his voyages. I am going to
be put exactly here. Them four stones I put to
mark it. And Peter hasn't any graveyard — don't
even know where his father is buried — so he's
going to lie over here in this corner. He's the
only one as ain't a Swift or a Bourne, and it's a
great honor to him. He's had to pay me for it,
though; he's written me an epitaph, and it's a good
one; it'll be the best one in the whole graveyard."

The Parting of the Ways.

Index

Barbadoes liquor, 101.
Barberries, superstitions about, 340–341.
Barge, use of word, 266–267.
Barnum, P. T., quoted, 130.
Barnum's Hotel, Baltimore, prices at, 88–89.
Barre, sign-board at, 168.
Barre, Colonel, 173.
Barre and Worcester Stage Line, 305.
Barrington, R.I., prices at, 79–80.
Bartlett, Eliphalet, tavern of, 47.
Bay Path, 224–225.
Beakers, glass, 44.
Beal, Thomas, coach line of, 271–272.
Bear, as a mark, 208.
Beaumont, quoted, 207.
Beehive Tavern, 154.
Beer, brewing regulated by law, 4; price established, 4; in New York, 121; in Virginia, 121–122.
Bell Savage, 141.
Bell teams, 247.
Bell, Tom, story of, 380–381.
Bellarmine jug, 44.
Bellows-top, 109.
Bells, on pack-horses, 243; on Conestoga wagons, 247–248.
Bennett, quoted, 103, 128, 256–257.
Berkeley, Governor, quoted, 122.
Bethlehem, Penn., tavern at, 57 et seq.
Beverige, 131–132.
Beverly, Mass., ordinary at, 2.
Bible and Key, 157.
Bible and Peacock, 157.
Biblical names, of towns, 58; of taverns, 157.
Bickerdyke, quoted, 132.
Bilboes, 8, 215.
Billiards, forbidden, 5.
Bills of fare, 87–88.
Bingham house a tavern, 53.
Birch, beer of, 123; vistas of, 346.
Bispham's Tavern, Trenton, 83–84.
Bissell's Tavern, 150–151.
"Bite," 327.
Black Ben, anecdote of, 332.

Black, William, quoted, 116.
Black Horse Tavern, Winchester, 180.
"Blacks," 373.
Bladensburgh, Md., tavern at, 32.
Black Horse Tavern, 39; shows at, 197.
Black jacks, 14.
Black Sam. See Samuel Fraunces.
Black strap, 104.
Bliss, Joseph, 311.
Bliss Tavern, Haverhill, N.H., 311, 314.
Blood, Sam, ghost story of, 420 et seq.
Blue Anchor Tavern, Boston, names of chambers, 18; landlord of, 62.
Blue Anchor Tavern, Cambridge, bills at, 81.
Bogus, 104.
Bonaparte, Jerome, 186.
Bonnets, bought by stage-drivers, 328; highway robbery of, 408.
Book auctions, 197.
Boreel Building, 35.
Boston, ordinaries in, 6, 9, 10–11, 13, 17–19; night watch in, 6; smoking fined in, 13; ale-houses in, 20; liquor sellers in, 25; disorder in, 26–27; taverns in, 154; oldest inn in, 180; pillory in, 218; bridges in, 228 et seq.; coaches in, 256 et seq.; stage-coach lines from, 271 et seq., 371 et seq.
Boston, Sarah, 96–99.
Boston and Hartford Stage Line, 291 et seq.
Boston and Lowell R. R., 287.
Boston and Providence R. R., 287.
Boston and Worcester R. R., first cars on, 287.
Boston Courier, objects to railroads, 289.
Boston Tea Party, 181.
Boston Traveller, 273.
Bound children, 221.
Bowen Inn, prices at, 79–80.
Bowls, forbidden, 5.
Box, fragrance of, 347.
Brackett, Landlord, 84–85.

Tar-bucket. *See* Tar-lodel.
Tar-lodel, 246–247.
Tarleton Arms, 310.
Tarleton Inn, story of, 309–310; sign-board of, 310, 312.
Tarleton, Wm., 309–310.
Tavern behind Nazareth, 57.
Taverns, use of word, 30; in Southern colonies, 30 *et seq*.; establishment of laws about, 31, 34–35; prices at, 31, 42, 118, 177–178; names of rooms in, 17; in New Netherlands, 33 *et seq*.; names of, 35; as war rendezvous, 172; as auction rooms, 197; as business exchanges, 198; as insurance offices, 198; as jails, 212, 303; on Albany Turnpike, 235; in Scotland, 283. Also see names of Towns and Ordinaries.
Taylor, M. M., milestone of, 351; tavern of, 352.
Taylor, the Water Poet, quoted, 255.
Taylorsville, Penn., bridge sign-board at, 239.
Teamsters, 249.
Thackeray, W. M., cited, 322.
Thief Detecting Societies, 393.
Thieves, band of, 388 *et seq*.
Thomas' Exchange Coffee-house, 300.
Thorburn, Grant, quoted, 72–73, 362–363.
Three Broiled Chickens, 183.
Three Crowns, Lancaster, Penn., 143–144.
Three Jolly Sailors, 158.
Three Loggerheads, 142.
Throat-lashing, 327.
Tipping, 326.
Tippling-houses, 31.
Tithing-man, duties of, 9.
Tobacco, restrictions on use of, 12–13; as payment, 31; drawers for, 45.
Toby Fillpots, 134.
Todd, Margaret, 40.
Todd, Robert, 39–40.
Toddy, derivation of word, 39–40; made of rum, 104; price of, 178.

Toddy-stick, description of, 114.
Toll-boards, 237, 238.
Toll-gates, on Mohawk Turnpike, 237.
Tolls, rates of 237–238: commuted, 298.
Tontine Association, 37.
Topsfield Bridge, 356.
"Towelling," 327.
Transportation, by water, 241; on horse-back, 241 *et seq*.
Travelling-bags, 331.
Trenton, N.J., tavern fare at, 83, 84; bridge at, 230.
Trout, boiled, 89.
Troy coaches, 269.
Trunks, old time, 330.
Tryer, on punch, 114.
"Tuck-a-nuck," 317.
Tufts, Henry, story of, 375 *et seq*.
Turkey-shoot, 207–209.
Turnpikes, 231 *et seq*., 297 *et seq*.; in Scotland, 284, 297; profits on, 297; desertion of, 297.
Turnspit dogs, 55–56.
Turtle, as gifts, 90.
Turtle-feasts, 90.
Tuttle, Sarah, love-making of, 216–217.
Twining, Thomas, quoted, 263, 326, 367.
Twist, slang term, 142.
Twitchell, Ginery, career of, 301 *et seq*.; coach of, 303; description of, 304; makes election returns, 304; obtains mail contracts, 305.
Tyler, Royall, 207.

Union Place Hotel, New York, fare at, 88.

Vardy, Luke, 204.
Veazie Road, 286.
Vendues, at coffee-houses, 49, 197; at taverns, 219; of thieves, 220; of paupers, 221 *et seq*.
Victuallyng-house, 2.
Virginia, ordinaries in, 30 *et seq*.; metheglin in, 125.

Wadsworth Inn, Springfield, 43–44.

Index